Modernity and the Holocaust

To Janina, and all the others
who survived to tell the truth

As I write, highly civilized human beings are flying overhead, trying to kill me. They do not feel any enmity to me as an individual, nor I against them. They are only 'doing their duty', as the saying goes. Most of them, I have no doubt, are kind-hearted law-abiding men who would never dream of committing murder in private life. On the other hand, if one of them succeeds in blowing me to pieces with a well-placed bomb, he will never sleep the worse for it. He is serving his country, which has the power to absolve him from evil.

George Orwell, *England your England* (1941)

Nothing is so sad as silence.

Leo Baeck, President of Reichsvertretung
der deutschen Juden, 1933–43

It is to our interest that the great historical and social question ... how could this happen? ... should retain all its weight, all its stark nakedness, all its horror.

Gershom Scholem, objecting
to the execution of Eichmann

Modernity and the Holocaust

ZYGMUNT BAUMAN

Cornell University Press
Ithaca, New York

First published in the United States in 1989 by Cornell University Press.

ISBN-13: 978-0-8014-8719-4 (pbk. : alk. paper)
ISBN-10: 0-8014-8719-6 (pbk. : alk. paper)

Librarians: A CIP catalog record for this book is available from the Library of Congress.

Cornell University Press strives to use environmentally responsible suppliers and materials to the fullest extent possible in the publishing of its books. Such materials include vegetable-based, low-VOC inks and acid-free papers that are recycled, totally chlorine-free, or partly composed of nonwood fibers. For further information, visit our website at www.cornellpress.cornell.edu.

Paperback printing: 10 9 8 7 6 5 4

Printed in the United States of America

Contents

Preface

Having written down her personal story of her life in the ghetto and in hiding, Janina thanked me, her husband, for putting up with her protracted absence during the two years of writing, when she dwelled again in that world 'that was not his'. Indeed, I escaped that world of horror and inhumanity when it reached out to the most remote corners of Europe. And like so many of my contemporaries, I never tried to explore it after it vanished from earth, leaving it to linger in the haunted memory and never-healing scars of those whom it bereaved or wounded.

I knew, of course, of the Holocaust. I shared my image of the Holocaust with so many other people of my own and younger generations: a horrible crime, visited by the wicked on the innocent. A world split into mad murderers and helpless victims, with many others helping the victims when they could, but unable to help most of the time. In that world, murderers murdered because they were mad and wicked and obsessed with a mad and wicked idea. Victims went to the slaughter because they were no match to the powerful and heavily armed enemy. The rest of the world could only watch, bewildered and agonized, knowing that only the final victory of the allied armies of the anti-Nazi coalition would bring an end to human suffering. With all this knowledge, my image of the Holocaust was like a picture on the wall: neatly framed, to set the painting apart from the wallpaper and emphasize how different it was from the rest of the furnishings.

Having read Janina's book, I began to think just how much I did not know – or rather, did not think about properly. It dawned on me that I did not really understand what had happened in that 'world which was not mine'. What did happen was far too complicated to be explained in that simple and intellectually comforting way I naively imagined sufficient. I realized that the Holocaust was not only sinister and horrifying, but also an event not at all easy to comprehend in habitual, 'ordinary' terms. This event had been written down in its own code which had to be broken first to make understanding possible.

I wanted historians and social scientists and psychologists to make sense of it and explain it to me. I explored library shelves that I had never inspected before, and I found these shelves tightly packed, overflowing with meticulous historical studies and profound theological tracts. There were a few sociological studies as well – skilfully researched and poignantly written. The evidence amassed by the historians was overwhelming in volume and content. Their analyses were cogent and profound. They showed beyond reasonable doubt that the Holocaust was a window, rather than a picture on the wall. Looking through that window, one can catch a rare glimpse of many things otherwise invisible. And the things one can see are of the utmost importance not just for the perpetrators, victims and witnesses of the crime, but for all those who are alive today and hope to be alive tomorrow. What I saw through this window I did not find at all pleasing. The more depressing the view, however, the more I was convinced that if one refused to look through the window, it would be at one's peril.

And yet I had not looked through that window before, and in not looking I did not differ from my fellow sociologists. Like most of my colleagues, I assumed that the Holocaust was, at best, something to be illuminated by us social scientists, but certainly not something that can illuminate the objects of our current concerns. I believed (by default rather than by deliberation) that the Holocaust was an interruption in the normal flow of history, a cancerous growth on the body of civilized society, a momentary madness among sanity. Thus I could paint for the use of my students a picture of normal, healthy, sane society, leaving the story of the Holocaust to the professional pathologists.

My complacency, and that of my fellow sociologists, was greatly helped (though not excused) by certain ways in which the memory of the Holocaust had been appropriated and deployed. It had been all-too-often sedimented in the public mind as a tragedy that occurred to the Jews and the Jews alone, and hence, as far as all the others were concerned, called for regret, commiseration, perhaps apology, but not much more than that. Time and again it had been narrated by Jews and non-Jews alike as a collective (and sole) property of the Jews, as something to be left to, or jealously guarded by, those who escaped the shooting and the gassing, and by the descendants of the shot and the gassed. In the end both views – the 'outside' and the 'inside' – complemented each other. Some self-appointed spokesmen for the dead went as far as warning against thieves who collude to steal the Holocaust from the Jews, 'christianize' it, or just dissolve its uniquely Jewish character in the misery of an indistinct 'humanity'. The Jewish state tried to employ the tragic memories as the certificate of its political legitimacy, a safe-conduct pass for its past and future policies, and above all as the advance payment for the injustices it might itself commit. Each for reasons of its own, such views contributed to the entrenchment of the Holocaust in public consciousness as an exclusively Jewish affair, of little significance to anyone else (including the Jews themselves as human beings) obliged to live in modern times and be members of modern society. Just how much and how perilously the significance of the Holocaust had been reduced to that of a private trauma and grievance of one nation was brought to me recently in a flash, by a learned and thoughtful friend of mine. I complained to him that I had not found in sociology much evidence of universally important conclusions drawn from the Holocaust experience. 'Is it not amazing,' my friend replied, 'considering how many Jewish sociologists there are?'

One read of the Holocaust on anniversaries, commemorated in front of mostly Jewish audiences and reported as events in the life of Jewish communities. Universities have launched special courses on the history of the Holocaust, which, however, were taught separately from courses in general history. The Holocaust has been defined by many as a specialist topic in Jewish history. It has attracted its own specialists, the professionals who kept meeting and lecturing to each other at specialist conferences and symposia. However, their impressively productive and crucially important work seldom finds it way back to the mainstream of scholarly discipline and cultural life in general – much like most other specialized interests in our world of specialists and specializations.

When it does find that way at all, more often than not it is allowed on the public stage in a sanitized and hence ultimately demobilizing and comforting form. Pleasantly resonant with public mythology, it can shake the public out of its indifference to human tragedy, but hardly out of its complacency – like the American soap-opera dubbed *Holocaust*, which showed well-bred and well-behaved doctors and their families (just like your Brooklyn neighbours), upright, dignified and morally unscathed, marched to the gas chambers by the revolting Nazi degenerates aided by uncouth and blood-thirsty Slav peasants. David G.

Roskies, an insightful and deeply empathetic student of Jewish reactions to the Apocalypse, has noted the silent yet relentless work of self-censorship – the 'heads bowed to the ground' of the ghetto poetry being replaced by the 'heads lifted in faith' in the later editions. 'The more the grey was eliminated,' Roskies concludes, 'the more the Holocaust as archetype could take on its specific contours. The Jewish dead were absolutely good, the Nazis and their collaborators were absolutely evil.'[1] Hannah Arendt was shouted down by the chorus of offended feelings when she suggested that the victims of an inhuman regime might have lost some of their humanity on the road to perdition.

The Holocaust was indeed a *Jewish tragedy*. Though Jews were not the only population subjected to a 'special treatment' by the Nazi regime (six million Jews were among more than 20 million people annihilated at Hitler's behest), only the Jews had been marked for total destruction, and allotted no place in the New Order that Hitler intended to install. Even so, the Holocaust was not simply a *Jewish problem*, and not an event in *Jewish history* alone. *The Holocaust was born and executed in our modern rational society, at the high stage of our civilization and at the peak of human cultural achievement, and for this reason it is a problem of that society, civilization and culture.* The self-healing of historical memory which occurs in the consciousness of modern society is for this reason more than a neglect offensive to the victims of the genocide. It is also a sign of dangerous and potentially suicidal blindness.

This self-healing process does not necessarily mean that the Holocaust vanishes from memory altogether. There are many signs to the contrary. Apart from a few revisionist voices denying the reality of the event (which seem, if inadvertently, only to add to the public awareness of the Holocaust through the sensational headlines they provoke), the cruelty of the Holocaust and its impact on the victims (and particularly on survivors) seem to occupy a growing place among public interests. Topics of this kind have become almost obligatory – if on the whole auxiliary – sub-plots in films, TV plays or novels. And yet there is little doubt that the self-healing does take place – through two intertwined processes.

One is the forcing of the Holocaust history into the status of a specialist industry left to its own scientific institutes, foundations and conference circuit. A frequent and well-known effect of the branching-off of scholarly disciplines is that the link of the new specialism with the main area of research becomes tenuous; the mainstream is little affected by the concerns and discoveries of the new specialists, and soon also by the peculiar language and imagery they develop. More often than not, the branching off means that the scholarly interests delegated to specialist institutions are thereby eliminated from the core canon of the discipline; they are, so to speak, particularized and marginalized, deprived in practice, if not necessarily in theory, of more general significance; thus mainstream scholarship is absolved from further preoccupation with them. And so we see that while the volume, depth and scholarly quality of specialist works in Holocaust history grow at an impressive pace, the amount of space and attention devoted to it in general accounts of modern history does not; if anything, it is easier now to be excused from a substantive analysis of the Holocaust by appending a respectably long list of scholarly references.

Another process is the already-noted sanitation of the Holocaust imagery sedimented in popular consciousness. Public information about the Holocaust has been all-too-often associated with commemorative ceremonies and the solemn homilies such ceremonies attract and legitimize. Occasions of this kind, however important in other respects, offer little room for the depth analysis of the Holocaust experience – and particularly of its more unsightly and disturbing aspects. Less still of this already limited analysis finds its way into public consciousness, served by the non-specialist and generally accessible information media.

When the public is called to think of the most awesome of questions – 'How was such a horror possible? How could it happen in the heart of the most civilized part of the world?' – its tranquility and balance of mind are seldom disturbed. Discussion of guilt masquerades as the analysis of causes; the roots of the horror, we are told, must be sought and will be found in Hitler's obsession, the obsequiousness of his henchmen, the cruelty of his followers and the moral corruption sown by his ideas; perhaps, if we search a little further, they may also be found in certain peculiar convolutions of German history, or in the particular moral indifference of ordinary Germans – an attitude only to be expected in view of their overt or latent antisemitism. What follows in most cases the call 'to try to understand how such things were possible' is a litany of revelations about the odious state called the Third Reich, and about Nazi bestiality or other aspects of 'the German malady' which, as we believe and are encouraged to go on believing, point to something 'that runs against the planet's grain'.[2] It is said as well that only once we are fully aware of the bestialities of Nazism and their causes 'will it ever be possible, if not to heal, at least to cauterize the wound which Nazism has made in Western civilization'.[3] One of the possible interpretations (not necessarily intended by the authors) of these and similar views, is that once the moral and material responsibility of Germany, Germans and the Nazis is established, the search for the causes will be completed. Like the Holocaust itself, its causes were enclosed in a confined space and a limited (now, fortunately, finished) time.

Yet the exercise in focusing on the *Germanness* of the crime as on that aspect in which the explanation of the crime must lie is simultaneously an exercise in exonerating everyone else, and particularly *everything* else. The implication that the perpetrators of the Holocaust were a wound or a malady of our civilization – rather than its horrifying, yet legitimate product – results not only in the moral comfort of self-exculpation, but also in the dire threat of moral and political disarmament. It all happened 'out there' – in another time, another country. The more 'they' are to blame, the more the rest of 'us' are safe, and the less we have to do to defend this safety. Once the allocation of guilt is implied to be equivalent to the location of causes, the innocence and sanity of the way of life of which we are so proud need not be cast in doubt.

The overall effect is, paradoxically, pulling the sting out of the Holocaust memory. The message which the Holocaust contains about the way we live today – about the quality of the institutions on which we rely for our safety, about the validity of the criteria with which we measure the propriety of our own conduct and of the patterns of interaction we accept and consider normal – is silenced, not listened to, and remains undelivered. If unravelled by the specialists and discussed inside the conference circuit, it is hardly ever heard elsewhere, and remains a mystery for all the outsiders. It has not entered as yet (at any rate not in a serious way) contemporary consciousness. Worse still, it has not as yet affected contemporary practice.

This study is intended as a small and modest contribution to what seems to be, in the circumstances, a long-overdue task of a formidable cultural and political importance; the task of bringing the sociological, psychological and political lessons of the Holocaust episode to bear on the self-awareness and practice of the institutions and the members of contemporary society. This study does not offer any new account of Holocaust history; in this respect, it relies entirely on the astounding achievement of recent specialist research, which I did my best to ransack and to which my debt is boundless. Instead, this study focuses on such revisions in various quite central areas of the social sciences (and possibly also social practices) as have been made necessary in view of the processes, trends and hidden potentials revealed in the course of the

Holocaust. *The purpose of the various investigations of the present study is not to add to specialist knowledge and to enrich certain marginal preoccupations of social scientists, but to open up the findings of the specialists to the general use of social science, to interpret them in a way that shows their relevance to the main themes of sociological inquiry, to feed them back into the mainstream of our discipline,* and thus to lift them up from their present marginal status into the central area of social theory and sociological practice.

Chapter 1 is a general survey of sociological responses (or, rather, of the glaring paucity of such responses) to certain theoretically crucial and practically vital issues raised by Holocaust studies. Some of these issues are then analysed separately and more fully in subsequent chapters. And so in chapters 2 and 3 are explored the tensions emanated by the boundary-drawing tendencies under the new conditions of modernization, the breakdown of the traditional order, the entrenchment of modern national states, the connections between certain attributes of modern civilization (the role of scientific rhetoric in the legitimization of social-engineering ambitions being most prominent among them), the emergence of the racist form of communal antagonism, and the association between racism and genocidal projects. Having thus proposed that the Holocaust was a characteristically modern phenomenon that cannot be understood out of the context of cultural tendencies and technical achievements of modernity, in chapter 4, I attempt to confront the problem of the truly dialectical combination of uniqueness and normality in the status occupied by the Holocaust among other modern phenomena; I suggest in the conclusion that *the Holocaust was an outcome of a unique encounter between factors by themselves quite ordinary and common; and that the possibility of such an encounter could be blamed to a very large extent on the emancipation of the political state, with its monopoly of means of violence and its audacious engineering ambitions, from social control – following the step-by-step dismantling of all non-political power resources and institutions of social self-management.*

Chapter 5 undertakes the unrewarding and painful task of analysing one of those things that we 'prefer to leave unspoken'[4] with particular zeal; the modern mechanisms that allow for the co-operation of victims in their own victimization and those which, contrary to the vaunted dignifying and moralizing effects of the civilizing process, condition a progressively dehumanizing impact of coercive authority. One of the 'modern connections' of the Holocaust, its intimate link with the pattern of authority developed to perfection in modern bureaucracy, is the subject of chapter 6 – an extended commentary to the crucial socio-psychological experiments conducted by Milgram and Zimbardo. Chapter 7, serving as the theoretical synthesis and conclusion, surveys the present status of morality in the dominant versions of social theory and argues in favour of its radical revision – which would focus on the revealed capacity of social manipulation of social (physical and spiritual) distance.

Diversity of their topics notwithstanding, I hope that all the chapters point in the same direction and reinforce one central message. *They are all arguments in favour of assimilating the lessons of the Holocaust in the mainstream of our theory of modernity and of the civilizing process and its effects.* They all proceed from the conviction that the experience of the Holocaust contains crucial information about the society of which we are members.

The Holocaust was a unique encounter between the old tensions which modernity ignored, slighted or failed to resolve – and the powerful instruments of rational and effective action that modern development itself brought into being. Even if their encounter was unique and called for a rare combination of circumstances, the factors that came together in that encounter were, and are still, ubiquitous and 'normal'. Not enough has been done after the Holocaust to fathom the awesome potential of these factors and less still to paralyse their potentially gruesome effects. I believe that much more can be done – and certainly should be done – in both respects.

While writing this book, I greatly benefited from the criticism and advice of Bryan Cheyette, Shmuel Eisenstadt, Ferenc Fehèr, Agnes Heller, Lukasz Hirszowicz and Victor Zaslavsky. I hope they will find in these pages more than a marginal evidence of their ideas and inspiration. I owe a particular debt to Anthony Giddens for the attentive reading of the successive versions of the book, thoughtful criticism and most valuable advice. To David Roberts goes my gratitude for all his editorial care and patience.

1

Introduction: Sociology after the Holocaust

Civilization now includes death camps and Muselmänner *among its material and spiritual products*
Richard Rubenstein and John Roth, *Approaches to Auschwitz*

There are two ways to belittle, misjudge, or shrug off the significance of the Holocaust for sociology as the theory of civilization, of modernity, of modern civilization.

One way is to present the Holocaust as something that happened to the Jews; as an event in *Jewish* history. This makes the Holocaust unique, comfortably uncharacteristic and sociologically inconsequential. The most common example of such a way is the presentation of the Holocaust as the culmination point of European-Christian antisemitism – in itself a unique phenomenon with nothing to compare it with in the large and dense inventory of ethnic or religious prejudices and aggressions. Among all other cases of collective antagonisms, antisemitism stands alone for its unprecedented systematicity, for its ideological intensity, for its supra-national and supra-territorial spread, for its unique mix of local and ecumenical sources and tributaries. In so far as it is defined as, so to speak, the continuation of antisemitism through other means, the Holocaust appears to be a 'one item set', a one-off episode, which perhaps sheds some light on the *pathology* of the society in which it occurred, but hardly adds anything to our understanding of this society's *normal* state. Less still does it call for any significant revision of the orthodox understanding of the historical tendency of modernity, of the civilizing process, of the constitutive topics of sociological inquiry.

Another way – apparently pointing in an opposite direction, yet leading in practice to the same destination – is to present the Holocaust as an extreme case of a wide and familiar category of social phenomena; a category surely loathsome and repellent, yet one we can (and must) live with. We must live with it because of its resilience and ubiquity, but above all because modern society has been all along, is and will remain, an organization designed to roll it back, and perhaps even to stamp it out altogether. Thus the Holocaust is classified as another item (however prominent) in a wide class that embraces many 'similar' cases of conflict, or prejudice, or aggression. At worst, the Holocaust is referred to a primeval and culturally inextinguishable, 'natural' predisposition of the human species – Lorenz's instinctual aggression or Arthur Koestler's failure of the neo-cortex to control the ancient, emotion-ridden part of the brain.[1] As pre-social and immune to cultural manipulation, factors responsible for the Holocaust are effectively removed from the area of sociological interest. At best, the Holocaust is cast inside the most awesome and sinister – yet still theoretically assimilable category – of genocide; or else simply dissolved in the broad, all-too-familiar class of ethnic, cultural or racial oppression and persecution.[2]

Whichever of the two ways is taken, the effects are very much the same. The Holocaust is shunted into the familiar stream of history:

> When viewed in this fashion, and accompanied with the proper citation of other historical horrors (the religious crusades, the slaughter of Albigensian heretics, the Turkish decimation of the Armenians, and even the British invention of concentration camps during the Boer War), it becomes all too convenient to see the Holocaust as 'unique' – but normal, after all.[3]

Or the Holocaust is traced back to the only-too-familiar record of the hundreds of years of ghettos, legal discrimination, pogroms and persecutions of Jews in Christian Europe – and so revealed as a uniquely horrifying, yet fully logical consequence of ethnic and religious hatred. One way or the other, the bomb is defused; no major revision of our social theory is really necessary; our visions of modernity, of its unrevealed yet all-too-present potential, its historical tendency, do not require another hard look, as the methods and concepts accumulated by sociology are fully adequate to handle this challenge – to 'explain it', to 'make sense of it', to understand. The overall result is theoretical complacency. Nothing, really, happened to justify another critique of the model of modern society that has served so well as the theoretical framework and the pragmatic legitimation of sociological practice.

Thus far, significant dissent with this complacent, self-congratulating attitude has been voiced mostly by historians and theologians. Little attention has been paid to these voices by the sociologists. When compared with the awesome amount of work accomplished by the historians, and the volume of soul-searching among both Christian and Jewish theologians, the contributions of professional sociologists to Holocaust studies seems marginal and negligible. Such sociological studies as have been completed so far show beyond reasonable doubt that *the Holocaust has more to say about the state of sociology than sociology in its present shape is able to add to our knowledge of the Holocaust*. This alarming fact has not yet been faced (much less responded to) by the sociologists.

The way the sociological profession perceives its task regarding the event called 'the Holocaust' has been perhaps most pertinently expressed by one of the profession's most eminent representatives, Everett C. Hughes:

> The National Socialist Government of Germany carried out the most colossal piece of 'dirty work' in history on the Jews. The crucial problems concerning such an occurrence are (1) who are the people who actually carry out such work and (2) what are the circumstances in which other 'good' people allow them to do it? What we need is better knowledge of the signs of their rise to power and better ways of keeping them out of power.[4]

True to the well-established principles of sociological practice, Hughes defines the problem as one of disclosing the peculiar combination of psycho-social factors which could be sensibly connected (as the determinant) with peculiar behavioural tendencies displayed by the 'dirty work' perpetrators; of listing another set of factors which detract from the (expected, though not forthcoming) resistance to such tendencies on the part of other individuals; and of gaining in the result a certain amount of explanatory–predictive knowledge which in this rationally organized world of ours, ruled as it is by causal laws and statistical probabilities, will allow its holders to prevent the 'dirty' tendencies from coming into existence, from expressing themselves in actual behaviour and achieving their deleterious, 'dirty' effects. The latter task will be presumably attained through the application of the same model of action that has made our world rationally organized, manipulable and 'controllable'. What we need is a better technology for the old – and in no way discredited – activity of social engineering.

In what has been so far the most notable among the distinctly sociological contributions to the study of the Holocaust, Helen Fein[5] has faithfully followed Hughes's advice. She defined her task as that of spelling out a number of psychological, ideological and structural variables which most strongly correlate with percentages of Jewish victims or survivors inside various state-national entities of Nazi-dominated Europe. By all orthodox standards, Fein produced a most impressive piece of research. Properties of national communities, intensity of local antisemitism, degrees of Jewish acculturation and assimilation, the resulting cross-communal solidarity have all been carefully and correctly indexed, so that correlations may be properly computed and checked for their relevance. Some hypothetical connections are shown to be non-existent or at least statistically invalid; some other regularities are statistically confirmed (like the correlation between the absence of solidarity and the likelihood that 'people would become detached from moral constraints'). It is precisely because of the impeccable sociological skills of the author, and the competence with which they are put in operation, that the weaknesses of orthodox sociology have been inadvertently exposed in Fein's book. Without revising some of the essential yet tacit assumptions of sociological discourse, one cannot do anything other than what Fein has done; conceive of the Holocaust as a unique yet fully determined product of a particular concatenation of social and psychological factors, which led to a temporary suspension of the civilizational grip in which human behaviour is normally held. On such a view (implicitly if not explicitly) one thing that emerges from the experience of the Holocaust intact and unscathed is the humanizing and/or rationalizing (the two concept are used synonymously) impact of social organization upon inhuman drives which rule the conduct of pre- or anti-social individuals. Whatever moral instinct is to be found in human conduct is socially produced. It dissolves once society malfunctions. 'In an anomic condition – free from social regulation – people may respond without regard to the possibility of injuring others.'[6] By implication, the presence of effective social regulation makes such disregard unlikely. The thrust of social regulation – and thus of modern civilization, prominent as it is for pushing regulative ambitions to limits never heard of before – is the imposition of moral constraints on otherwise rampant selfishness and inborn savagery of the animal in man. Having processed the facts of the Holocaust through the mill of that methodology which defines it as a scholarly discipline, orthodox sociology can only deliver a message bound more by its presuppositions than by 'the facts of the case': the message that the Holocaust was a failure, not a product, of modernity.

In another remarkable sociological study of the Holocaust, Nechama Tec attempted to explore the opposite side of the social spectrum; the rescuers – those people who did not allow the 'dirty work' to be perpetrated, who dedicated their lives to the suffering others in the world of universal selfishness; people who, in short, remained moral under immoral conditions. Loyal to the precepts of sociological wisdom, Tec tried hard to find the social determinants of what by all standards of the time was an aberrant behaviour. One by one, she put to the test all hypotheses that any respectable and knowledgeable sociologist would certainly include in the research project. She computed correlations between the readiness to help on the one hand, and various factors of class, educational, denominational, or political allegiance on the other – only to discover that there was none. In defiance of her own – and her sociologically trained readers' – expectations, Tec had to draw the only permissible conclusion: 'These rescuers acted in ways that were natural to them – spontaneously they were able to strike out against the horrors of their times.'[7] In other words, the rescuers were willing to rescue because this was their nature. They came from all corners and sectors of 'social structure', thereby calling the bluff of there being 'social determinants' of moral behaviour. If anything, the contribution of such determinants expressed itself in their failure to extinguish the rescuers' urge to help others in their distress. Tec came closer than most sociologists to the discovery that the real point at issue is not; 'What can we, the sociologists, say about the Holocaust?', but, rather, 'What has the Holocaust to say about us, the sociologists, and our practice?'

While the necessity to ask this question seems both a most urgent and a most ignobly neglected part of the Holocaust legacy, its consequences must be carefully considered. It is only too easy to over-react to the apparent bankruptcy of established sociological visions. Once the hope to contain the Holocaust experience in the theoretical framework of malfunction (modernity incapable of suppressing the essentially alien factors of irrationality, civilizing pressures failing to subdue emotional and violent drives, socialization going awry and hence unable to produce the needed volume of moral motivations) has been dashed, one can be easily tempted to try the 'obvious' exit from the theoretical impasse; to proclaim the Holocaust a 'paradigm' of modern civilization, its 'natural', 'normal' (who knows – perhaps also *common*) product, its 'historical tendency'. In this version, the Holocaust would be promoted to the status of *truth* of modernity (rather than recognized as a *possibility* that modernity contains) – the truth only superficially concealed by the ideological formula imposed by those who benefit from the 'big lie'. In a perverse fashion, this view (we shall deal with it in more detail in the fourth chapter) having allegedly elevated the historical and theoretical significance of the Holocaust, can only belittle its importance, as the horrors of genocide will have become virtually indistinguishable from other sufferings that modern society does undoubtedly generate daily – and in abundance.

The Holocaust as the test of modernity

A few years ago a journalist of *Le Monde* interviewed a sample of former hijack victims. One of the most interesting things he found was an abnormally high incidence of divorce among the couples who went jointly through the agony of hostage experience. Intrigued, he probed the divorcees for the reasons for their decision. Most interviewees told him that they had never contemplated a divorce before the hijack. During the horrifying episode, however, 'their eyes opened', and 'they saw their partners in a new light'. Ordinary good husbands, 'proved to be' selfish creatures, caring only for their own stomachs; daring businessmen displayed disgusting cowardice; resourceful 'men of the world' fell to pieces and did little except bewailing their imminent perdition. The journalist asked himself a question; which of the two incarnations each of these Januses was clearly capable of was the true face, and which was the mask? He concluded that the question was wrongly put. Neither was 'truer' than the other. Both were possibilities that the character of the victims contained all along – they simply surfaced at different times and in different circumstances. The 'good' face seemed normal only because normal conditions favoured it above the other. Yet the other was always present, though normally invisible. The most fascinating aspect of this finding was, however, that were it not for the hijackers' venture, the 'other face' would probably have remained hidden forever. The partners would have continued to enjoy their marriage, unaware of the unprepossessing qualities some unexpected and extraordinary circumstances might still uncover in persons they seemed to know, liking what they knew.

The paragraph we quoted before from Nechama Tec's study ends with the following observation; 'were it not for the Holocaust, most of these helpers might have continued on their independent paths, some pursuing charitable actions, some leading simple, unobtrusive lives. They were dormant heroes, often indistinguishable from those around them.' One of the most powerfully (and convincingly) argued conclusions of the study was the impossibility of 'spotting in advance' the signs, or symptoms, or indicators, of individual readiness for sacrifice, or of cowardice in the face of adversity; that is, to decide, outside the context that calls them into being or just 'wakes them up', the probability of their later manifestation.

John R. Roth brings the same issue of potentiality versus reality (the first being a yet-undisclosed mode of the second, and the second being an already-realized – and thus empirically accessible – mode of the first) in a direct contact with our problem:

> Had Nazi Power prevailed, authority to determine what ought to be would have found that no natural laws were broken and no crimes against God and humanity were committed in the Holocaust. It would have been a question, though, whether the slave labour operations should continue, expand, or go out of business. Those decisions would have been made on rational grounds.[8]

The unspoken terror permeating our collective memory of the Holocaust (and more than contingently related to the overwhelming desire not to look the memory in its face) is the gnawing suspicion that the Holocaust could be more than an aberration, more than a deviation from an otherwise straight path of progress, more than a cancerous growth on the otherwise healthy body of the civilized society; that, in short, the Holocaust was not an antithesis of modern civilization and everything (or so we like to think) it stands for. We suspect (even if we refuse to admit it) that the Holocaust could merely have uncovered another face of the same modern society whose other, more familiar, face we so admire. And that the two faces are perfectly comfortably attached to the same body. What we perhaps fear most, is that each of the two faces can no more exist without the other than can the two sides of a coin.

Often we stop just at the threshold of the awesome truth. And so

Henry Feingold insists that the episode of the Holocaust was indeed a new development in a long, and on the whole blameless, history of modern society; a development we had no way to expect and predict, like an appearance of a new malign strain of an allegedly tamed virus:

> The Final Solution marked the juncture where the European industrial system went awry; instead of enhancing life, which was the original hope of the Enlightenment, it began to consume itself. It was by dint of that industrial system and the ethos attached to it that Europe was able to dominate the world.

As if the skills needed and deployed in the service of world domination were qualitatively different from those which secured the effectiveness of the Final Solution. And yet Feingold is staring the truth in the face:

> [Auschwitz] was also a mundane extension of the modern factory system. Rather than producing goods, the raw material was human beings and the end-product was death, so many units per day marked carefully on the manager's production charts. The chimneys, the very symbol of the modern factory system, poured forth acrid smoke produced by burning human flesh. The brilliantly organized railroad grid of modern Europe carried a new kind of raw material to the factories. It did so in the same manner as with other cargo. In the gas chambers the victims inhaled noxious gas generated by prussic acid pellets, which were produced by the advanced chemical industry of Germany. Engineers designed the crematoria; managers designed the system of bureaucracy that worked with a zest and efficiency more backward nations would envy. Even the overall plan itself was a reflection of the modern scientific spirit gone awry. What we witnessed was nothing less than a massive scheme of social engineering ... [9]

The truth is that every 'ingredient' of the Holocaust – all those many things that rendered it possible – was normal; 'normal' not in the sense of the familiar, of one more specimen in a large class of phenomena long ago described in full, explained and accommodated (on the contrary, the experience of the Holocaust was new and unfamiliar), but in the sense of being fully in keeping with everything we know about our civilization, its guiding spirit, its priorities, its immanent vision of the world – and of the proper ways to pursue human happiness together with a perfect society. In the words of Stillman and Pfaff,

There is more than a wholly fortuitous connection between the applied technology of the mass production line, with its vision of universal material abundance, and the applied technology of the concentration camp, with its vision of a profusion of death. We may wish to deny the connection, but Buchenwald was of our West as much as Detroit's River Rouge – we cannot deny Buchenwald as a casual aberration of a Western world essentially sane.[10]

Let us also recall the conclusion Raul Hilberg has reached at the end of his unsurpassed, magisterial study of the Holocaust's accomplishment: 'The machinery of destruction, then, was structurally no different from organized German society as a whole. The machinery of destruction *was* the organized community in one of its special roles.'[11]

Richard L. Rubenstein has drawn what seems to me the ultimate lesson of the Holocaust. 'It bears,' he wrote, 'witness to the *advance of civilization*.' It was an advance, let us add, in a double sense. In the Final Solution, the industrial potential and technological know-how boasted by our civilization has scaled new heights in coping successfully with a task of unprecedented magnitude. And in the same Final Solution our society has disclosed to us it heretofore unsuspected capacity. Taught to respect and admire technical efficiency and good design, we cannot but admit that, in the praise of material progress which our civilization has brought, we have sorely underestimated its true potential.

The world of the death camps and the society it engenders reveals the progressively intensifying night side of Judeo-Christian civilization. Civilization means slavery, wars, exploitation, and death camps. It also means medical hygiene, elevated religious ideas, beautiful art, and exquisite music. It is an error to imagine that civilization and savage cruelty are antithesis ... In our times the cruelties, like most other aspects of our world, have become far more effectively administered than ever before. They have not and will not cease to exist. Both creation and destruction are inseparable aspects of what we call civilization.[12]

Hilberg is a historian, Rubenstein is a theologian. I have keenly searched the works of sociologists for statements expressing similar awareness of the urgency of the task posited by the Holocaust; for evidence that the Holocaust presents, among other things, a challenge to sociology as a profession and a body of academic knowledge. When measured against the work done by historians or theologians, the bulk of academic sociology looks more like a collective exercise in forgetting and eye-closing. By and large, the lessons of the Holocaust have left little trace on sociological common sense, which includes among many others such articles of faith as the benefits of reason's rule over the emotions, the superiority of rationality over (what else?) irrational action, or the endemic clash between the demands of efficiency and the moral leanings with which 'personal relations' are so hopelessly infused. However loud and poignant, voices of the protest against this faith have not yet penetrated the walls of the sociological establishment.

I do not know of many occasions on which sociologists, *qua* sociologists, confronted publicly the evidence of the Holocaust. One such occasion (though on a small scale) was offered by the symposium on *Western Society after the Holocaust*, convened in 1978 by the Institute for the Study of Contemporary Social Problems.[13] During the symposium, Richard L. Rubenstein presented an imaginative, though perhaps over-emotional attempt to re-read, in the light of the Holocaust experience, some of the best-known of Weber's diagnoses of the tendencies of modern society. Rubenstein wished to find out whether the things we know about, but of which Weber was naturally unaware, could have been anticipated (by Weber himself and his readers), at least as a possibility, from what Weber knew, perceived or theorized about. He thought he had found a positive answer to this question, or at least so he suggested: that in Weber's exposition of modern bureaucracy, rational spirit, principle of efficiency, scientific mentality, relegation of values to the realm of subjectivity etc. no mechanism was recorded that was capable of excluding the possibility of Nazi excesses; that, moreover, there was nothing in Weber's ideal types that would necessitate the description of the activities of the Nazi state as *excesses*. For example, 'no horror perpetrated by the German medical profession or German technocrats was inconsistent with the view that values are inherently subjective and that science is intrinsically instrumental and value-free'. Guenther Roth, the eminent Weberian scholar and a sociologist of high and deserved repute, did not try to hide his displeasure: 'My disagreement with Professor Rubenstein is total. There is just no sentence in his presentation that I can accept.' Probably incensed by the possible harm to Weber's memory (a harm lurking, as it were, in the very idea of 'anticipation'), Guenther Roth reminded the gathering that Weber was a liberal, loved the constitution and approved of the working class's voting rights (and thus, presumably, could not be recalled in conjunction with a thing so abominable as the Holocaust). He refrained, however, from confronting the substance of Rubenstein's suggestion. By the same token, he deprived himself of the possibility of seriously considering the 'unanticipated consquences' of the growing rule of reason which Weber identified as the central attribute of modernity and to which analysis he made a most seminal contribution. He did not use the occasion to face point-blank the 'other side' of the perceptive visions bequeathed by the classic of the sociological tradition; nor the opportunity to ponder whether our sad knowledge, unavailable to the classics, may enable us to find out in their insights things the full consequences of which they themselves could not be, except dimly, aware.

In all probability, Guenther Roth is not the only sociologist who would rally to the defence of the hallowed truths of our joint tradition at the expense of the adverse evidence; it is just that most other sociologists have not been forced to do so in such an outspoken way. By and large, we need not bother with the challenge of the Holocaust in our daily professional practice. As a profession, we have succeeded in all but forgetting it, or shelving it away into the 'specialist interests' area, from where it stands no chance of reaching the mainstream of the discipline. If at all discussed in sociological texts, the Holocaust is at best offered as a sad example of what an untamed innate human aggressiveness may do, and then used as a pretext to exhort the virtues of taming it through an increase in the civilizing pressure and another flurry of expert problem-solving. At worst, it is remembered as a private experience of the Jews, as a matter between the Jews and their haters (a 'privatization' to which many spokesmen of the State of Israel, guided by other than eschatological concerns, has contributed more than a minor share).[14]

This state of affairs is worrying not only, and not at all primarily, for the professional reasons – however detrimental it may be for the cognitive powers and societal relevance of sociology. What makes this situation much more disturbing is the awareness that if 'it could happen on such a massive scale elsewhere, then it can happen anywhere; it is all within the range of human possibility, and like it or not, Auschwitz expands the universe of consciousness no less than landing on the moon'.[15] The anxiety can hardly abate in view of the fact that none of the societal conditions that made Auschwitz possible has truly disappeared, and no effective measures have been undertaken to prevent such possibilities and principles from generating Auschwitz-like catastrophes; as Leo Kuper has recently found out, 'the sovereign territorial state claims, as an integral part of its sovereignty, the right to commit genocide, or engage in genocidal massacres, against people under its rule, and ... the UN, for all practical purposes, defends this right.'[16]

One posthumous service the Holocaust can render is to provide an insight into the otherwise unnoticed 'other aspects' of the societal principles enshrined by modern history. I propose that the experience of the Holocaust, now thoroughly researched by the historians, should be looked upon as, so to speak, a sociological 'laboratory'. The Holocaust has exposed and examined such attributes of our society as are not revealed, and hence are not empirically accessible, in 'non-laboratory' conditions. In other words, *I propose to treat the Holocaust as a rare, yet significant and reliable, test of the hidden possibilities of modern society.*

The meaning of the civilizing process

The etiological myth deeply entrenched in the self-consciousness of our Western society is the morally elevating story of humanity emerging from pre-social barbarity. This myth lent stimulus and popularity to, and in turn was given a learned and sophisticated support by, quite a few influential sociological theories and historical narratives; the link most recently illustrated by the burst of prominence and overnight success of the Elias's presentation of the 'civilizing process'. Contrary opinions of contemporary social theorists (see, for instance, the thorough analyses of multifarious civilizing processes: historical and comparative by Michael Mann, synthetic and theoretical by Anthony Giddens), which emphasize the growth of military violence and untrammelled use of coercion as the most crucial attributes of the emergence and entrenchment of great civilizations, have a long way to go before they succeed in displacing the etiological myth from public consciousness, or even from the diffuse folklore of the profession. By and large, lay opinion resents all challenge to the myth. Its resistance is backed, moreover, by a broad coalition of respectable learned opinions which contains such powerful authorities as the 'Whig view' of history as the victorious struggle between reason and superstition; Weber's vision of rationalization as a movement toward achieving more for less effort; psychoanalytical promise to debunk, prise off and tame the animal in man; Marx's grand prophecy of life and history coming under full control of the human species once it is freed from the presently debilitating parochialities; Elias's portrayal of recent history as that of eliminating violence from daily life; and, above all, the chorus of experts who assure us that human problems are matters of wrong policies, and that right policies mean elimination of problems.

Behind the alliance stands fast the modern 'gardening' state, viewing the society it rules as an object of designing, cultivating and weed-poisoning.

In view of this myth, long ago ossified into the common sense of our era, the Holocaust can only be understood as the failure of civilization (i.e. of human purposive, reason-guided activity) to contain the morbid natural predilections of whatever has been left of nature in man. Obviously, the Hobbesian world has not been fully chained, the Hobbesian problem has not been fully resolved. In other words, we do not have as yet enough civilization. The unfinished civilizing process is yet to be brought to its conclusion. If the lesson of mass murder does teach us anything it is that the prevention of similar hiccups of barbarism evidently requires still more civilizing efforts. There is nothing in this lesson to cast doubt on the future effectivenes of such efforts and their ultimate results. We certainly move in the right direction; perhaps we do not move fast enough.

As its full picture emerges from historical research, so does an alternative, and possible more credible, interpretation of the Holocaust as an event which disclosed the weakness and fragility of human nature (of the abhorrence of murder, disinclination to violence, fear of guilty conscience and of responsibility for immoral behaviour) when confronted with the matter-of-fact efficiency of the most cherished among the products of civilization; its technology, its rational criteria of choice, its tendency to subordinate thought and action to the pragmatics of economy and effectiveness. The Hobbesian world of the Holocaust did not surface from its too-shallow grave, resurrected by the tumult of irrational emotions. It arrived (in a formidable shape Hobbes would certainly disown) in a factory-produced vehicle, wielding weapons only the most advanced science could supply, and following an itinerary designed by scientifically managed organization. Modern civilization was not the Holocaust's *sufficient* condition; it was, however, most certainly its *necessary* condition. Without it, the Holocaust would be unthinkable. It was the rational world of modern civilization that made the Holocaust thinkable. 'The Nazi mass murder of the European Jewry was not only the technological achievement of an industrial society, but also the organizational achievement of a bureaucratic society.'[17] Just consider what was needed to make the Holocaust unique among the many mass murders which marked the historical advance of the human species.

The civil service infused the other hierarchies with its sure-footed planning and bureaucratic thoroughness. From the army the machinery of destruction acquired its military precision, discipline, and callousness. Industry's influence was felt in the great emphasis upon accounting, penny-saving, and salvage, as well as in factory-like efficiency of the killing centres. Finally, the party contributed to the entire apparatus an 'idealism', a sense of 'mission', and a notion of history-making ...

It was indeed the organized society in one of special roles. Though engaged in mass murder on a gigantic scale, this vast bureaucratic apparatus showed concern for correct bureaucratic procedure, for the niceties of precise definition, for the minutiae of bureaucratic regulation, and the compliance with the law.[18]

The department in the SS headquarters in charge of the destruction of European Jews was officially designated as the Section of Administration and Economy. This was only partly a lie; only in part can it be explained by reference to the notorious 'speech rules', designed to mislead both chance observers and the less resolute among the perpetrators. To a degree much too high for comfort, the designation faithfully reflected the organizational meaning of activity. Except for the moral repulsiveness of its goal (or, to be precise, the gigantic scale of the moral odium), the activity did not differ in any formal sense (the only sense that can be expressed in the language of bureaucracy) from all other organized activities designed, monitored and supervised by 'ordinary' administrative and economic sections. Like all other activities amenable to bureaucratic rationalization, it fits well the sober description of modern administration offered by Max Weber:

> Precision, speed, unambiguity, knowledge of the files, continuity, discretion, unity, strict subordination, reduction of friction and of material and personal costs – these are raised to the optimum point in the strictly bureaucratic administration ... Bureaucratization offers above all the optimum possibility for carrying through the principle of specializing administrative functions according to purely objective considerations ... The 'objective' discharge of business primarily means a discharge of business according to *calculable rules* and 'without regard for persons.'[19]

There is nothing in this description that warrants questioning the bureaucratic definition of the Holocaust as either a simply travesty of truth or a manifestation of a particularly monstrous form of cynicism. And yet the Holocaust is so crucial to our understanding of the modern bureaucratic mode of rationalization not only, and not primarily, because it reminds us (as if we need such a reminder) just how formal and ethically blind is the bureaucratic pursuit of efficiency. Its significance is not fully expressed either once we realize to what extent mass murder on an unprecedented scale depended on the availability of well-developed and firmly entrenched skills and habits of meticulous and precise division of labour, of maintaining a smooth flow of command and information, or of impersonal, well-synchronized co-ordination of autonomous yet complementary actions: on those skills and habits, in short, which best grow and thrive in the atmosphere of the office. The light shed by the Holocaust on our knowledge of bureaucratic rationality is at its most dazzling once we realize the extent to which *the very idea of the* Endlösung *was an outcome of the bureaucratic culture.*

We owe to Karl Schleuner[20] the concept of the twisted road to physical extermination of European Jewry: a road which was neither conceived in a single vision of a mad monster, nor was a considered choice made at the start of the 'problem-solving process' by the ideologically motivated leaders. It did, rather, emerge inch by inch, pointing at each stage to a different destination, shifting in response to ever-new crises, and pressed forward with a 'we will cross that bridge once we come to it' philosophy. Schleuner's concept summarizes best the findings of the 'functionalist' school in the historiography of the Holocaust (which in recent years rapidly gains strength at the expense of the 'intentionalists', who in turn find it increasingly difficult to defend the once dominant single-cause explanation of the Holocaust – that is, a vision that ascribes to the genocide a motivational logic and a consistency it never possessed).

According to the functionalists' findings, 'Hitler set the objective of Nazism: "to get rid of the Jews, and above all to make the territory of the Reich *judenfrei*, i.e., clear of Jews" – but without specifying how this was to be achieved.'[21] Once the objective had been set, everything went on exactly as Weber, with his usual clarity, spelled out: 'The "political master" finds himself in the position of the "dilettante" who stands opposite the "expert", facing the trained official who stands within the management of administration.'[22] The objective had to be implemented; how this was to be done depended on the circumstances, always judged by the 'experts' from the point of view of feasibility and the costs of alternative opportunities of action. And so the emigration of German Jews was chosen first as the practical solution to Hitler's objective; it would resulted in a *judenfrei* Germany, were other countries more hospitable to Jewish refugees. When Austria was annexed, Eichmann earned his first accolade for expediting and streamlining the mass emigration of Austrian Jewry. But then the territory under Nazi rule began to swell. At first the Nazi bureaucracy saw the conquest and appropriation of quasi-colonial territories as the dreamt-of opportunity to fulfil the *Führer's* command in full: *Generalgouvernment* seemed to provide the sought-after dumping ground for the Jewry still inhabiting lands of Germany proper, destined for racial purity. A separate reserve for the future 'Jewish principality' was designated around Nisko, in what was, before the conquest, central Poland. To this, however, German bureaucracy saddled with the management of the former Polish territories objected: it had already enough trouble with policing its own local Jewry. And so Eichmann spent a full year working on the Madagascar project: with France defeated, her far-away colony could be transformed into the Jewish principality that failed to materialize in Europe. The Madagascar project, however, proved to be similarly ill-fated, given the enormous distance, the volume of necessary ship-space, and the British navy presence on the high seas. In the meantime the size of the conquered territory, and so the number of Jews under German jurisdiction continued to grow. A Nazi-dominated Europe (rather than simply the 'reunited *Reich*') seemed a more and more tangible prospect. Gradually yet relentlessly, the thousand-year *Reich* took up, ever more distinctly, the shape of a German-ruled Europe. Under the circumstances, the goal of a *judenfrei* Germany could not but follow the process. Almost imperceptibly, step by step, it expanded into the objective of *judenfrei* Europe. Ambitions on such a scale could not be satisfied by a Madagascar, however accessible (though according to Eberhard Jäckel there is some evidence that still in July 1941, when Hitler expected the USSR to be defeated in a matter of weeks, the vast expanses of Russia beyond the Archangel–Astrakhan line were seen as the ultimate dumping ground for all Jews inhabiting Europe unified under German rule). With the downfall of Russia reluctant to materialize, and the alternative solutions unable to keep pace with the fast-growing problem, Himmler ordered on 1 October 1941 the final stop to all further Jewish emigration. The task of 'getting rid of the Jews' had been found another, more effective means of implementation: physical extermination was chosen as the most feasible and effective means to the original, and newly expanded, end. The rest was the matter of co-operation between various departments of state bureaucracy; of careful planning, designing proper technology and technical equipment, budgeting, calculating and mobilizing necessary resources: indeed, the matter of dull bureaucratic routine.

The most shattering of lessons deriving from the analysis of the 'twisted road to Auschwitz' is that – in the last resort – *the choice of physical extermination as the right means to the task of* Entfernung *was a product of routine bureaucratic procedures*: means–ends calculus, budget balancing, universal rule application. To make the point sharper still – the choice was an effect of the earnest effort to find rational solutions to successive 'problems', as they arose in the changing circumstances. It was also affected by the widely described bureaucratic tendency to goal-displacement – an affliction as normal in all bureaucracies as their routines. The very presence of functionaries charged with their specific tasks led to further initiatives and a continuous expansion of original purposes. Once again, expertise demonstrated its self-propelling capacity, its proclivity to expand and enrich the target which supplied its *raison d'être*.

> The mere existence of a corpus of Jewish experts created a certain bureaucratic momentum behind Nazi Jewish policy. Even when deportations and mass murder were already under way, decrees appeared in 1942 prohibiting German Jews from having pets, getting their hair cut by Aryan barbers, or receiving the Reich sport badge! It did not require orders from above, merely the existence of the job itself, to ensure that the Jewish experts kept up the flow of discriminating measures.[23]

At no point of its long and tortuous execution did the Holocaust come in conflict with the principles of rationality. The 'Final Solution' did not clash at any stage with the rational pursuit of efficient, optimal goal-implementation. On the contrary, *it arose out of a genuinely rational concern, and it was generated by bureaucracy true to its form and purpose.* We know of many massacres, pogroms, mass murders, indeed instances not far removed from genocide, that have been perpetrated without modern bureaucracy, the skills and technologies it commands, the scientific principles of its internal management. The Holocaust, however, was clearly unthinkable without such bureaucracy. The Holocaust was not an irrational outflow of the not-yet-fully-eradicated residues of pre-modern barbarity. It was a legitimate resident in the house of modernity; indeed, one who would not be at home in any other house.

This is not to suggest that the incidence of the Holocaust was *determined* by modern bureaucracy or the culture of instrumental rationality it epitomizes; much less still, that modern bureaucracy *must* result in Holocaust-style phenomena. I do suggest, however, that the rules of instrumental rationality are singularly incapable of preventing such phenomena; that there is nothing in those rules which disqualifies the Holocaust-style methods of 'social-engineering' as improper or, indeed, the actions they served as irrational. I suggest, further, that the bureaucratic culture which prompts us to view society as an object of administration, as a collection of so many 'problems' to be solved, as 'nature' to be 'controlled', 'mastered' and 'improved' or 'remade', as a legitimate target for 'social engineering', and in general a garden to be designed and kept in the planned shape by force (the gardening posture divides vegetation into 'cultured plants' to be taken care of, and weeds to be exterminated), was the very atmosphere in which the idea of the Holocaust could be conceived, slowly yet consistently developed, and brought to its conclusion. And I also suggest that it was the spirit of instrumental rationality, and its modern, bureaucratic form of institutionalization, which had made the Holocaust-style solutions not only possible, but eminently 'reasonable' – and increased the probability of their choice. This increase in probability is more than foruitously related to the ability of modern bureaucracy to co-ordinate the action of great number of moral individuals in the pursuit of any, also immoral, ends.

Social production of moral indifference

Dr Servatius, Eichmann's counsel in Jerusalem, pointedly summarized his line of defence: Eichmann committed acts for which one is decorated if one wins, and goes to the gallows if one loses. The obvious message of this statement – certainly one of the most poignant of the century not at all short of striking ideas – is trivial; might does make right. Yet there is also another message, not so evident, though no less cynical and much more alarming; Eichmann did nothing essentially different from things done by those on the side of the winners. Actions have no intrinsic moral value. Neither are they immanently immoral. Moral evaluation is something external to the action itself, decided by criteria other than those that guide and shape the action itself.

What is so alarming in the message of Dr Servatius is that – once detached from the circumstances under which it was uttered, and considered in depersonalized universal terms – it does not differ significantly from what sociology has been saying all along; or indeed, from the seldom-questioned, and still less frequently assailed, common sense of our modern, rational society. Dr Servatius's statement is shocking precisely for this reason. It brings home a truth that on the whole we prefer to leave unspoken: that as long as the commonsensical truth in question is accepted as evident, there is no sociologically legitimate way of excluding Eichmann's case from its application.

It is common knowledge by now that the initial attempts to interpret the Holocaust as an outrage committed by born criminals, sadists, madmen, social miscreants or otherwise morally defective individuals failed to find any confirmation in the facts of the case. Their refutation by historical research is today all but final. The present drift of historical thinking has been aptly summed up by Kren and Rappoport:

> By conventional clinical criteria no more than 10 per cent of the SS could be considered 'abnormal'. This observation fits the general trend of testimony by survivors indicating that in most of the camps, there was usually one, or at most a few, SS men known for their intense outbursts of sadistic cruelty. The others were not always decent persons, but their behaviour was at least considered comprehensible by the prisoners ...
>
> Our judgement is that the overwhelming majority of SS men, leaders as well as rank and file, would have easily passed all the psychiatric tests ordinarily given to American army recruits or Kansas City policemen.[24]

That most of the perpetrators of the genocide were normal people, who will freely flow through any known psychiatric sieve, however dense, is morally disturbing. It is also theoretically puzzling, particularly when seen conjointly with the 'normality' of those organizational structures that co-ordinated the actions of such normal individuals into an enterprise of the genocide. We know already that the institutions responsible for the Holocaust, even if found criminal, were in no legitimate sociological sense pathological or abnormal. Now we see that the people whose actions they institutionalized did not deviate either from established standards of normality. There is little choice left, therefore, but to look again, with eyes sharpened by our new knowledge, at the allegedly fully understood, normal patterns of modern rational action. It is in these patterns that we can hope to uncover the possibility so dramatically revealed in the times of the Holocaust.

In the famous phrase of Hannah Arendt, the most difficult problem that the initiators of the *Endlösung* encountered (and solved with astounding success, as it were) was 'how to overcome ... the animal pity by which all normal men are affected in the presence of physical suffering'.[25] We know that people enlisted into the organizations most directly involved in the business of mass murder were neither abnormally sadistic nor abnormally fanatical. We can assume that they shared in the well-nigh instinctual human aversion to the affliction of physical suffering, and even more universal inhibition against taking life. We know even that when, for instance, members of the *Einsatzgruppen* and other units similarly close to the scene of actual killings were enlisted, special care was taken to weed out – bar or discharge – all particularly keen, emotionally charged, ideologically over-zealous individuals. We know that individual initiatives were discouraged, and much effort was made to keep the whole task in a businesslike and strictly impersonal framework. Personal gains, and personal motives in general, were censured and penalized. Killings induced by desire or pleasure, unlike those following orders and perpetrated in an organized fashion, could lead (at least in principle) to trial and conviction, like ordinary murder or manslaughter. On more than one occasion Himmler expressed deep, and in all likelihood genuine, concern with maintaining the mental sanity and upholding the moral standards of his many subordinates engaged daily in inhuman activity; he also expressed pride that, in his belief, both sanity and morality emerged unscathed from the test. To quote Arendt again, 'by its "objectivity' (*Sachlichkeit*), the SS dissociated itself from such "emotional" types as Streicher, that "unrealistic fool" and also from certain "Teutonic-Germanic Party bigwigs who behaved as though they were clad in horns and pelts"'.[26] The SS leaders counted (rightly, it would appear) on organizational routine, not on individual zeal; on discipline, not ideological dedication. Loyalty to the gory task was to be – and was indeed – a derivative of loyalty to the organization.

The 'overcoming of animal pity' could not be sought and attained through release of other, base animal instincts; the latter would be in all probability dysfunctional regarding the organizational capacity to act; a multitude of vengeful and murderous individuals would not match the effectiveness of a small, yet disciplined and strictly co-ordinated bureaucracy. And then it was not at all clear whether the killing instincts can be relied on to surface in all those thousands of ordinary clerks and professionals, who, because of the sheer scale of the enterprise, must have been involved at various stages of the operation. In Hilberg's words,

The German perpetrator was not a special kind of German ... We know that the very nature of administrative planning, of the jurisdictional structure and of the budgetary system precluded the special selection and special training of personnel. Any member of the Order Police could be a guard at a ghetto or on a train. Every lawyer in the Reich Security Main Office was presumed to be suitable for leadership in the mobile killing units; every finance expert to the Economic-Administrative Main Office was considered a natural choice for service in a death camp. In other words, all necessary operations were accomplished with whatever personnel were at hand.[27]

And so, how were these ordinary Germans transformed into the German perpetrators of mass crime? In the opinion of Herbert C. Kelman,[28] moral inhibitions against violent atrocities tend to be eroded once three conditions are met, singly or together; the violence is *authorized* (by official orders coming from the legally entitled quarters), actions are *routinized* (by rule-governed practices and exact specification of roles), and the victims of the violence are *dehumanized* (by ideological definitions and indoctrinations). With the third condition we shall deal separately. The first two, however, sound remarkably familiar. They have been spelled out repeatedly in those principles of rational action that have been given universal application by the most representative institutions of modern society.

The first principle most obviously relevant to our query is that of organizational discipline; more precisely, the demand to obey commands of the superiors to the exclusion of all other stimuli for action, to put the devotion to the welfare of the organization, as defined in the commands of the superiors, above all other devotions and commitments. Among these other, 'external' influences, interfering with the spirit of dedication and hence marked for suppression and extinction, personal views and preferences are the most prominent. The ideal of discipline points towards total identification with the organization – which, in its turn, cannot but mean readiness to obliterate one's own separate identity and sacrifice one's own interests (by definition, such interests as do not overlap with the task of the organization). In organizational ideology, readiness for such an extreme kind of self-sacrifice is articulated as a moral virtue; indeed, as the moral virtue destined to put paid to all other moral demands. The selfless observance of that moral virtue is then represented, in Weber's famous words, as the honour of the civil servant; 'The honour of the civil servant is vested in his ability to execute conscientiously the order of superior authorities, exactly as if the order agreed with his own conviction. This holds even if the order seems wrong to him and if, despite the civil servant's remonstrances, the authority insists on the order'. This kind of behaviour means, for a civil servant, 'moral discipline and self-denial in the highest sense'.[29] Through honour, discipline is substituted for moral responsibility. The delegitimation of all but inner-organizational rules as the source and guarantee of propriety, and thus denial of the authority of private conscience, become now the highest moral virtue. The discomfort that the practising of such virtues may cause on occasion, is counterbalanced by the superior's insistence that he and he alone bears the responsibility for his subordinates' actions (as long, of course, as they conform to his command). Weber completed his description of the civil servant's honour by emphasizing strongly the 'exclusive personal responsibility' of the leader, 'a responsibility he cannot and must not reject or transfer'. When pressed to explain, during the Nuremberg trial, why he did not resign from the command of the *Einsatzgruppe* of whose actions he, as a person, disapproved, Ohlendorf invoked precisely this sense of responsibility: were he to expose the deeds of his unit in order to obtain release from duties he said he resented, he would have let his men be 'wrongly accused'. Obviously, Ohlendorf expected that the same paternalistic responsibility he observed towards 'his men' would be practised by his own superiors towards himself; this absolved him from worry about the moral evaluation of his actions – a worry he could safely leave to those who commanded him to act. 'I do not think I am in a position to judge whether his measures ... were moral or immoral ... I surrender my moral conscience to the fact I was a soldier, and therefore a cog in a relatively low position of a great machine.'[30]

If Midas's touch transformed everything into gold, SS administration transformed everything which had come into its orbit – including its victims – into an integral part of the chain of command, an area subject to the strictly disciplinary rules and freed from moral judgement. The genocide was a composite process; as Hilberg observed, it included things done by the Germans, and things done – on German orders, yet often with dedication verging on self-abandonment – by their Jewish victims. This is the technical superiority of a purposefully designed, rationally organized mass murder over riotous outbursts of orgy killing. Co-operation of the victims with the perpetrators of a pogrom is inconceivable. The victims' co-operation with the bureaucrats of the SS was part of the design: indeed, it was a crucial condition of its success. 'A large component of the entire process depended on Jewish participation – the simple acts of individuals as well as organized activity in councils ... German supervisors turned to Jewish councils for information, money, labour, or police, and the councils provided them with these means every day of the week.' This astonishing effect of successfully extending the rules of bureaucratic conduct, complete with the delegitimation of alternative loyalties and moral motives in general to encompass the intended victims of bureaucracy, and thereby deploying their skills and labour in the implementation of the task of their destruction, was achieved (much as in the mundane activity of every other, sinister or benign, bureacracy) in a twofold way. First, the external setting of the ghetto life was so designed that all actions of its leaders and inhabitants could not but remain objectively 'functional' to German purposes. 'Everything that was designed to maintain its [ghetto] viability was simultaneously promoting a German goal ... Jewish efficiency in allocating space or in distributing rations was an extension of German effectiveness. Jewish rigour in taxation or labour utilization was a reinforcement of German stringency, even Jewish incorruptibility could be a tool of German administration.' Second, particular care was taken that at every stage of the road the victims should be put in a situation of choice, to which criteria or rational action apply, and in which the rational decision invariably agrees with the 'managerial design'. 'The Germans were notably successful if deporting Jews by stages, because these that remained behind would reason that it was necessary to sacrifice the few in order to serve the many.'[31] As a matter of fact, even those already deported were left with the opportunity to deploy their rationality to the very end. The gas chambers, temptingly dubbed 'bathrooms', presented a welcome sight after days spent in overcrowded, filthy cattle trucks. Those who already knew the truth and entertained no illusions still had a choice between a 'quick and painless' death, and one preceded by extra sufferings reserved for the insubordinate. Hence not only the external articulations of the ghetto setting, on which the victims had no control, were manipulated so as to transform the ghetto as a whole into an extension of the murdering machine; also the rational faculties of the 'functionaries' of that extension were deployed for the elicitation of behaviour motivated by loyalty and co-operation with the bureaucratically defined ends.

Social production of moral invisibility

So far we have tried to reconstruct the social mechanism of 'overcoming the animal pity'; a social production of conduct contrary to innate moral inhibitions, capable of transforming individuals who are not 'moral degenerates' in any of the 'normal' senses, into murderers or conscious collaborators in the murdering process. The experience of the Holocaust brings into relief, however, another social mechanism; one with a much more sinister potential of involving in the perpetration of the genocide a much wider number of people who never in the process face consciously either difficult moral choices or the need to stifle inner resistance of conscience. The struggle over moral issues never takes place, as the moral aspects of actions are not immediately obvious or are deliberately prevented from discovery and discussion. In other words, the moral character of action is either invisible or purposefully concealed.

To quote Hilberg again, 'It must be kept in mind that most of the participants [of genocide] did not fire rifles at Jewish children or pour gas into gas chambers ... Most bureaucrats composed memoranda, drew up blueprints, talked on the telephone, and participated in conferences. They could destroy a whole people by sitting at their desk.'[32] Were they aware of the ultimate product of their ostensibly innocuous bustle – such knowledge would stay, at best, in the remote recesses of their minds. Causal connections between their actions and the mass murder were difficult to spot. Little moral opprobrium was attached to the natural human proclivity to avoid worrying more than necessity required – and thus to abstain from examining the whole length of the causal chain up to its furthest links. To understand how that astounding moral blindness was possible, it is helpful to think of the workers of an armament plant who rejoice in the 'stay of execution' of their factory thanks to big new orders, while at the same time honestly bewailing the massacres visited upon each other by Ethiopians and Eritreans; or to think how it is possible that the 'fall in commodity prices' may be universally welcomed as good news while 'starvation of African children' is equally universally, and sincerely, lamented.

A few years ago John Lachs singled out the *mediation of action* (the phenomenon of one's action being performed for one by someone else, by an intermediate person, who 'stands between me and my action, making it impossible for me to experience it directly') as one of the most salient and seminal features of modern society. There is a great distance between intentions and practical accomplishments, with the space between the two packed with a multitude of minute acts and inconsequential actors. The 'middle man' shields off the outcomes of action from the actors' sight.

> The result is that there are many acts no one consciously appropriates. For the person on whose behalf they are done, they exist only verbally or in the imagination; he will not claim them as his own since he never lived through them. The man who has actually done them, on the other hand, will always view them as someone else's and himself as but the blameless instrument of an alien will ...
>
> Without first hand acquaintance with his actions, even the best of humans moves in a moral vacuum: the abstract recognition of evil is neither a reliable guide nor an adequate motive ... [W]e shall not be surprised at the immense and largely unintentional cruelty of men of good will ...
>
> The remarkable thing is that we are not unable to recognize wrong acts or gross injustices when we see them. What amazes us is how they could have come about when each of us did none but harmless acts ... It is difficult to accept that often there is no person and no group that planned or caused it all. It is even more difficult to see how our own actions, through their remote effects, contributed to causing misery.[33]

The increase in the physical and/or psychic distance between the act and its consequences achieves more than the suspension of moral inhibition; it quashes the moral significance of the act and thereby pre-empts all conflict between personal standard of moral decency and immorality of the social consequences of the act. With most of the socially significant actions mediated by a long chain of complex causal and functional dependencies, moral dilemmas recede from sight, while the occasions for more scrutiny and conscious moral choice become increasingly rare.

A similar effect (on a still more impressive scale) is achieved by rendering the victims themselves psychologically invisible. This has been certainly one of the most decisive among the factors responsible for the escalation of human costs in modern warfare. As Philip Caputo observed, war ethos 'seems to be a matter of distance and technology. You could never go wrong if you killed people at long range with sophisticated weapons.'[34] With killing 'at a distance', the link between the carnage and totally innocent acts - like pulling a trigger, or switching on the electric current, or pressing a button on a computer keyboard – is likely to remain a purely theoretical notion (the tendency enormously helped by the mere discrepancy of scale between the result and its immediate cause – an incommensurability that easily defies comprehension grounded in commonsensical experience). It is therefore possible to be a pilot delivering the bomb to Hiroshima or to Dresden, to excel in the duties assigned at a guided missile base, to design ever more devastating specimens of nuclear warheads – and all this without detracting from one's moral integrity and coming anywhere near moral collapse (invisibility of victims was, arguably, an important factor also in Milgram's infamous experiments). With this effect of the invisibility of victims in mind, it is perhaps easier to understand the successive improvements in the technology of the Holocaust. At the *Einsatz-gruppen* stage, the rounded-up victims were brought in front of machine guns and killed at point-blank range. Though efforts were made to keep the weapons at the longest possible distance from the ditches into which the murdered were to fall, it was exceedingly difficult for the shooters to overlook the connection between shooting and killing. This is why the administrators of genocide found the method primitive and inefficient, as well as dangerous to the morale of the perpetrators. Other murder techniques were therefore sought – such as would optically separate the killers from their victims. The search was successful, and led to the invention of first the mobile, then the stationary gas chambers; the latter – the most perfect the Nazis had time to invent – reduced the role of the killer to that of the 'sanitation officer' asked to empty a sackful of 'disinfecting chemicals' through an aperture in the roof of a building the interior of which he was not prompted to visit.

The technical-administrative success of the Holocaust was due in part to the skilful utilization of 'moral sleeping pills' made available by modern bureaucracy and modern technology. The natural invisibility of causal connections in a complex system of interaction, and the 'distancing' of the unsightly or morally repelling outcomes of action to the point of rendering them invisible to the actor, were most prominent among them. Yet the Nazis particularly excelled in a third method, which they did not invent either, but perfected to an unprecedented degree. This was the method of making invisible the very humanity of the victims. Helen Fein's concept of the *universe of obligation* ('the circle of people with reciprocal obligations to protect each other whose bonds arise from their relation to a deity or sacred source of authority')[35] goes a long way towards illuminating the socio-psychological factors that stand behind the awesome effectiveness of this method. The 'universe of obligation' designates the outer limits of the social territory inside which moral questions may be asked at all with any sense. On the other side of the boundary, moral precepts do not bind, and moral evaluations are meaningless. To render the humanity of victims invisible, one needs merely to evict them from the universe of obligation.

Within the Nazi vision of the world, as measured by one superior and uncontested value of the rights of Germanhood, to exclude the Jews from the universe of obligation it was only necessary to deprive them of the membership in the German nation and state community. In another of Hilberg's poignant phrases, 'When in the early days of 1933 the first civil servant wrote the first definition of "non-Aryan" into a civil service ordinance, the fate of European Jewry was sealed.'[36] To induce the co-operation (or just inaction or indifference) of non-German Europeans, more was needed. Stripping the Jews of their Germanhood, sufficient for the German SS, was evidently not enough for nations which, even if they liked the ideas promoted by the new rulers of Europe, had reasons to fear and resent their claims to the monopoly of human virtue. Once the objective of *judenfrei* Germany turned into the goal of *judenfrei* Europe, the eviction of the Jews from the German nation had to be supplanted by their total dehumanization. Hence Frank's favourite conjunction of 'Jews and lice', the change in rhetoric expressed in the transplanting of the 'Jewish question' form the context of racial self-defence into the linguistic universe of 'self-cleansing' and 'political hygiene', the typhus-warning posters on the walls of the ghettos, and finally the commissioning of the chemicals for the last act from the Deutsche Gesellschaft für Schädlingsbekämpung – the German Fumigation Company.

Moral consequences of the civilizing process

Although other sociological images of the civilizing process are available, the most common (and widely shared) is one that entails, as its two centre points, the suppression of irrational and essentially antisocial drives, and the gradual yet relentless elimination of violence from social life (more precisely: concentration of violence under control of the state, where it is used to guard the perimeters of national community and conditions of social order). What blends the two centre points into one is the vision of the civilized society – at least in our own, Western and modern, form – as, first and foremost, a moral force; as a system of institutions that co-operate and complement each other in the imposition of a normative order and the rule of law, which in turn safeguard conditions of social peace and individual security poorly defended in pre-civilized settings.

This vision is not necessarily misleading. In the light of the Holocaust, however, it certainly looks one-sided. While it opens for scrutiny important trends of recent history, it forecloses the discussion of no less crucial tendencies. Focusing on one facet of the historical process, it draws an arbitrary dividing line between norm and abnormality. By de-legitimizing some of the resilient aspects of civilization, it falsely suggests their fortuitous and transitory nature, simultaneously concealing the striking resonance between most prominent of their attributes and the normative assumptions of modernity. In other words, it diverts attention from the permanence of the alternative, destructive potential of the civilizing process, and effectively silences and marginalizes the critics who insist on the double-sidedness of modern social arrangement.

I propose that the major lesson of the Holocaust is the necessity to treat the critique seriously and thus to expand the theoretical model of the civilizing process, so as to include the latter's tendency to demote, exprobate and delegitimize the ethical motivations of social action. We need to take stock of the evidence that *the civilizing process is, among other things, a process of divesting the use and deployment of violence from moral calculus, and of emancipating the desiderata of rationality from interference of ethical norms or moral inhibitions*. As the promotion of rationality to the exclusion of alternative criteria of action, and in particular the tendency to subordinate the use of violence to rational calculus, has been long ago acknowledged as a constitutive feature of modern civilization – the Holocaust-style phenomena must be recognized as legitimate outcomes of civilizing tendency, and its constant potential.

Read again, with the benefit of hindsight, Weber's elucidation of the conditions and the mechanism of rationalization reveals these important, yet thus far the underrated, connections. We see more clearly that the conditions of the rational conduct of business – like the notorious separation between the household and the enterprise, or between private income and the public purse – function at the same time as powerful factors in isolating the end-orientated, rational action from interchange with processes ruled by other (by definition, irrational) norms, and thus rendering it immune to the constraining impact of the postulates of mutual assistance, solidarity, reciprocal respect etc., which are sustained in the practices of non-business formations. This general accomplishment of rationalizing tendency has been codified and institutionalized, not unexpectedly, in modern bureaucracy. Subjected to the same retrospective re-reading, it reveals the silencing of morality as it major concern; as, indeed, the fundamental condition of its success as an instrument of rational coordination of action. And it also reveals its capacity of generating the Holocaust-like solution while pursuing, in impeccably rational fashion, its daily problem-solving activity.

Any rewriting of the theory of civilizing process along the suggested lines would involve by necessity a change in sociology itself. The nature and style of sociology has been attuned to the selfsame modern society it theorized and investigated; sociology has been engaged since its birth in a mimetic relationship with its object – or, rather, with the imagery of that object which it constructed and accepted as the frame for its own discourse. And so sociology promoted, as its own criteria of propriety, the same principles of rational action it visualized as constitutive of its object. It also promoted, as binding rules of own discourse, the inadmissibility of ethical problematics in any other form but that of a communally-sustained ideology and thus heterogenous to sociological (scientific, rational) discourse. *Phrases like 'the sanctity of human life' or 'moral duty' sound as alien in a sociology seminar as they do in the smoke-free, sanitized rooms of a bureaucratic office.*

In observing such principles in its professional practice, sociology did no more than partake in the scientific culture. As part and parcel of the rationalizing process, that culture cannot escape a second look. The self-imposed moral silence of science has, after all, revealed some of its less advertised aspects when the issue of production and disposal of corpses in Auschwitz has been articulated as a 'medical problem'. It is not easy to dismiss Franklin M. Littell's warnings of the credibility crisis of the modern university: 'What kind of a medical school trained Mengele and his associates? What departments of anthropology prepared the staff of Strasbourg University's "Institute of Ancestral Heredity"?'[37] Not to wonder for whom this particular bell tolls, to avoid the temptation to shrug off these questions as of merely historical significance, one needs search no further than Colin Gray's analysis of the momentum behind the contemporary nuclear arms race: 'Necessarily, the scientists and technologists on each side are "racing" to diminish their own ignorance (the enemy is not Soviet technology; it is the physical unknowns that attract scientific attention) ... Highly motivated, technologically competent and adequately funded teams of research scientists will inevitably produce an endless series of brand new (or refined) weapon ideas'.[38]

An early version of this chapter was published in *The British Journal of Sociology*, December 1988.

2

Modernity, Racism, Extermination I

There appear few causal links more transparent than that between antisemitism and the Holocaust. The Jews of Europe have been murdered because the Germans who did it, and their local helpers, were Jew-haters. The Holocaust was the spectacular climax of a centuries-long history of religious, economic, cultural and national resentment. This is the explanation of the Holocaust that first comes to mind. It 'stands to reason' (if one is allowed to indulge in paradoxes). And yet the apparent clarity of the causal link does not survive closer examination.

Thanks to the thorough historical research conducted over the last decades, we know now that before the Nazi ascent to power, and long after the entrenchment of their rule over Germany, German popular antisemitism came a poor second to Jew-hatred in quite a few other European countries. Long before the Weimar Republic put the finishing touches to the long process of Jewish emancipation, Germany was widely conceived by international Jewry as the haven of religious and national equality and tolerance. Germany entered this century with many more Jewish academics and professionals than contemporary America or Britain. Popular resentment of Jews was neither deep-seated nor widespread. Hardly ever did it manifest itself in outbursts of public violence, so common in other parts of Europe. Nazi attempts to bring popular antisemitism to the surface by staging public spectacles of anti-Jewish violence proved counterproductive and had to be foiled. One of the most prominent historians of the Holocaust, Henry L. Feingold, has concluded that had we had public opinion polls designed to measure intensity of antisemitic attitudes 'during Weimar, we probably would have discovered that the Germans' distaste for Jews was less than that of the French'.[1] Never during the process of destruction did popular antisemitism become an active force. At most it is suggested that it obliquely contributed to the perpetration of mass murder by inducing the apathy with which most Germans viewed the fate of the Jews when they knew of it, or resigned themselves to ignorance. In Norman Cohn's words, 'people were unwilling to bestir themselves on behalf of the Jews. The very widespread indifference, the ease with which people dissociated themselves from the Jews and their fate, was certainly in part a result of a vague feeling that ... Jews were somehow uncanny and dangerous'.[2] Richard L. Rubenstein goes a step or two further still and suggests that German apathy – the ordinary Germans' co-operation by default, so to speak – cannot be fully understood unless a question has been asked: 'Did the majority of the Germans regard the elimination of the Jews to be a benefit?'[3] There are other historians, however, who have convincingly explained the 'co-operation by non-resistance' by factors which do not necessarily include any beliefs as to the nature or essence of Jews. Thus, Walter Laqueur emphasizes the fact that [v]ery few people had an interest in the fate of the Jews. Most individuals faced a great many more important problems. It was an unpleasant topic, speculations were unprofitable, discussions of the fate of the Jews were discouraged. Consideration of this question was pushed aside, blotted out for the duration.'[4]

There is one more problem which the explanation of the Holocaust by antisemitism is ill-prepared to face. Antisemitism – religious or economic, cultural or racial, virulent or mild – has been for millenia an almost ecumenical phenomenon. And yet the Holocaust has been an event without precedents. In virtually every one of its many aspects it stands alone and bears no meaningful comparison with other massacres, however gory, visited upon groups previously defined as foreign, hostile or dangerous. Clearly, being perpetual and ubiquitous, antisemitism cannot by itself account for the Holocaust's uniqueness. To make the issue more complex still, it is far from obvious that the presence of antisemitism, admittedly a necessary condition of anti-Jewish violence, can be seen as its sufficient condition. In Norman Cohn's opinion, an organized group of 'professional Jew-killers' (itself a phenomenon not unconnected with antisemitism, yet in no way identical with it) is the very material and operative cause of violence; without it, resentment of the Jews, however strong, had hardly ever erupted into physical assaults against Jewish neighbours.

Pogroms as spontaneous outbreaks of popular fury seem to be a myth, and there is in fact no established case where the inhabitants of a town or village have simply fallen upon their Jewish neighbours and slaughtered them. This was true even in the Middle Ages ... In modern times popular initiative has been still less in evidence, for the organizing groups themselves have been effective only when they were carrying out the policy and enjoying the sponsorship of some kind of government.[5]

In other words, the case for the anti-Jewish violence in general, and particularly for the unique event of the Holocaust, being a 'culmination of anti-Jewish sentiments', 'antisemitism at its most intense', or the 'eruption of the popular resentment against Jews' is weak and poorly grounded in historical or contemporary evidence. Alone, antisemitism offers no explanation of the Holocaust (more generally, we would argue, *resentment is not in itself a satisfactory explanation of any genocide*). If it is true that antisemitism was functional, and perhaps indispensable, for the conception and implementation of the Holocaust, it is equally true that the antisemitism of the designers and the managers of mass murder must have differed in some important respects from the anti-Jewish sentiments, if any, of the executors, collaborators and complaisant witnesses. It is also true that to make the Holocaust possible, antisemitism of whatever kind had to be fused with certain factors of an entirely different character. Rather than look into the mysteries of individual psychology, we need to unravel social and political mechanisms capable of manufacturing such extra factors and examine their potentially explosive reaction with the traditions of inter-group antagonisms.

Some peculiarities of Jewish estrangement

Once the term 'antisemitism' had been coined and come into general use toward the end of the nineteenth century, it was acknowledged that the phenomenon that the newly forged term tried to capture had a long past, reaching deep into antiquity; virtually unbroken continuity was recognized in historical evidence of resentment and discrimination towards Jews extending over two millenia. Near-consensus of the historians tied the beginnings of antisemitism to the destruction of the Second Temple (70 *AD*) and the start of the massive diaspora, though much interesting research was done of, so to speak, proto-antisemitic opinions and practices reaching as far back as the Babylonian exile. (A provoking and controversial study of 'pagan' antisemitism was published in the early 1920s by a Soviet historian, Salomo Luria.)

Etymologically, 'antisemitism' is not a felicitous term, as it leaves its referent poorly (on the whole, too broadly) defined, and misses the true object of the practices it purports to set apart. (The Nazis, the most dedicated practitioners of antisemitism in known history, grew increasingly cool towards the term, particularly during the war, when the semantic clarity of the concept turned into a politically dangerous issue, as the term was ostensibly targeted also against some of the most devoted German allies.) In practical applications, however, semantic controversy has been by and large avoided, and the concept has been focused unerringly on its intended target. 'Antisemitism' stands for the resentment of Jews. It refers to the conception of the Jews as an alien, hostile and undesirable group, and to the practices that derive from, and support, such a conception.

From other cases of long-standing inter-group enmity, antisemitism differs in one important respect; social relations of which the ideas and practices of antisemitism can be an aspect are never relations between two territorially established groups that confront each other on an equal footing; they are, instead, relations between majority and minority, between a 'host' population and a smaller group that lives in its midst yet retains its separate identity, and for this reason – being the weaker partner – is the marked member of the opposition, the 'they' who are set apart from the native 'we'. The objects of antisemitism occupy as a rule the semantically confusing and psychologically unnerving status of foreigners inside, thereby striding a vital boundary which ought to be clearly drawn and kept intact and impregnable; and the intensity of antisemitism is most likely to remain proportional to the urgency and ferocity of the boundary-drawing and boundary-defining drive.[6] More often than not, antisemitism has been an outer manifestation of the boundary-keeping urge and the emotional tensions and practical concerns it prompted.

It is obvious that such unique features of antisemitism have been inextricably linked to the phenomenon of the diaspora. The Jewish diaspora, however, differs again from most other known instances of migrations and group resettlement. A most spectacular distinctive feature of the Jewish diaspora was the sheer length of historical time through which these particular 'foreigners in our midst' retained their separation, both in the sense of diachronic continuity and synchronic self-identity. Unlike in most other cases of resettlement, therefore, boundary-clearing responses to the Jewish presence had enough time to sediment and institutionalize as codified rituals with an in-built self-reproducing capacity, which in its turn further reinforced the resilience of the separation. Another peculiar feature of the Jewish diaspora was the universality of Jewish homelessness, a quality that the Jews shared perhaps only with the Gypsies. The original link of the Jews with the land of Israel grew increasingly tenuous over the centuries, losing all but the spiritual dimension. The latter, moreover, was contested by the host population once the land of Israel had become the Holy Land claimed by the hosts in the name of their own spiritual ancestry. However resentful of the Jewish presence in their own country, the hosts would resent even more hotly the repossession of the Holy Land by the people whom they saw as illegitimate pretenders.

The permanent and irremedial homelessness of the Jews was an integral part of their identity virtually from the beginning of their diasporic history. Indeed, this fact was used as a main argument in the Nazi case against the Jews, and was employed by Hitler to substantiate the claim that hostility against the Jews is of a radically different kind from ordinary antagonisms between rival nations or races.

(As Eberhard Jäckel[7] demonstrated, it was the perpetual and unbiquitous homelessness of the Jews that more than anything else set them apart in the eyes of Hitler from all other nations he hated and wished to enslave or destroy. Hitler believed[8] that having no territorial state, the Jews could not participate in the universal power-struggle in its ordinary form of a war aimed at land conquest, and thus had to reach instead for indecent, surreptitious and underhand methods which made them a particularly formidable and sinister enemy; an enemy, moreover, unlikely ever to be satiated or pacified, and hence bound to be destroyed in order to be rendered harmless.)

And yet in pre-modern Europe the peculiar flavour of Jewish *otherness* did not on the whole prevent their accommodation into the prevailing social order. The accommodation was possible because of the relatively low intensity of tension and conflict generated by the boundary-drawing and boundary-maintaining processes. But it was also made easier by the segmentary structure of pre-modern society and the normality of separation between the segments. In a society divided into estates or castes, the Jews were just one estate or one caste among many. The individual Jew was defined by the caste to which he belonged, and by the specific privileges and burdens the caste enjoyed or bore. But the same applied to every other member of the same society. The Jews were set apart, but the state of being set apart in no way made them unique. Their status, like the status of the rest of caste-like groupings, has been shaped and effectively perpetuated and defended by the general practices related to the maintenance of purity and prevention of pollution. However varied, these practices were united by a common function; that of creating a safe distance and making it, as far as possible, unbridgeable. The separation of groups was achieved by keeping them physically apart (reducing to a minimum all but strictly controlled and ritualized encounters), marking individual members of the group to make them visible as aliens, or inducing spiritual separation between the groups in order to preclude inter-group cultural osmosis and the levelling up of the cultural oppositions it could effect. For centuries the Jew was someone who lived in a separate quarter of the town and wore a strikingly distinct dress (occasionally prescribed by the law – particularly when the communal tradition failed to guard the uniformity of distinction). Separation of the domicile did not suffice, however, as in most cases the economies of the ghetto and of the host community were intertwined and thus necessitated regular physical contacts. Territorial distance had to be therefore supplemented by a thoroughly codified ritual aimed at formalizing and functionalizing such relations as could not be avoided. Relations that resisted formalization and functional reduction were by and large forbidden, or at least discouraged. As in the most caste-maintaining, pollution-fighting rituals, prohibitions of *connubium* and commensality (as well as all, except strictly functional, *commercium*) were among the most forcibly imposed and observed.

An important point to remember is that all such apparently antagonistic measures were at the same time vehicles of social integration. Between them, they defused the danger that a 'foreigner inside' cannot but present to the self-identity and self-production of the host group. They set up conditions under which cohabitation without friction was conceivable. They spelled out behavioural rules which, if closely observed, could guarantee peaceful coexistence in a potentially conflict-ridden and explosive situation. As Simmel explained, ritualistic institutionalization transformed the conflict into an instrument of sociation and social cohesion. As long as they are effective, practices of separation do not need the support of attitudinal hostility. Reduction of commerce to strictly ritualized exchanges required solely devotion to the rules and a trained revulsion against their transgression. It also required, certainly, the acceptance by the objects of the separation of a status inferior to that of the host community, and their consent to the hosts' entitlement to define, enforce or alter that status. Throughout most of Jewish diaspora history, however, law in general remained a network of privileges and dispossessions, while the idea of legal, and particularly social, equality was unheard of, or at any rate not considered as a practical proposition. Until the advent of modernity, estrangement of the Jews was little more than an instance of the universal separateness of the units of the preordained chain of being.

Jewish incongruity from Christendom to modernity

This does not mean, of course, that the separation of the Jews was not singled out from other instances of segregation and theorized upon as a special case with significance fully of its own. For the learned elites of pre-modern Europe – Christian clergy, theologians and philosophers – busy as all learned elites are with unearthing sense in randomness and logic in the spontanteity of life experience, Jews were an oddity; an entity that defied cognitive clarity and the moral harmony of the universe. They belonged neither with the not-yet-converted heathens, nor with the fallen-from-grace heretics, who marked the two zealously defended, and defensible, frontiers of Christendom. The Jews, so to speak, sat awkwardly astride the barricade, thereby compromising its impregnability. Simultaneously, they were venerable fathers of Christendom and its hateful, execrable detractors. Their rejection of Christian teachings could not be dismissed as a manifestation of pagan ignorance without serious harm to the truth of Christianity. Neither could it be written off as an – in principle – rectifiable error of a lost sheep. Jews were not simply pre- or post-conversion infidels, but people who in full consciousness refused to accept the truth when given the chance to admit it. Their presence constituted a permanent challenge to the certainty of Christian evidence. The challenge could be repelled, or at least rendered less dangerous, only by explaining Jewish obstinacy by a malice aforethought, ill intentions and moral corruption. Let us add a factor that will again and again figure in our argument as one of the most salient and seminal aspects of antisemitism: Jews were so to speak, co-extensive and co-terminal with Christianity. For this reason, they were unlike any other disturbing and unassimilated parts of the Christian world. Unlike any other heresy, they were neither a local trouble nor an episode with clearly defined beginning and hence, hopefully, with an end. Instead, they constituted an ubiquitous and constant concomitant of Christianity, a virtual *alter ego* of the Christian Church.

The coexistence of Christianity and the Jews was not, therefore, an instance of conflict and enmity. It was certainly that but more as well. Christianity could not reproduce itself, and certainly could not reproduce its ecumenical domination, without guarding and reinforcing the foundations of Jewish estrangement – the view of itself as the heir *and* the overcoming of Israel. The self-identity of Christianity was, in fact, estrangement of the Jews. It was born of the rejection *by the Jews*. It drew its continuous vitality from the rejection *of the Jews*. Christianity could theorize its own existence only as an on-going opposition to the Jews. Continuing Jewish stubbornness bore evidence that the Christian mission remained as yet unfinished. Jewish admission of error, surrender to Christian truth, and perhaps a future massive conversion, served as the model of Christianity's ultimate triumph. Again in a truly *alter ego* fashion, Christianity assigned to the Jews an eschatological mission. It magnified Jewish visibility and importance. *It endowed the Jews with a powerful and sinister fascination* they would otherwise hardly possess.

The presence of Jews in Christendom, in its lands and its history, was therefore neither marginal nor contingent. Their distinctiveness was not like that of any other minority group; it was an aspect of Christian self-identity. The Christian theory of the Jews stepped therefore beyond the generalization of the practices of exclusion; it was more than an attempt at systemization of that vague and diffuse experience of distinctiveness which emanates from, and informs, practices of caste-style separation. Rather than a reflection of grass roots, neighbourly exchanges or frictions, Christian theory of the Jews was subject to a different logic – that of the self-reproduction of the Church and its ecumenical domination. Hence the relative autonomy of the 'Jewish question' regarding the popular social, economic and cultural experience. Hence also the relative facility with which this question could be set apart from the context of daily life and made immune against the test of daily experience. To their Christian hosts, Jews were simultaneously concrete objects of daily intercourse and exemplars of a category defined independently of such intercourse. The latter characteristic of the Jews was neither indispensable nor inevitable from the point of view of the first. It was precisely for this reason that it could be relatively easily separated from the first and deployed as a resource in actions only loosely, if at all, related to the practices of quotidianity. In the Church theory of the Jews, antisemitism acquired a form in which it 'can exist almost regardless of the real situation of Jews in society ... Most striking of all, it can be found among people who have never set eyes on a Jew and in countries where there have been no Jews for centuries.'[9] This form proved able to persist long after the spiritual dominion of the Church waned, and its grip on the popular world-view faded. *The age of modernity inherited 'the Jew' already firmly separated from the Jewish men and women who inhabited its towns and villages.* Having successfully played the role of the *alter ego* of the Church, it was prepared to be cast in a similar role in relation to the new, secular, agencies of social integration.

The most spectacular, and pregnant, aspect of the concept of 'the Jew' as constructed by the practices of the Christian Church was its inherent illogicality. The concept brought together elements that neither belonged nor could be reconciled with one another. The sheer incoherence of their conflation marked the mythical entity deemed to reconcile them as a demonic, potent force; a force simultaneously intensely fascinating and repulsive, and above all frightening. The conceptual Jew was the battle ground on which the never-ending struggle for the self-identity of the Church, for the clarity of its temporal and spatial boundaries, was fought. The conceptual Jew was a semantically overloaded entity, comprising and blending meanings which ought to be kept apart, and for this reason a natural adversary of any force concerned with drawing borderlines and keeping them watertight. The conceptual Jew was *visqueux* (in Sartrean terms), slimy (in Mary Douglas's terms) – an image construed as compromising and defying the order of things, as the very epitome and embodiment of such defiance (of the mutual relation between the universal cultural activity of boundary-drawing, and the equally universal production of sliminess, I wrote extensively in the third chapter of *Culture as Praxis*). Construed in such a way, the conceptual Jew performed a function of prime importance; he visualized the horrifying consequences of boundary-transgression, of not remaining fully in the fold, of any conduct short of unconditional loyalty and unambiguous choice; he was the prototype and arch-pattern of all nonconformity, heterodoxy, anomaly and abberation. As an evidence of the mind-boggling, uncanny unreason of deviation, the conceptual Jew discredited in advance the alternative to that order of things which had been defined, narrated and practised by the Church. For this reason, he was a most reliable frontier-guard of that order. *The conceptual Jew carried a message; alternative to this order here and now is not another order, but chaos and devastation.*

I believe that the production of Jewish incongruity as a by-product of the self-constitution and self-reproduction of the Christian Church has been a major cause of the prominence of the Jews among those of *Europe's Inner Demons* that Norman Cohn so vividly described in his memorable study of European witch-hunt. Most remarkable among Cohn's findings (and one that has found ample confirmation in numerous other studies of the problem) is the apparent lack of correlation between the intensity of witch scare and irrational fears in general, and the advances of scientific knowledge and general level of daily rationality. As a matter of fact, the explosion of modern scientific method and the powerful strides towards the rationalization of daily life in the early years of modern history coincided with the most fierce and vicious episode of witch-hunting in history. It appears that the irrationality of witchcraft myths and witch persecution was very loosely related to the retardation of Reason. It was, on the other hand, most intimately related to the intensity of anxieties and tensions provoked or generated by the collapse of the *ancien régime* and the advent of the modern order. The old securities disappeared, while the new ones were slow to emerge and unlikely to attain the solidity of the old. Age-long distinctions were ignored, safe distances shrank, strangers emerged from their reserves and moved next door, secure identities lost durability and conviction. Whatever remained of old boundaries needed desperate defence, and new boundaries had to be built around new identities – this time, moreover, under conditions of universal movement and accelerating change. Fighting the 'slime', the archetypal enemy of clarity and security of borderlines and identities, had to be a major instrument in the implementation of both tasks. It was bound to reach an unprecedented ferocity, as the tasks themselves were of an unprecedented magnitude.

It is the assertion of this study that the active or passive, direct or oblique involvement in the intense concerns of the modern era with boundary-drawing and boundary-maintenance was to remain the most distinctive and defining feature of the conceptual Jew. I propose that the conceptual Jew has been historically construed as the universal 'viscosity' of the Western world. He has been located astride virtually every barricade erected by the successive conflicts that tore apart the Western society at its various stages and in various dimensions. The very fact that the conceptual Jew straddled so many different barricades, built on so many, ostensibly unrelated, front lines, endowed his sliminess with the elsewhere unknown, exorbitant intensity. His was a multi-dimensional unclarity and *the very multi-dimensionality was an extra cognitive incongruence* unencountered in all other (simple, because confined, isolated and functionally specialized) 'viscous' categories spawned by boundary conflicts.

Astride the barricades

For the reasons discussed above, the phenomenon of antisemitism cannot be really conceived as a case of a wider category of national, religious or cultural antagonisms. Neither was antisemitism a case of conflicting economic interests (though the latter has been frequently deployed in arguments supporting the antisemitic case in our modern competitive era, which thinks of itself in terms of interest groups locked in a zero-sum game) – it was sustained entirely by the self-definitional and self-assertive interests of its carriers. It was a case of boundary-drawing, not of boundary-contest. Because of all that, it defies the explanation in terms of a local and coincidental cluster of factors. Its incredible capacity of servicing so many different and mutually unrelated concerns and pursuits is rooted precisely in its unique universality, ex-temporality and ex-territoriality. *It fits so well so many local issues because it is not causally connected with any.* Adaptation of the conceptual Jew to the circumstances of dissimilar, often mutually contradictory, but always hotly contentious issues, has been continuously exacerbating its innate incoherence. This has rendered it, however, ever more suitable and convincing as an explanation, adding, as it were, to its demonic potency. Of no other social category of the Western world could it be said what Leo Pinsker wrote of the Jews in 1882: 'For the living, the Jew is a dead man; for the natives an alien and a vagrant; for the poor and exploited a millionaire; for patriots a man without country.'[7] Or what was said again, in an updated yet virtually unchanged form, in 1946: 'The Jew could be represented as the embodiment of everything to be resented, feared, or despised. He was a carrier of bolshevism but, curiously enough, he simultaneously stood for the liberal spirit of rotten Western democracy. Economically, he was both capitalist and socialist. He was blamed as the indolent pacificist but, by strange coincidence, he was also the eternal instigator to wars.'[11] Or even what W. D. Rubinstein has recently written in reference to just one of the innumerable dimensions of Jewish sliminess: the combination of anti-semitism aimed at the Jewish masses 'with these variants of antisemitism aimed at the Jewish elite may have lent to European anti-semitism its peculiar virulence: while other groups have been resented as either elites or as masses, perhaps only the Jews were resented as both simultaneously.'[12]

The prismatic group

Anna Żuk, of Lublin University, has recently suggested that Jews can be considered a 'mobile class', 'since they are the subject of emotions usually directed by the more highly-placed social groups to the lower classes, and, conversely, by the lower strata to groups of higher social ranking'.[13] Żuk examines in much detail this clash of cognitive perspectives in eighteenth-century Poland, which she treats as an example for a more general sociological phenomenon of great importance for the explanation of antisemitism. In the last century before the partitions, Polish Jews were by and large servants of nobility and gentry. They performed all sorts of highly unpopular public functions that the political and economic domination of landed nobility required, like rent-collecting and administering the disposition of the peasant produce – serving as 'middle man' and in socio-psychological terms as a shield, for the real lords of the land. The Jews fitted the role better than any other category, as they themselves did not (could not) aspire to the social advancement that their important role could offer. Unable to compete socially and politically with their masters, they settled instead for purely financial rewards. Hence not only were they socially and politically inferior to their masters, but were bound to remain so. The lords could, and did, treat them as they treated all other servants tied to the lower classes; with social contempt and cultural distaste. The image of the Jews upheld by nobility did not differ from the general stereotype of social inferiors. Like peasants and petty urban folk, Jews were seen by the gentry as uncivilized, dirty, ignorant and greedy. Like other commoners, they were kept at a distance. As, in view of their economic roles, some contact could not be avoided, the rules of their social separation were observed all the more meticulously and articulated more explicitly and with greater precision, and on the whole were paid more attention than such other class relations as occasioned no ambiguity and thus could be perpetuated unproblematically.

To peasants and the urban folk, however, Jews presented an entirely different image. The service they rendered to the rulers of the land and the exploiters of primary producers was, after all, not just economic, but protective; they insulated the nobility and gentry from popular wrath and fury. Instead of reaching its real target, the discontent stopped and discharged itself at the middlemen. For the lower classes, the Jews were the enemy; they were the only exploiters those classes met in person. It was only Jewish ruthlessness of which they had first-hand experience. For all they knew, Jews were the ruling classes. No wonder that 'Jews who occupied an equally low and underprivileged position in society as those who attacked them became the object of aggression directed against the upper classes'. Jews were cast in a 'mediating position as a highly visible link which became the focus for the aggression of the lower and oppressed classes'.

On both sides, it seems, the Jews were entangled in class struggle, a phenomenon in no way related to the specificity of Jews and by itself insufficient to account for the distinctive features of Judeophobia. What made the Jewish placement in the class war truly special was that *they had become objects of two mutually opposed and contradictory class antagonisms*. Each of the adversaries locked in the mutual class battle perceived of the Jewish mediators as sitting on the opposite side of the barricade. The metaphor of the prism, and hence the concept of a *prismatic category*, seems to convey this situation better than that of the 'mobile class'. Depending on the side from which the Jews were looked at, they – like all prisms – unwittingly refracted altogether different sights; one of crude, unrefined and brutal lower classes, another of ruthless and haughty social superiors.

Żuk's investigation has been confined to a period that stops at the threshold of Polish modernization. The full consequences of the duality of vision which she has so brilliantly captured are not, therefore, revealed. There was little communication between the ranks in pre-modern times. There was hence little opportunity for the two perspectives, and the two stereotypes they generated, to converge and eventually to merge into the incongruous mixture typical of modern antisemitism. Due to the paucity of inter-class exchange, each of the antagonists waged, so to speak, its own 'private war' against the Jews, which – particularly in the case of the lower classes – could be wedded by the Church to ideological elaborations only tenuously related to the true causes of the conflict. (Not only during the massacre instigated by Peter the Hermit in the townships of the Rhineland, local princes, counts and bishops attempted to defend 'their Jews' against charges blatantly irrelevant to such grievances as Jews were meant to attract upon themselves and defuse.)

It was only with the advent of modernity that the various, logically inconsistent sightings of the conspicuously alien (i.e. already estranged by systematic segregating practices) Jewish 'caste' had been brought together, confronted and eventually blended. Modernity meant, among other things, a new role for ideas – because of the state relying for its functional efficiency on ideological mobilization, because of its pronounced tendency to uniformity (manifested most spectacularly in the practices of cultural crusades), because of its 'civilizing' mission and sharp proselytizing edge,[14] and because of the attempt to bring previously peripheral classes and localities into an intimate spiritual contact with the idea-generating centre of the body politic. The overall result of all these new developments was a sharp increase in the scope and intensity of inter-class communication; in addition to its traditional facets, class domination took the form of spiritual guidance, as well as of the supply and dissemination of cultural ideals and formulae for political allegiance. An encounter and confrontation between previously separated images of the Jew was one of the consequences. Their previously unnoted incompatability had now become a problem and a challenge. Like everything else in the rapidly modernizing society, the problem had to be 'rationalized'. The contradiction had to be resolved; either by total rejection of inherited imagery, as hopelessly incongruent, or by rational argument providing new and acceptable grounds for the same incongruence.

Indeed, both strategies were tried in early modern Europe. On the one hand, the blatant irrationality of the status of the Jews was represented as another example of the general absurdity of the feudal order and one of the superstitions that barred the advance of reason. As for the salient distinctiveness and idiosyncracy of the Jews, it was seen as being in no way different from innumerable particularisms that the *ancien régime* tolerated and the new order was set to explode. Like many other local eccentricities, this one was understood as mainly a cultural problem – that is, a feature which diligent educational effort was able and bound to eradicate. There was no shortage of prophecies that once the newly fashioned legal equality was extended to the Jews, their distinctiveness would fast evaporate, and the Jews – that is, Jews as so many free individuals and bearers of citizen rights – would soon dissolve in the now culturally and legally uniform society.

On the other hand, however, the rise of modernity was accompanied by processes pointing in an exactly opposite direction. It seemed as if the already entrenched incongruity, having marked its carrier as a 'viscous', semantically disturbing and subversive factor in the otherwise transparent and orderly reality, tended to accommodate to new conditions and to expand itself through attacking new incongruities; it acquired new, modern dimensions, and the lack of mutual connection between them turned into an incongruity in its own right, a meta-incongruity of sorts. The Jews, already construed as 'slimy' in religious and class dimensions, were more than any other category vulnerable to the impact of new tensions and contradictions which the social upheavals of the modernizing revolution could not fail to generate. For most members of society, the advent of modernity meant the destruction of order and security; and once again, the Jews were perceived as standing close to the centre of the destructive process. Their own rapid and incomprehensible social advancement and transformation seemed to epitomize the havoc visited by advancing modernity upon everything familiar, habitual and secure.

For centuries, Jews were safely isolated in partly enforced, partly freely chosen enclosures; now they emerged from their seclusion, bought property and rented houses in once uniformly Christian districts, became part of daily reality and partners of diffuse discourse unconfined to ritualized exchanges. For centuries the Jews were distinguishable on sight: they wore their segregation, so to speak, on their sleeves, symbolically and literally. Now they dressed like all the others, according to social station rather than caste membership. For centuries Jews were a pariah caste, legitimately looked down upon by even the lowliest of the low among the Christians. Now some of the pariah moved into positions of social influence and prestige – through intellectual skills or through money, now accorded full status-determining force and ostensibly unconstrained and unqualified by considerations of rank and pedigree. Truly, *the fate of the Jews epitomized the awesome scope of social upheaval and served as a vivid, obtrusive reminder of the erosion of old certainties*, of melting and evaporating of everything once deemed solid and lasting. Whoever felt thrown out of balance, threatened or displaced, could easily – and rationally – make sense of his own anxiety through articulating the experienced turbulence as an imprint of Jewish subversive incongruity.

And so the Jews were caught in the most ferocious of historical conflicts: that between the pre-modern world and advancing modernity. The conflict found its first expression in the overt resistance of the classes and strata of the *ancien régime* about to be uprooted, disinherited and ploughed out of their secure social locations by the new social order which they could not but perceive as a chaos. With the initial anti-modernist rebellion defeated and the triumph of modernity no longer in doubt, the conflict would move underground, and in its new latent state would signal its presence in the acute fear of the void, the never-satiated lust for certainty, paranoic mythologies of conspiracy and the frantic search for ever-elusive identity. Eventually, modernity would supply its enemy with sophisticated weapons only his defeat made possible. *The irony of history would allow the anti-modernist phobias to be unloaded through channels and forms only modernity could develop.* Europe's inner demons were to be exorcised with the sophisticated products of technology, scientific management and the concentrated power of the state – all modernity's supreme achievements.

Jewish incongruity was made to measure this historical act of exquisite incongruence. The Jews remained visible embodiments of inner demons when the exorcisms were officially disallowed and forced underground. Through most of modern history the Jews were the principal carriers of tensions and anxieties modernity declared out of existence, brought to an unprecedented intensity and supplied with formidable tools of expression.

Modern dimensions of incongruity

Rich yet contemptible, the Jews provided a natural lightning-rod to divert early discharges of the anti-modernist energy. They provided the point where formidable powers of money met with social disdain, moral condemnation and aesthetic disgust. This was exactly what hostility to modernity, and particularly to its capitalist form, needed for an anchor. If only capitalism could be connected to the Jew, it would stand condemned as simultaneously alien, unnatural, inimical, dangerous and ethically repulsive. The connection was easy to establish: money power was confined to the margins and (under the contemptuous name of *usury*) writhed under the burden of authoritative condemnation as long as the Jews stayed enclosed in the ghetto: it moved to the centre of life and (under the prestigious name of *capital*) claimed authority and social respect once the Jews appeared on the streets of the city centre.

The first impact of modernity on the situation of European Jews was their selection as *the prime target of anti-modernist resistance*. The first modern antisemites were spokesmen for anti-modernity, people like Fourier, Proudhon, Toussenel – united in their implacable hostility to the power of money, capitalism, technology and the industrial system. The most virulent antisemitism of early industrial society was associated with anti-capitalism in its pre-capitalist version; such opposition to the advancing capitalist order as could still hope to stem the tide, to arrest the development, to restore the real or imaginary 'natural' order which the new money barons were set to dismantle. For reasons briefly sketched above, money power and the Jews were conflated. A causal link between the two was suggested, and for all practical purposes corroborated, by the metaphorical correspondence between them – their, so to speak, 'spiritual kinship', or, to use Weber's favourite term, *elective affinity*. That capitalism which had cast its sinister shadow over the craftsman's work ethic and cherished independence was so much easier to resist if identified with the admittedly alien and disreputable force. For Fourier and Toussenel, the Jew stood for everything they hated in the advancing capitalism and sprawling urban metropolis. The venom spattered over the Jew was meant to spill over the new, frightening and repelling order of society. According to Proudhon, the Jew 'is by temperament an anti-producer, neither a farmer, nor even a true merchant'.[15]

By definition, the anti-modernist version of antisemitism could retain its appearance of rationality, and its popular appeal, as long as the hope to arrest the advance of the new order and to replace it with a petty-bourgeois utopia masquerading as the lost paradise, seemed feasible and realistic. Indeed, that form of antisemitism all but petered out towards the middle of the nineteenth century when the last massive attempt to change the tracks of history failed, and victory of the new order had to be, however grudgingly, accepted as definite and irreversible. The link between money power and the Jewish temperament or spirit, established in the early, anti-modern and petty-bourgeois, form of anti-capitalist opposition, was destined to be absorbed and inventively refashioned by its later forms. Sometimes concealed, occasionally bursting into prominence, it was never far removed from the mainstream of anti-capitalist resistance. It played a prominent role in the history of European socialism.

It was indeed Karl Marx, the father of scientific socialism (i.e., socialism that set itself an aim of overcoming and leaving behind, rather than arresting the capitalist development; which acknowledged the irrevocability of capitalist transformation and accepted its progressive nature; and which promised to start building a new, better society at the point to which capitalist progress brought universal human progress), who turned the anti-capitalist antisemitism from backward-looking into forward-looking. Having done so, he made it potentially usable for the anti-capitalist opposition at a time when the last illusion that capitalism was a temporary disease which could be cured or exorcised would have been dashed and rejected. Marx accepted the elective affinity between the 'spirit of Judaism' and that of capitalism; both were prominent for promoting self-interest, haggling, the money-chase. Both had to be pushed out of the way if human cohabitation was to be placed on a safer and saner basis. Capitalism and Judaism shared their fate. They triumphed together, and they will perish together. One cannot survive the other; each has to be destroyed for the other to disappear. Emancipation from capitalism will mean emancipation from Judaism, and vice versa.

The tendency to conflate Judaism with money and power and, indeed, with the ills of the capitalism one resented and condemned, was to remain endemic in the socialist movements of Europe, often hiding just below the surface. Antisemitic sallies were frequent in the largest social democracies of the continent – the German and the Austro-Hungarian. In 1874 the leader of German social democracy, August Bebel, lavished praise on the virulently antisemitic teachings of Karl Eugen Dührer – an act that prompted Engels to produce two years later a book-sized response to the self-appointed prophet of German socialism; he did this not to defend the Jews, however, but to save the position of Marx as the ideological authority of the growing labour movement. Yet, on a number of occasions, efforts to hold the anti-Jewish sentiments in their intended role – that of an inescapable yet minor concomitant of the anti-capitalist stance – did not help, and the priorities were reversed: capitalism was degraded to a derivative of the Jewish threat. Thus most of the followers of August Blanqui, indomitable French martyr of the anti-capitalist war, had been led by his most intimate friend, Ernest Granger, straight from the barricades of the Paris Commune to the ranks of the budding national-socialist movement. It was not until the emergence of the Nazi movement that popular opposition to capitalism finally split and polarized, and the socialist branch adopted the uncompromising struggle against antisemitism as one of the necessary elements in its attempt to stem the rising tide of fascism.

If in the West the most stubborn resistance to the new industrial order came mostly from the ranks of urban and rural smallholders, in the East a broad anti-capitalist, anti-urban and anti-liberal front was a standard response. With social influence and political domination of landed aristocracy still virtually intact, urban occupations were kept at the lowest end of the prestige scale and treated with a mixture of disgust and contempt. All means of enrichment except by marriage or farming were seen as unworthy of true nobility; even farming, alongside the rest of economic activities, was traditionally left to hired servants or leased to persons of admittedly inferior status and personal quality. With native elites indifferent or hostile to the challenge of modernization, the Jews – accepted as culturally alien – were one of the few categories free from the deadly grip of genteel values, and hence able and willing to pick up the opportunities opened by industrial, financial and technological revolutions in the West. Their initiative, however, was met by nobility-dominated opinion with unqualified hostility. From his thorough study of nineteenth-century industrialization in Poland (a process not untypical for the rest of European East), Joseph Marcus concluded that the arrival of industry was treated by the native, nobility-dominated elites, as national calamity.

> While Jewish entrepreneurs were constructing the railroads, a leading Polish economist, J. Supiński, was complaining that 'the railways are an abyss in which enormous resources are being sunk, not leaving other traces than the raised dyke and the rail lying on it'. When Jews built industrial plants, landowners accused them of destroying agriculture, which allegedly was short of labour. When the factories began working, their owners were not only hated by the Polish literary and social elite, but also pitied, for having left the life of country delights and bohemian liberty and pleasure for the dreary surroundings of a factory, which enslaves man and destroys him.
>
> It should be clear that a society that largely shared such attitudes, which held material welfare unimportant and money-making contemptuous, could not produce the entrepreneurial qualities that are required in an era of capitalist industrialization. It is also not surprising that the sole promoters of industrial progress in Poland were the indigenous Jews and foreign settlers.
>
> The Jewish bourgeoisie also became the main propagators of western ideas of liberalism. Aristocratic and Catholic-conservative Polish opinion regarded this, and 'western materialism' in general, as a threat to the Polish tradition and 'national spirit'.[16]

The indigenous Jews who in the eyes of the dumbfounded nobility were turning into the Jewish bourgeoisie, threatened the established elites in more than one way. They exemplified the competition of a new, financially- and industrially-based, social power – against the traditional power grounded in land ownership and hereditary landed patronage. They also epitomized the dissembling of the once close co-ordination between the scale of prestige and that of influence; a servant group, held in the lowest of esteems, reached for positions of power while climbing a ladder it picked from the junk-heap of discarded values. To the nobility eager to retain national leadership, industrialization presented a double threat; because of what was being done, and because of who was doing it. The economic initiative of the Jews conflated the danger to the established social domination with a blow to the total social order which that domination sustained and was sustained by. It was easy, therefore, to conflate the Jews themselves with the new turmoil and instability. Jews were perceived as a sinister and destructive force, as agents of chaos and disorder; typically, as that glutinous substance which blurs the boundary between things which ought to be kept apart, which renders all hierarchical ladders slippery, melts all solids and profanes everything sacred.

Indeed, as the Jewish assimilatory drive approached the absorptive limits of their host societies, Jewish educational elites leaned more heavily toward social criticism, and were seen by many a native conservative as an inherently destabilizing force. In David Biale's perceptive summary, as the twentieth century approached, 'Jewish liberals, nationalists, and revolutionaries, who differed on anything else, all agreed that the societies of Europe in their contemporay form were inhospitable to Jews. Only by changing society in some way or by changing the Jews' relationship to it could the problems of the Jews in Europe be solved ... "Normality" now signified social experiments, utopian ideals that had never existed.'[17]

Attachment to the liberal heritage of Enlightenment supplied an additional dimension to Jewish 'viscosity'. Like no other group, the Jews had vested interests in the citizenship that liberalism promoted. In Hannah Arendt's memorable phrase, 'In contrast to all other groups, the Jews were defined and their position determined by the body politic. Since, however, this body politic had no other social reality, they were, socially speaking, in the void.'[18] This remained true of Jews throughout the pre-modern history of Europe. Jews were *Königjuden*, property and wards of the King, of the Prince, or the local warlord, depending on the stage or variety of the feudal order. Their status was politically born and politically sustained. By the same token, they were collectively exempt from social entanglements; they remained outside the social structure, which in practical terms meant the irrelevance or near-irrelevance of class affinities or conflicts in defining their existence. As an extension of the state in the midst of society, the Jews were inherently exterritorial in the social sense. Because of that, they could not but serve, for both sides, as a buffer in the often tense and conflict-ridden intercourse between society and its political masters, always bearing the first and the hardest blows once the conflicts approached boiling point. Whatever protection they could count on came from the state, yet it was precisely this fact that made them and kept them so implacably dependent on the benevolence of political rulers, and so impotent when faced with royal malice or greed. The incongruence of their location – in the void between state and society – was duly reflected in equally incongruent reaction to social and political dislocations that marked the advent of modernity. Breaking the age-long dependence on political rulers required an acquisition of a non-political, social basis and hence political autonomy. Liberalism promised exactly this, with its emphasis on the self-construction and self-assertion of free individuals. And yet the right to practise liberal commandments seemed to depend, like all other privileges the Jews happened to enjoy in the past, on political decisions. Emancipation from the state could come – so it seemed – from the state alone. While other groups were satisfied with defending their social powers from excessive intrusiveness of the state, the Jews could not acquire such rights without an intrusive state, prepared to go all the way towards dismantling monopolies and closely guarded enclosures of the old rank system. To established elites, the Jews seemed therefore seeds of destruction – not merely because of their own sudden career, but because of the collapse of security which that career symbolized. P. G. J. Pulzer quotes typical voices of alarm: 'The strongest weapon of Judaism is the democracy of the non-Jews'; 'The Jew needs merely to get hold of the party of enlightenment and individualism in order to undermine from within the structure of German social framework. Thus he does not have to fawn his way to the peaks of society, instead he has forced on the Germans a social theory which was bound to help the Jews up to the towering heights.'[19] On the other hand, the intense preoccupation of the Jews with the new variety of political protection enabled the native, self-reliant and self-made bourgeoisie to project the Jews against the camp of the enemies of social self-assertion and political freedom. Thus, simultaneously, 'a brand of liberal antisemitism' could emerge 'which lumped Jews and nobility together and pretended that they were some kind of financial alliance against the rising bourgeoisie.'[20]

The non-national nation

Hardly any dimension of the endemic Jewish incongruence, however, has influenced the shape of modern antisemitism more strongly and in more durable fashion than the fact that the Jews were, to quote Arendt again, a 'non-national element in a world of growing or existing nations'.[21] By the very fact of their territorial dispersion and ubiquity, the Jews were an inter-national nation, a non-national nation. Everywhere, they served as a constant reminder of the relativity and limits of individual self-identity and communal interest, which the criterion of nationhood was meant to determine with absolute and final authority. Inside every nation, they were the 'enemy inside'. The boundaries of the nation were too narrow to define them; the horizons of national tradition were too short to see through their identity. *The Jews were not just unlike any other nation; they were also unlike any other foreigners.* In short, they undermined the very difference between hosts and guests, the native and the foreign. And as nationhood became the paramount basis of group self-constitution, they came to undermine the most basic of differences: the difference between 'us' and 'them'. Jews were flexible and adaptable; an empty vehicle, ready to be filled with whatever despicable load 'them' were charged of carrying. Thus Toussenel saw the Jews as the bearers of anti-French Protestant poison, while Liesching, the prominent detractor of *Das junge Deutschland*, accused the Jews of smuggling into Germany the pestilent Gallic spirit.

The supra-national quality of the Jews was sharply brought into relief at an early stage of the nation-formation process – when the inter-dynastic boundary conflicts, prompted by, or at least complicated by, new, unprecedented claims made in the name of various national unities, put a premium on the Jewish non-involvement in local particularism and Jewish ability to communicate above the heads of the warring states and across the front lines. Jewish mediating capacity was eagerly used by the rulers encumbered, often against their will, into conflicts they ill understood and wished to put paid to, while dreaming of nothing else but of a compromise, or at least a mode of coexistence, acceptable to their adversaries as much as to their own obstreperous nation-minded subjects. In the wars aimed mostly, or solely, at a more agreeable *modus coexistendi*, the Jews – the natural internationalists, so to speak – were cast in the role of the harbingers of peace and extinguishers of belligerence. This originally praised achievement rebounded on them with a vengeance once dynastic heirlooms turned into truly national, and nationalistic, states: the purpose of the war became the destruction of the enemy, and patriotism replaced loyalty to the king, while the dream of supremacy silenced the craving for peace. In a world fully and exhaustively divided into national domains, there was no space left for internationalism, and each scrap of the no-man's-land had become a standing invitation to aggression. *The world tightly packed with nations and nation-states abhorred the non-national void. Jews were in such a void: they were such a void.* They were suspect for the very reason of being able to negotiate where the only permissibile communication was to be conducted through the barrel of the gun. (Suspicion that their own Jews lacked patriotism and enthusiasm for slaughtering the nation's enemies, was well-nigh the only point of agreement between the warring camps of the Great War.) Though already smacking of high treason, this quality however was a minor irritant when compared with the Jewish inborn and evidently irreparable cosmopolitanism.

The worst suspicions were readily confirmed by the pronounced tendency of the Jews to reflect their exterritorial status in their infuriating bias for 'human values', 'men as such', universalism and other, similarly demobilizing, hence un-patriotic, slogans. At the very start of the nationalist age, Heinrich Leo warned that

> The Jewish nation stands out conspicuously among all other nations of this world in that it possesses a truly corroding and decomposing mind. In the same way as there exist some fountains that would transmute every object thrown into them into stone, thus the Jews, from the very beginning until this very day, have transmuted everything that fell into the orbit of their spiritual activity into an abstract generality.'

Jews, indeed, were the very epitome of Simmel's *strangers* – always on the outside even when inside, examining the familiar as if it was a foreign object of study, asking questions no one else asked, questioning the unquestionable and challenging the unchallengeable. From Heine's companion Ludwig Börne, through Karl Krauss on the eve of Hapsburg collapse and up to Kurt Tucholsky on the eve of the Nazi triumph, they made light of what they thought to be a parochial pettiness and prejudice, ridiculed local mixtures of backwardness with conceit and bravado, fought provincial sluggishness of mind and philistinism of taste. No one with such an outside vision could be truly admitted into the nation, defined as it was by taking itself for granted and by readiness to live with itself in peace. Friedrich Rühs's verdict, the first in a long row of grievances that particularity must raise against all abstract generality, came as no surprise: 'The Jew does not truly belong to the country in which he lives, for as the Jew from Poland is not a Pole, the Jew from England is not an Englishman, and the Jew from Sweden is not a Swede, so the Jew from Germany cannot be a German and the Jew from Prussia a Prussian.'[22]

The fate of Jewish incongruity among the nations was not made any easier by the fact that nationalistic claims were often themselves incongruous and mutually incompatible. As a rule, nations had their oppressors, whom they feared, and their oppressed, whom they disdained. Few known nations enthusiastically endorsed the right of the others to the same treatment they claimed for themselves. Throughout the turbulent, and yet unfinished period of national self-production, the national game has been a zero-sum game; sovereignty of the other has been an assault against one's own. One nation's rights were another nation's aggression, intransigence or arrogance.

Nowhere were the consequences of this more daunting than in the East-Central part of Europe – in the nineteenth century a veritable cauldron of nationalisms – either old yet still unsatiated, or up-and-coming and hungry. It was virtually impossible to side with one nationalist claim without making enemies of several other established or aspiring nations. This put the Jews in a particularly awkward position. In Pulzer's opinion,

> their occupational structure, their generally higher standards of literacy, and their need for political security made it easier to associate with the dominant, 'historic' nationalities (Poles, Magyars, Russians) than with the submerged, peasant, 'non-historic' nationalities (Czechs, Slovaks, Ukrainians, Lithuanians, for example). In Galicia and Hungary, therefore, they rid themselves of the stigma of being German, though this did not help them much with the races whom the Poles and Magyars were in turn oppressing.[23]

In quite a few cases the elites of established or budding nations were eager to deploy Jewish zeal and talent to promote developments unlikely to endear them with the masses marked (often against their will) as the objects of national proselytism and economic modernization. In Hungary under Hapsburg rule, the joyously self-acculturalizing Jews were welcomed by the landed aristocracy as the most dedicated and efficient agents of magyarization in peripheral, mostly Slav, areas which the nobility hoped to take under its rule in the future independent Hungary; and as the perpetrators of ruthless modernization of stagnant and backward peasant economy. Weak Lithuanian elites eagerly co-opted Jewish enthusiasm to promote their claims to government over the complex mixture of ethnic, linguistic and religious communities that populated the ancient lands of historic Great Lithuania they dreamed of resurrecting. On the whole, political elites were fond of deploying the Jews in all sorts of unpleasant and dangerous jobs they deemed necessary, yet preferred not do themselves. This was convenient in more than one respect. Once the need of Jewish services lost its urgency, they could be easily disposed of; 'putting the Jews in their place' would be applauded by the masses that the Jews had bossed on behalf of the elites, and would provide a sweetener for a bitter brew the elites, now firmly in the saddle, wanted the masses to taste.

Even the elites, however, and even temporarily, could not fully trust Jewish allegiances. Unlike the membership of those 'born into' a national community, for the Jews the membership was a matter of choice, and hence in principle revokable, 'until further notice'. Boundaries of national communities (even more so of their territorial holdings) were still uncertain and in contention, complacency was impermissible, vigilance was the order of the day. The barricades are erected to divide, and woe to those who use them as passageways. The sight of a large group of people free to flip at will from one national fortress to another must have aroused deep anxiety. It defied the very truth on which all nations, old and new alike, rested their claims; the ascribed character of nationhood, heredity and naturalness of national entities. The short-lived liberal dream of assimilation (and, more generally, the conception of the 'Jewish problem' as mostly a cultural one, as thus bound to be solved through voluntary, and readily accepted, acculturation) foundered on *the essential incompatability between nationalism and the idea of free choice*. However paradoxical this may sound, consistent nationalists must in the end resent the absorptive powers of their own nations. They can gladly accept praise lavished on the nation's virtues by its admirers. Such an accolade they would made a condition for granting to the admirers – the more zealous and vociferous the better – that benevolence of the patrons which comes with the clientship status. They would hardly forgive, however, taking the admiration (even a practised admiration, an imitation tantamount to self-dissolution) for a title to membership. As Geoff Dench's pithy advice to all client nations goes, 'By all means declare a belief in future justice and equality. This is part of the role. But do not expect it to materialize.'[24]

As this brief survey of the long list of Jewish incongruities shows, there was hardly a single door slammed on the road to modernity in which the Jews did not put their fingers. From the process which brought their emancipation from the ghetto, they could not but emerge heavily bruised. *They were the opacity of the world fighting for clarity, the ambiguity of the world lusting for certainty.* They bestrode all the barricades and invited bullets from every side. The conceptual Jew has been, indeed, construed as the archetypal 'viscosity' of the modern dream of order and clarity; as the enemy of all order: old, new, and particularly the desired one.

The modernity of racism

An important thing happened to the Jews on the road to modernity. They had embarked on that road while set securely aside, segregated and enclosed behind stony or imaginary walls of the *Judengasse*. Their estrangement was a fact of life, like air or mortality. It did not call for mobilization of popular feelings, sophisticated arguments or alertness of self-appointed vigilantes; diffuse and often uncodified, yet on the whole well-co-ordinated habits, sufficed to reproduce the mutual repellence which guarded the permanence of separation. All this changed with the advent of modernity, with its dismantling of legislated differences, its slogans of legal equality and the strangest of its novelties; citizenship. As Jacob Katz put it,

> When Jews lived in the ghetto, and immediately after they left it, accusation against them came from citizens who enjoyed the legal status denied the Jews. These accusations were designed only to justify and reconfirm the status quo and provide a rationale for keeping Jews in an inferior legal and social position. Now, however, the accusations were levelled by citizens as citizens who were equal before the law, and the purpose of these indictments was to show that Jews were unworthy of the legal and social position conferred upon them.[25]

As it were, it was not just moral or social worth that was at stake. The problem was infinitely more intricate. No less was involved than the designing of previously unpractised mechanisms, and acquiring of hitherto unthought-of skills – both necessary to produce *artificially* what was in the past given *naturally*. In pre-modern times, Jews were a caste among castes, a rank among ranks, an estate among estates. Their distinctiveness was not an issue, and habitual, virtually unreflective, practices of segregation effectively prevented it from becoming one. With the rise of modernity, separation of the Jews did become an issue. Like everything else in modern society, it had now to be manufactured, built up, rationally argued, technologically designed, administered, monitored and managed. Those in charge of pre-modern societies could assume the leisurely and confident attitude of gamekeepers: left to its own resources, society would reproduce itself year by year, generation after generation, with scarcely a noticeable change. Not so its modern successor. Here, nothing could be taken for granted any more. Nothing should grow unless planted, and whatever would have grown on its own must have been the wrong thing, and hence a dangerous thing, jeopardizing or confounding the overall plan. The gamekeeper-like complacency would be a luxury one could ill afford. What was needed instead was the posture, and skills, of a gardener; one armed with a detailed design of the lawn, of the borders and of the furrow dividing the lawn from the borders; with a vision of harmonious colours and of the difference between pleasing harmony and revolting cacophony; with determination to treat as weeds every self-invited plant which interferes with his plan and his vision of order and harmony; and with machines and poisons adequate to the task of exterminating the weeds and altogether preserve the divisions as required and defined by the overall design.

Separation of the Jews had lost its naturalness, suggested in the past by the territorial segregation and reinforced by profuse and obtrusive warning signs. It seemed instead hopelessly artificial and brittle. What used to be an axiom, a tacitly accepted assumption, became now a truth one had to demonstrate and prove; and 'essence of things' hidden behind phenomena that apparently contradicted it. New *naturalness* now had to be laboriously *constructed* and grounded in an authority different from that of the evidence of sensual impressions. As Patrick Girard put it,

> The Jewish assimilation into surrounding society and the disappearance of social and religious distinctions had led to a situation in which Jews and Christians could not be differentiated. Having become a citizen like any other and mixing with Christians through marriage, the Jew was no longer recognizable. This fact

had significant weight for anti-Semitic theorists. Edouard
Drumont, the author of the pamphlet *Jewish France*, wrote: 'A Mr
Cohen, who goes to synagogue, who keeps kosher is a respectable
person. I don't hold anything against him. I do have it in for the
Jew who is not obvious'.

One finds similar ideas in Germany, where Jews in ritual curls
and caftans were less scorned ... than their coreligionists, the
German patriots of Jewish persuasion who imitated their Christian
countryman ... [M]odern anti-Semitism was born not from the
great difference between groups but rather from the threat of
absence of differences, the homogenization of Western society and
the abolition of the ancient social and legal barriers between Jews
and Christians.[26]

Modernity brought the levelling of differences – at least of their
outward appearances, of the very stuff of which symbolic distances
between segregated groups are made. With such differences missing, it
was not enough to muse philosophically over the wisdom of reality as it
was – something Christian doctrine had done before when it wished to
make sense out of the factual Jewish separation. Differences had to be
created now, or retained against the awesome eroding power of social
and legal equality and cross-cultural exchange.

The inherited religious explanation of the boundary – the rejection of
Christ by the Jews – was singularly unfit for the new task. Such an
explanation inevitably entailed the possibility of exit from the
segregated field. As long as the boundary remained clearly drawn and
well marked, that explanation served a good purpose. It provided the
needed element of flexibility which tied the fate of men to their assumed
freedom to earn salvation or commit a sin, to accept or to reject the
Divine grace; and it achieved it all without in the slightest detracting
from the solidity of the boundary itself. The same element of flexibility,
however, would prove disastrous once the practices of segregation had
become too half-hearted and lackadaisical to sustain the 'naturalness' of
the boundary – making it instead a hostage to human self-determination.
The modern world-view, after all, proclaimed the unlimited potential of
education and self-perfection. Everything was possible, with due effort
and good will. Man was at birth a *tabula rasa*, an empty cabinet, later to
be covered and filled, in the course of the civilizing process, with
contents supplied by the levelling-up pressure of shared cultural ideas.
Paradoxically, referring the differences between the Jews and their

Christian hosts solely to the distinction of creed and connected rituals, appeared well geared to the modern vision of human nature. Alongside the renunciation of other prejudices, the abandonment of Judaist superstitions, and the conversion to a superior faith, seemed to be proper and sufficient vehicles of self-improvement; a drive only to be expected, and on a massive scale, on the road to the final victory of reason over ignorance.

What truly threatened the solidity of old boundaries was not, of course, the ideological formula of modernity (though it did not strengthen it either), but the refusal of the secularized modern state to legislate differentiated social practices. This was all right as long as the Jews (Drumont's 'Mr Cohen') themselves refused to follow the state in its drive towards uniformity, and stuck to their own discriminating practices. Real confusion was caused by those ever-more-numerous Jews, who did take up the offer and accomplish the conversion, either in its bequeathed, religious form, or in its modern form of cultural assimilation. In France, Germany, in the German-dominated part of Austro-Hungary, the likelihood that all Jews would sooner or later be 'socialized', or would 'self-socialize', into non-Jews, and hence would become culturally indistinguishable and socially invisible, was quite real. In the absence of old customary and legally supported practices of segregation, such absence of visible marks of difference could only be tantamount to wiping out the boundary itself.

Under conditions of modernity, segregation required a modern method of boundary-building. A method able to withstand and neutralize the levelling impact of allegedly infinite powers of educatory and civilizing forces; a method capable of designating a 'no-go' area for pedagogy and self-improvement, of drawing an unencroachable limit to the potential of cultivation (a method applied eagerly, though with mixed success, to all groups intended to be kept permanently in a subordinate position – like the working classes or women). If it was to be salvaged from the assault of modern equality, *the distinctiveness of the Jews had to be re-articulated and laid on new foundations, stronger than human powers of culture and self-determination*. In Hannah Arendt's terse phrase, Judaism has to be replaced with Jewishness: 'Jews had been able to escape from Judaism into conversion; from Jewishness there was no escape.'[27]

Unlike Judaism, Jewishness had to be, emphatically, stronger than human will and human creative potential. It had to be located at the level of natural law (the kind of law that ought to be discovered, and then taken account of and exploited for human benefit, but which cannot be wished away, tampered with, or neglected – at least, not without terrible consequences). It is of such a law that Drumont's anecdote was meant to remind his readers: '"Do you want to see how blood speaks?" a French duke once asked his friends. He had married a Rothschild from Frankfurt in spite of his mother's tears. He called his little son, pulled a golden louis from his pocket and showed it to him. The child's eyes lit up. "You see," continued the duke, "the semitic instinct reveals itself straight away".' Some time later Charles Maurras would insist that 'what one is determines one's attitude from the beginning. The illusion of choice, of reason, can only lead to personal *déracinement* and political disaster.' To neglect such a law may only be done at one's own, and common, peril – or so we learn from Maurice Barrès: 'Caught up in mere words a child is cut off from all reality: Kantian doctrine uproots him from the soil of his ancestors. A surplus of diplomas creates what we may call, after Bismarck, a "proletariat of graduates". This is our indictment of the universities; what happens to their product, the "intellectual", is that he becomes an enemy of society.'[28] The product of conversion – be it religious or cultural – is not the change, but *loss* of quality. On the other side of conversion lurks a void, not another identity. The convert loses his identity without acquiring anything instead. Man *is* before he *acts*; nothing he does may change what he is. This is, roughly, the philosophical essence of racism.

3

Modernity, Racism, Extermination II

There is an apparent paradox in the history of racism, and Nazi racism in particular.

In the by far most spectacular and the best known case in this history, racism was instrumental in the mobilization of anti-modernist sentiments and anxieties, and was apparently effective primarily because of this connection. Adolf Stöcker, Dietrich Eckart, Alfred Rosenberg, Gregor Strasser, Joseph Goebbels, and virtually any other prophet, theorist and ideologue of National Socialism used the phantom of the Jewish race as a lynch-pin binding the fears of the past and prospective victims of modernization, which they articulated, and the ideal *volkisch* society of the future which they proposed to create in order to forestall further advances of modernity. In their appeals to the deep-seated horror of the social upheaval that modernity augured, they identified modernity as the rule of economic and monetary values, and charged Jewish racial characteristics with responsibility for such a relentless assault on the *volkisch* mode of life and standards of human worth. Elimination of the Jews was hence presented as a synonym of the rejection of modern order. This fact suggests an essentially pre-modern character of racism; its natural affinity, so to speak, with anti-modern emotions and its selective fitness as a vehicle for such emotions.

On the other hand, however, as a conception of the world, and even more importantly as an effective instrument of political practice, racism is unthinkable without the advancement of modern science, modern technology and modern forms of state power. As such, racism is strictly a modern product. Modernity made racism possible. It also created a demand for racism; an era that declared achievement to be the only measure of human worth needed a theory of ascription to redeem boundary-drawing and boundary-guarding concerns under new conditions which made boundary-crossing easier than ever before. Racism, in short, is a thoroughly modern weapon used in the conduct of pre-modern, or at least not exclusively modern, struggles.

From heterophobia to racism

Most commonly (though wrongly), racism is understood as a variety of inter-group resentment or prejudice. Sometimes racism is set apart from other sentiments or beliefs of the wider class by its emotional intensity; at other times, it is set apart by reference to hereditary, biological and extra-cultural attributes which, unlike the non-racist variants of group animosity, it normally contains. In some cases writers about racism point out the scientific pretensions that other, non-racist yet similarly negative stereotypes of foreign groups, do not usually possess. Whatever the feature chosen, however, the habit of analysing and interpreting racism in the framework of a larger category of prejudice is seldom breached.

As racism gains in saliency among contemporary forms on inter-group resentment, and alone among them manifests a pronounced affinity with the scientific spirit of the age, a reverse interpretive tendency becomes ever more prominent; a tendency to extend the notion of racism so as to embrace all varieties of resentment. All kinds of group prejudice are then interpreted as so many expressions of innate, natural racist predispositions. One can probably afford not to be too excited by such an exchange of places and view it, philosophically, as just a question of the definitions, which can, after all, be chosen or rejected at will. On a closer scrutiny, however, complacency appears ill-advised. Indeed, if all inter-group dislike and animosity are forms of racism, and if the tendency to keep strangers at a distance and resent their proximity has been amply documented by historical and ethnological research as a well-nigh universal and perpetual attribute of human groupings, then there is nothing essentially and radically novel about the racism that has acquired such a prominence in out time; just a rehearsal of the old scenario, though admittedly staged with somewhat updated dialogues. In particular, the intimate link of racism with other aspects of modern life is either denied outright or left out of focus.

In his recent impressively erudite study of prejudice,[1] Pierre-André Taguieff writes synonimically of racism and heterophobia (resentment of the different). Both appear, he avers, 'on three levels', or in three forms distinguished by the rising level of sophistication. The 'primary racism' is in his view universal. It is a natural reaction to the presence of an unknown stranger, to any form of human life that is foreign and puzzling. Invariably, the first response to strangeness is antipathy, which more often than not leads to aggressiveness. Universally goes hand-in-hand with spontaneity. The primary racism needs no inspiring or fomenting; nor does it need a theory to legitimize the elemental hatred – though it can be, on occasion, deliberately beefed up and deployed as an instrument of political mobilization.[2] At such a time it can be lifted to another level of complexity and turn into a 'secondary' (or rationalized) racism. This transformation happens when a theory is supplied (and internalized) that provides logical foundations for resentment. The repelling Other is represented as ill-willed or 'objectively' harmful – in either case threatening to the well-being of the resenting group. For instance, the resented category can be depicted as conspiring with the forces of evil in the form construed by the resenting group's religion, or it can be portrayed as an unscrupulous economic rival; the choice of the semantic field in which 'harmfulness' of the resented Other is theorized is presumably dictated by the current focus of social relevance, conflicts and divisions. Xenophobia, or more particularly ethnocentrism (both coming into their own in the age of rampant nationalism, when one of the most closely defended lines of division is argued in terms of shared history, tradition and culture), is a most common contemporary case of 'secondary racism'. Finally, the 'tertiary', or mystifactory, racism, which presupposes the two 'lower' levels, is distinguished by the deployment of a quasi-biological argument.

In the form in which it has been constructed and interpreted by Taguieff, the tri-partite classification seems logically flawed; if the secondary racism is already characterized by the theorizing of primary resentment, there seem to be no good reason for setting aside just one of the many possible ideologies that can (and are) used for this purpose as a distinctive feature of a 'higher-level' racism. The third-level racism looks much like a unit in the second-level set. Perhaps Taguieff could defend his classification against this charge were he, instead of separating biological theories because of their supposedly 'mystifactory' nature (one can argue without end about the degree of mystification in all the rest of the second-level racist theories), pointing to the tendency of biological argument to emphasize the irreversibility and incurability of the damaging 'otherness' of the Other. One could indeed point out that – in our age of artificiality of the social order, of the putative omnipotence of education and, more generally, of social engineering – biology in general, and heredity in particular, stand in public consciousness for the area still off-limits for cultural manipulation; something we do not know yet how to tinker with and to mould and reshape according to our will. Taguieff, however, insists that the modern biological-scientific form of racism does not appear 'different in nature, operation and function, from traditional discourses of disqualifying exclusion',[3] and focuses instead on the degree of 'deliric paranoia' or extreme 'speculativess' as on distinctive features of the 'tertiary racism'.

I suggest, on the contrary, that *it is precisely the nature, function and the mode of operation of racism that sharply differ from heterophobia* – that diffuse (and sentimental rather than practical) unease, discomfort, or anxiety that people normally experience whenever they are confronted with such 'human ingredients' of their situation as they do not fully understand, cannot communicate with easily and cannot expect to behave in a routine, familiar way. Heterophobia seems to be a focused manifestation of a still wider phenomenon of anxiety aroused by the feeling that one has no control over the situation, and that thus one can neither influence its development, nor foresee the consequences of one's action. Heterophobia may appear as either a realistic or an irrealistic objectification of such anxiety – but it is likely that the anxiety in question always seeks an object on which to anchor, and that consequently heterophobia is a fairly common phenomenon at all times and more common still in an age of modernity, when occasions for the 'no control' experience become more frequent, and their interpretation in terms of the obtrusive interference by an alien human group becomes more plausible.

I suggest as well that, so described, *heterophobia ought to be analytically distinguished from contestant enmity*, a more specific antagonism generated by the human practices of identity-seeking and boundary-drawing. In the latter case, sentiments of antipathy and resentment seem more like emotional appendages to the activity of separation; separation itself demands an activity, an effort, a sustained action. The alien of the first case, however, is not merely a too-close-for-comfort, yet clearly separate category of people easy to spot and keep at a required distance, but a collection of people whose 'collectiveness' is not obvious or generally recognized; its collectiveness may be even contested and is often concealed or denied by the members of the alien category. The alien in this case threatens to penetrate the native group and fuse with it – if preventive measures are not set out and vigilantly observed. The alien, therefore, threatens the unity and the identity of the alien group, not so much by confounding its control over a territory or its freedom to act in the familiar way, but by blurring the boundary of the territory itself and effacing the difference between the familiar (right) and the alien (wrong) way of life. This is the 'enemy in our midst' case – one that triggers a vehement boundary-drawing bustle, which in its turn generates a thick fall-out of antagonism and hatred to those found or suspected guilty of double loyalty and sitting astride the barricade.

Racism differs from both heterophobia and contestant enmity. The difference lies neither in the intensity of sentiments nor in the type of argument used to rationalize it. *Racism stands apart by a practice of which it is a part and which it rationalizes: a practice that combines strategies of architecture and gardening with that of medicine – in the service of the construction of an artificial social order, through cutting out the elements of the present reality that neither fit the visualized perfect reality, nor can be changed so that they do.* In a world that boasts the unprecedented ability to improve human conditions by reorganizing human affairs on a rational basis, racism manifests the conviction that a certain category of human beings cannot be incorporated into the rational order, whatever the effort. In a world notable for the continuous rolling back of the limits to scientific, technological and cultural manipulation, racism proclaims that certain blemishes of a certain category of people cannot be removed or rectified – that they remain beyond the boundaries of reforming practices, and will do so for ever. In a world proclaiming the formidable capacity of training and cultural conversion, racism sets apart a certain category of people that cannot be reached (and thus cannot be effectively cultivated) by argument or any other training tools, and hence must remain perpetually alien. To summarize: in the modern world distinguished by its ambition to self-control and self-administration racism declares a certain category of people endemically and hopelessly resistant to control and immune to all efforts at amelioration. To use the medical metaphor; one can train and shape 'healthy' parts of the body, but not cancerous growth. The latter can be 'improved' only by being destroyed.

The consequence is that *racism is inevitably associated with the strategy of estrangement*. If conditions allow, racism demands that the offending category ought to be removed beyond the territory occupied by the group it offends. If such conditions are absent, racism requires that the offending category is physically exterminated. Expulsion and destruction are two mutually exchangeable methods of estrangement.

Of the Jews, Alfred Rosenberg wrote: 'Zunz calls Judaism the whim of [the Jewish] soul. Now the Jew cannot break loose from this "whim" even if he is baptized ten times over, and the necessary result of this influence will always be the same: lifelessness, anti-Christianity and materialism.'[4] What is true about religious influence applies to all the other cultural interventions. Jews are beyond repair. Only a physical distance, or a break of communication, or fencing them off, or annihilation, may render them harmless.

Racism as a form of social engineering

Racism comes into its own only in the context of a design of the perfect society and intention to implement the design through planned and consistent effort. In the case of the Holocaust, the design was the thousand-year *Reich* – the kingdom of the liberated German Spirit. It was that kingdom which had no room for anything but the German Spirit. It had no room for the Jews, as the Jews could not be spiritually converted and embrace the *Geist* of the German *Volk*. This spiritual inability was articulated as the attribute of heredity or blood – substances which at that time at least embodied the other side of culture, the territory that culture could not dream of cultivating, a wilderness that would be never turned into the object of gardening. (The prospects of genetic engineering were not as yet seriously entertained.)

The Nazi revolution was an exercise in social engineering on a grandiose scale. 'Racial stock' was the key link in the chain of engineering measures. In the collection of official plaidoyers of Nazi policy, published in English on Ribbentrop's initiative for the purposes of international propaganda and for this reason expressed in a carefully tempered and cautious language, Dr Arthur Gütt, the Head of the National Hygiene Department in the Ministry of Interior, described as the major task of the Nazi rule 'an active policy consistently aiming at the preservation of racial health', and explained the strategy such policy had necessarily to involve: 'If we facilitate the propagation of healthy stock by systematic selection and by elimination of the unhealthy elements, we shall be able to improve the physical standards not, perhaps, of the present generation, but of those who will succeed us.' Gütt had no doubt that the selection-cum-elimination such a policy envisaged 'go along the lines universally adopted in conformity with the researches of Koch, Lister, Pasteur, and other celebrated scientists'[5] and thus constituted a logical extension – indeed, a culmination – of the advancement of modern science.

Dr Walter Gross, the Head of the Bureau for Enlightenment on Population Policy and Racial Welfare, spelled out the practicalities of the racial policy: reversing the current trend of 'declining birth-rate among the fitter inhabitants and unrestrained propagation among the hereditary unfit, the mentally deficient, imbeciles and hereditary criminals, etc.'[6] As he writes for an international audience unlikely to applaud the determination of the Nazis, unencumbered as they were by things so irrational as public opinion or political pluralism, to see the accomplishment of modern science and technology to their logical end, Gross does not venture beyond the necessity to sterilize the hereditary unfit.

The reality of racial policy was, however, much more gruesome. Contrary to Gütt's suggestion, the Nazi leaders saw no reason to restrict their concerns to 'those who will succeed us'. As the resources allowed, they set about to improve the *present* generation. The royal road to this goal lead through the forceful removal of *unwertes Leben*. Every vehicle would do to secure progress along this road. Depending on circumstances, references were made to 'elimination', 'ridding', 'evacuation', or 'reduction' (read 'extermination'). Following Hitler's command of 1 September 1939, centres had been created in Brandenburg, Hadamar, Sonnenstein and Eichberg, which hid under a double lie: they called themselves, in hushed conversations between the initiated, 'euthanasia institues', while for the wider consumption they used still more deceitful and misleading names of a Charitable Foundation for 'Institutional Care' or the 'the Transport of the Sick' – or even the bland 'T4' code (from 4 Tiergartenstrasse, Berlin, where the co-ordinating office of the whole killing operation was located).[7] When the command had to be rescinded on 28 August 1941 as the result of an outcry raised by a number of prominent luminaries of the Church, the principle of 'actively managing the population trends' was in no way abandoned. Its focus, together with the gassing technologies that the euthanasia campaign had helped to develop, was merely shifted to a different target: the Jews. And to different places, like Sobibór or Chelmno.

Unwertes Leben remained the target all along. For the Nazi designers of the perfect society, the project they pursued and were determined to implement through social engineering split human life into worthy and unworthy; the first to be lovingly cultivated and given *Lebensraum*, the other to be 'distanced', or – if the distancing proved unfeasible – exterminated. Those simply alien were not the objects of strictly racial policy: to them, old and tested strategies traditionally associated with contestant enmity could be applied: the aliens ought to be kept beyond closely guarded borders. Those bodily and mentally handicapped made a more difficult case and called for a new, original policy: they could not be evicted or fenced off as they did not rightfully belong to any of the 'other races', but they were unworthy to enter the thousand-year *Reich* either. The Jews offered an essentially similar case. They were not a race like the others; they were an anti-race, a race to undermine and poison all other races, to sap not just the identity of any race in particular, but the racial order itself. (Remember the Jews as the 'non-national nation', the incurable enemy of the nation-based order as such.) With approval and relish, Roseberg quoted Weiniger's self-deprecatory verdict on the Jews as 'an invisible cohesive web of slime fungus (plasmodium), existing since time immemorial and spread over the entire earth'.[8] Thus the separation of the Jews could only be a half-measure, a station on the road to the ultimate goal. The matter could not possibly end with the cleansing of Germany of the Jews. Even residing far from the German borders, the Jews would continue to erode and disintegrate the natural logic of the universe. Having had ordered his troops to fight for the supremacy of the *German* race, Hitler believed that the war he kindled was waged in the name of *all races*, a service rendered to racially organized humankind.

In this conception of social engineering as a scientifically founded work aimed at the institution of a new, and better, order (a work which necessarily entails the containment, or preferably elimination, of any disruptive factors), racism was indeed resonant with the world-view and practice of modernity. And this, at least, in two vital respects.

First, with the Enlightenment came the enthronement of the new deity, that of Nature, together with the legitimation of science as its only orthodox cult, and of scientists as its prophets and priests. Everything, in principle, had been opened to objective inquiry; everything could, in principle, be known – reliably and truly. Truth, goodness and beauty, that which is and that which ought to be, had all become legitimate objects of systematic, precise observation. In turn, they could legitimize themselves only through objective knowledge which would result from such observation. In George L. Mosse's summary of his most convincingly documented history of racism, 'it is impossible to separate the inquiries of the Enlightenment philosophies into nature from their examination of morality and human character ... [From] the outset ... natural science and the moral and aesthetic ideals of the ancient joined hands.' In the form in which it was moulded by the Enlightenment, scientific activity was marked by an 'attempt to determine man's exact place in nature through observation, measurements, and comparisons between groups of men and animals' and 'belief in the unity of body and mind'. The latter 'was supposed to express itself in a tangible, physical way, which could be measured and observed'.[9] Phrenology (the art of reading the character from the measurements of the skull) and physiognomy (the art of reading the character from facial features) captured most fully the confidence, strategy and ambition of the new scientific age. Human temperament, character, intelligence, aesthetic talents, even political inclinations, were seen as determined by Nature; in what way exactly, one could find out through diligent observation and comparison of the visible, material 'substratum' of even the most elusive or concealed spiritual attributes. Material sources of sensual impressions were so many clues to Nature's secrets; signs to be read, records written down in a code which science must crack.

What was left to racism was merely to postulate a systematic, and genetically reproduced distribution of such material attributes of human organism as bore responsibility for characterological, moral, aesthetic or political traits. Even this job, however, had already been done for them by respectable and justly respected pioneers of science, seldom if ever listed among the luminaries of racism. Observing *sine ira et studio* the reality as they found it, they could hardly miss the tangible, material, indubitably 'objective' superiority that the West enjoyed over the rest of the inhabited world. Thus the father of scientific taxonomy, Linnaeus, recorded the division between the residents of Europe and inhabitants of Africa with the same scrupulous precision as that which he applied while describing the difference between crustacea and fishes. He could not, and he did not, describe the white race otherwise than 'as inventive, full of ingenuity, orderly, and governed by laws ... By contrast the Negroes were endowed with all the negative qualities which made them a counterfoil for the superior race: they were regarded as lazy, devious, and unable to govern themselves.'[10] The father of 'scientific racism', Gobineau, did not have to exercise much inventiveness to describe the black race as of little intelligence, yet of overdeveloped sensuality and hence a crude, terrifying power (just as the mob on the loose), and the white race as in love with freedom, honour and everything spiritual.[11]

In 1938, Walter Frank described the persecution of Jews as the saga of 'German scholarship in a struggle against World Jewry'. From the very first day of the Nazi rule, scientific institutes, run by distinguished university professors of biology, history and political science, had been set up to investigate 'the Jewish question' according to the 'international standards of advanced science'. Reichinstitut für Geschichte des neuen Deutschlands, Institut zum Studium der Judenfrage, Institut zur Erforschung des jüdischen Einflusses auf das deutsche kirchliche Leben, and the notorious Rosenberg's Institut zur Enforschung der Judenfrage were just a few of the many scientific centres that tackled theoretical and practical issues of 'Jewish policy' as an application of scholarly methodology, and never were they short of qualified staff with academically certified credentials. According to a typical rationale of their activity, the

> whole cultural life for decades has been more or less under the influence of biological thinking, as it was begun particularly around the middle of the last century, by the teachings of Darwin, Mendel and Galton and afterwards has been advanced by the studies of Plötz, Schallmayer, Correns, de Vries, Tschermak, Baur, Rüdin, Fischer, Lenz and others ... It was recognized that the natural laws discovered for plants and animals ought also be valid for man ...[12]

Second – from the Enlightenment on, the modern world was distinguished by its activist, engineering attitude toward nature and toward itself. Science was not to be conducted for its own sake; it was seen as, first and foremost, an instrument of awesome power allowing its holder to improve on reality, to re-shape it according to human plans and designs, and to assist it in its drive to self-perfection. Gardening and medicine supplied the archetypes of constructive stance, while normality, health, or sanitation offered the archmetaphors for human tasks and strategies in the management of human affairs. Human existence and cohabitation became objects of planning and administration; like garden vegetation or a living organism they could not be left to their own devices, lest should they be infested by weeds or overwhelmed by cancerous tissues. Gardening and medicine are functionally distinct forms of the same activity of *separating and setting apart useful elements destined to live and thrive, from harmful and morbid ones, which ought to be exterminated.*

Hitler's language and rhetoric were fraught with images of disease, infection, infestation, putrefaction, pestilence. He compared Christianity and bolshevism to syphilis or plague; he spoke of Jews as bacilli, decomposing germs, or vermin. 'The discovery of the Jewish virus', he told Himmler in 1942, 'is one of the greatest revolutions that have taken place in the world. The battle in which we are engaged today is of the same sort as the battle waged, during the last century, by Pasteur and Koch. How many diseases have their origin in the Jewish virus ... We shall regain our health only by eliminating the Jew.'[13] In October of the same year, Hitler proclaimed: 'By exterminating the pest, we shall do humanity a service.'[14] The executors of Hitler's will spoke of the extermination of Jews as *Gesundung* (healing) of Europe, *Selbsttreinigung* (self-cleansing), *Judensäuberung* (cleansing-of-Jews). In an article in *Das Reich*, published on 5 November 1941, Goebbels hailed the introduction of the Star of David badge as a measure of 'hygienic prophylactic'. The isolation of the Jews from a racially pure community was 'an elementary rule of racial, national, and social hygiene'. There were, Goebbels argued, good people and bad people, as much as there are good and bad animals. 'The fact that the Jew still lives among us is no proof that he also belongs with us, just as a flea does not become a domestic animal because it lives in the house.'[15] The Jewish question, in the words of the Foreign Office Press Chief, was 'eine Frage der politischen Hygiene'.[16]

Two German scientists of world-wide reputation, the biologist Erwin Baur and the anthropologist Martin Stämmler, put in the exact and matter-of-fact language of applied science what the leaders of Nazi Germany repeatedly expressed in an emotive and passionate vocabulary of politics:

> Every farmer knows that should he slaughter the best specimens of his domestic animals without letting them procreate and should instead continue breeding inferior individuals, his breeds would degenerate hopelessly. This mistake, which no farmer would commit with his animals and cultivated plants, we permit to go on in our midst to a large extent. As a recompense for our humanness of today, we must see to it that these inferior people do not procreate. A simple operation to be executed in a few minutes makes this possible without further delay ... No one approves of the new sterilization laws more than I do, but I must repeat over and over that they constitute only a beginning ...
>
> Extinction and salvation are the two poles around which the whole race cultivation rotates, the two methods with which it has

to work ... Extinction is the biological destruction of the hereditary inferior through sterilization, the quantative repression of the unhealthy and the undesirable ... The task consists of safeguarding the people from an overgrowth of the weeds.[17]

To sum up: well before they built the gas chambers, the Nazis, on Hitler's orders, attempted to exterminate their own mentally insane or bodily impaired compatriots through 'mercy killing' (falsely nicknamed 'euthanasia'), and to breed a superior race through the organized fertilization of racially superior women by racially superior men (eugenics). Like these attempts, the murder of Jews was an exercise in the rational management of society. And a systematic attempt to deploy in its service the stance, the philosophy and the precepts of applied science.

From repellence to extermination

'Christian theology never advocated extermination of the Jews', writes George L. Mosse, 'but rather their exclusion from society as living witnesses to deicide. The pogroms were secondary to isolating Jews in ghettos.'[18] 'A crime', Hannah Arendt asserts, 'is met with punishment; a vice can only be exterminated.'[19]

Only in its modern, 'scientific', racist form, the age-long repellence of the Jews has been articulated as an exercise in sanitation; only with the modern reincarnation of Jew-hatred have the Jews been charged with an ineradicable vice, with an immanent flaw which cannot be separated from its carriers. Before that, the Jews were sinners; like all sinners, they were bound to suffer for their sins, in an earthly or other-worldly purgatory – to repent and, possibly, to earn redemption. Their suffering was to be seen so that the consequences of sin and the need for repentance are seen. No such benefit can possibly be derived from watching vice, even if complete with its punishment. (If in doubt, consult Mary Whitehouse.) Cancer, vermin or weed cannot repent. They have not sinned, they just lived according to their nature. There is nothing to punish them for. By the nature of their evil, they have to be exterminated. Alone with himself, in his diary, Joseph Goebbels spelled this out with the same clarity we previously noted in the abstract historiosophy of Rosenberg: 'There is no hope of leading the Jews back into the fold of civilized humanity by exceptional punishments. They will forever remain Jews, just as we are forever members of the Aryan race.'[20] Unlike the 'philosopher' Rosenberg, Goebbels was, however, a minister in a government wielding an awesome and unchallenged power; a government, moreover, which – thanks to the achievements of modern civilization – could conceive of the possibility of life without cancer, vermin or weeds, and had at its disposal material resources to make such a possibility into a reality.

It is difficult, perhaps impossible, to arrive at the idea of extermination of a whole people without race imagery; that is, without a vision of endemic and fatal defect which is in principle incurable and, in addition, is capable of self-propagation unless checked. It is also difficult, and probably impossible, to arrive at such an idea without the entrenched practice of medicine (both of medicine proper, aimed at the individual human body, and of its numerous allegorical applications), with its model of health and normality, strategy of separation and technique of surgery. It is particularly difficult, and well-nigh impossible, to conceive of such an idea separately from the engineering approach to society, the belief in artificiality of social order, institution of expertise and the practice of scientific management of human setting and interaction. For these reasons, *the exterminatory version of anti-Semitism ought to be seen as a thoroughly modern phenomenon*; that is, something which could occur only in an advanced state of modernity.

These were not, however, the only links between exterminatory designs and the developments rightly associated with modern civilization. Racism, even when coupled with the technological predisposition of the modern mind, would hardly suffice to accomplish the feat of the Holocaust. To do that, it would have had to be capable of securing the passage from theory to practice – and this would probably mean energizing, by sheer mobilizing power of ideas, enough human agents to cope with the scale of the task, and sustaining their dedication to the job for as long as the task would require. By ideological training, propaganda or brainwashing, racism would have to imbue masses of non-Jews with the hatred and repugnance of Jews so intense as to trigger a violent action against the Jews whenever and wherever they are met.

According to the widely shared opinion of the historians, this did not happen. In spite of the enormous resources devoted by the Nazi regime to racist propaganda, the concentrated effort of Nazi education, and the real threat of terror against resistance to racist practices, the popular acceptance of the racist programme (and particularly of its ultimate logical consequences) stopped well short of the level an emotion-led extermination would require. As if a further proof was needed, this fact demonstrates once again *the absence of continuity or natural progression between heterophobia or contestant enmity and racism.* Those Nazi leaders who hoped to capitalize on the diffuse resentment of the Jews to obtain popular support for the racist policy of extermination were soon forced to realize their mistake.

Yet even if (an unlikely case, indeed) the racist creed was more successful, and volunteers for lynching and throat-cutting were many times more numerous, mob violence should strike us as a remarkably inefficient, blatantly pre-modern form of social engineering or of the thoroughly modern project or racial hygiene. Indeed, as Sabini and Silver have convincingly put it, the most successful – widespread and materially effective – episode of mass anti-Jewish violence in Germany, the infamous *Kristallnacht*, was

> a pogrom, an instrument of terror ... typical of the long-standing tradition of European anti-Semitism not the new Nazi order, not the systematic extermination of European Jewry. Mob violence is a primitive, ineffective technique of extermination. It is an effective method of terrorizing a population, keeping people in their place, perhaps even of forcing some to abandon their religious or political convictions, but these were never Hitler's aims with regard to the Jews: he meant to destroy them.[21]

There was not enough 'mob' to be violent; the sight of murder and destruction put off as many as it inspired, while the overwhelming majority preferred to close their eyes and plug their ears, but first of all to gag their mouths. Mass destruction was accompanied not by the uproar of emotions, but the dead silence of unconcern. It was not public rejoicing, but public indifference which 'became a reinforcing strand in the noose inexorably tightening around hundreds of thousands of necks.'[22] *Racism is a policy first, ideology second. Like all politics, it needs organization, managers and experts.* Like all policies, it requires for its implementation a division of labour and an effective isolation of the task from the disorganizing effect of improvization and spontaneity. It demands that the specialists are left undisturbed and free to proceed with their task.

Not that indifference itself was indifferent; it surely was not, as far as the success of the Final Solution was concerned. It was the paralysis of that public which failed to turn into a mob, a paralysis achieved by the fascination and fear emanating from the display of power, which permitted the deadly logic of problem-solving to take its course unhampered. In Lawrence Stoke's words, 'The failure when the regime first set insecurely in power to protest its inhumane measures made prevention of their logical culmination all but impossible, however unwanted and disapproved this undoubtedly was.'[23] The spread and the depth of heterophobia was apparently sufficient for the German public not to protest against violence, even if the majority did not like it and remained immune to racist indoctrination. Of the latter fact the Nazis found numerous occasions to convince themselves. In her impeccably balanced account of German attitudes Sarah Gordon quotes an official Nazi report which vividly expressed Nazi disappointment with public responses to the *Kristallnacht*:

> One knows that anti-Semitism in Germany today is essentially confined to the party and its organizations, and that there is a certain group in the population who have not the slightest understanding for anti-Semitism and in whom every possibility of empathy is lacking.
>
> In the days after *Kristallnacht* these people ran immediately to Jewish businesses ...
>
> This is to a great extent because we are, to be sure, an anti-Semitic people, an anti-Semitic state, but nevertheless in all manifestations of life in the state and people anti-Semitism is as good as unexpressed ... There are still groups of *Spiessern* among the German people who talk about the poor Jews and who have no understanding for the anti-Semitic attitudes of the German people and who interceded for Jews at every opportunity. It should not be that only the leadership and party are anti-Semitic.[24]

Dislike of violence – particularly of such violence as could be seen and was meant to be seen – coincided, however, with a much more sympathetic attitude towards administrative measures taken against Jews. A great number of Germans welcomed an energetic and vociferously advertised action aimed at the segregation, separation, and disempowering of the Jews – those traditional expressions and instruments of heterophobia or contestant enmity. In addition, many Germans welcomed the measures portrayed as the punishment of the Jew (as long as one could pretend that the punished was indeed the conceptual Jew) as an imaginary (yet plausible) solution to quite real (if subconscious) anxieties and fears of displacement and insecurity. Whatever the reasons of their satisfaction, they seemed to be radically different from those implied by the Streicher-style exhortations to violence as an all-too-realistic way of repaying imaginary economic or sexual crimes. From the point of view of those who designed and commanded the mass murder of the Jews, Jews were to die not because they were resented (or at least not primarily for this reason); *they were seen as deserving death (and resented for that reason) because they stood between this one imperfect and tension-ridden reality and the hoped-for world of tranquil happiness.* As we shall see in the next chapter, the disappearance of the Jews was instrumental in bringing about the world of perfection. The absence of Jews was precisely the difference between that world and the imperfect world here and now.

Examining neutral and critical sources in addition to official reports, Gordon has documented a widespread and growing approval of 'ordinary Germans' for the exclusion of Jews from positions of power, wealth and influence.[25] The gradual disappearance of Jews from public life was either applauded or studiously overlooked. Unwillingness of the public to partake personally of the persecution of the Jews was, in short, combined with the readiness to go along with, or at least not to interfere with, the action of the State. 'If most Germans were not fanatical or "paranoid" anti-Semites, they were "mild", "latent", or passive anti-Semites, for whom the Jews had become a "depersonalized", abstract, and alien entity beyond human empathy and the "Jewish Question" a legitimate subject of state policy deserving solution.'[26]

These considerations demonstrate once more the paramount importance of the other, operational rather than ideological, link between the exterminatory form of antisemitism and modernity. The *idea* of extermination, discontinuous with the traditional heterophobia and dependent for that reason on the two implacably modern phenomena of racist theory and the medical-therapeutic syndrome, provided the first link. But the modern idea needed also suitably modern means of implementation. It found such means in modern bureaucracy.

The only adequate solution to problems posited by the racist world-view is a total and uncompromising isolation of the pathogenic and infectious race – the source of disease and contamination – through its complete spatial separation or physical destruction. By its nature, this is a daunting task, unthinkable unless in conjunction with the availability of huge resources, means of their mobilization and planned distribution, skills of splitting the overall task into a great number of partial and specialized functions and skills to co-ordinate their performance. In short, the task is inconceivable without modern bureaucracy. To be effective, modern exterminatory antisemitism had to be married to modern bureaucracy. And in Germany it was. In his famous Wandsee briefing, Heydrich spoke of the 'approval' or 'authorization' of the RSHA Jewish policy by the *Führer*.[27] Face with the *problems* arising from the idea and the purpose this idea determined (Hitler himself preferred to speak of 'prophecy' rather than of a purpose or a task), the bureaucratic organization called *Reichsicherheithauptamt* set about designing proper practical *solutions*. It went about it the way all bureaucracies do: counting costs and measuring them against available resources, and then trying to determine the optimal combination. Heydrich underlined the need to accumulate practical experience, stressed the graduality of the process, and the provisional character of each step, confined by as-yet-limited practical know-how; RSHA was actively to seek the best solution. The *Führer* expressed his romantic vision of the world cleansed of the terminally diseased race. The rest was the matter of a not at all romantic, coolly rational bureaucratic process.

The murderous compound was made of a typically modern ambition of social design and engineering, mixed with the typically modern concentration of power, resources and managerial skills. In Gordon's terse and unforgettable phrase, 'when the millions of Jewish and other victims pondered their own imminent deaths and wondered "why must I die, since I have done nothing to deserve it?" probably the simplest answer would have been that power was totally concentrated in one man, and that man happened to hate their "race".'[28] The man's hatred and the concentrated power did not have to meet (indeed, no satisfactory theory has been offered to date which proves that antisemitism is functionally indispensable for a totalitarian regime; or, *vice versa*, that the presence of antisemitism in its modern, racialist, form, inevitably results in such a regime. Klaus von Beyme has found in his recent study that, for instance, Spanish falangists took particular pride in the absence of a single antisemitic remark in all the writings of Antonio Primo de Rivera, while even such a 'classical' Fascist as Franco's brother-in-law Serrano Suñer declared racism in general as a heresy for a good Catholic. French neo-Fascist Maurice Bardech stated that the persecution of the Jews was Hitler's greatest error and remained *hors du contrat fasciste*.[29]) But they did. And they may meet again.

Looking ahead

The story of modern antisemitism – in both its heterophobic and in its modern, racist, forms – is unfinished, as is the history of modernity in general and the modern state in particular. Modernization processes seem to move in our days away from Europe. Though some sort of boundary-defining device seemed to be necessary in the passage to modern, 'garden-type' culture, as well as during the most traumatic dislocations in societies undergoing the modernizing change, the selection of Jews for the role of such a device was in all probability dictated by the particular vicissitudes of European history. The connection between Judeophobia and European modernity was historical – and, one may say, historically unique. On the other hand, we know only too well that cultural stimuli travel relatively freely, if also unaccompanied by structural conditions closely related to them in their place of origin. Stereotype of the Jew as an order-disturbing force, as an incongruous cluster of oppositions that saps all identities and threatens all efforts at self-determination, has been long ago sedimented in the highly authoritative European culture and is available for export and import transactions, like everything else in that culture which is widely recognized as superior and trustworthy. This stereotype, like so many other culturally framed concepts and items before, can be adopted as a vehicle in the solution of local problems even if historical experience of which it was born has been locally missing; even if (or perhaps particularly if) societies which adopt it have had no previous first-hand knowledge of the Jews.

It has been recently noted that antisemitism survived the populations it had been ostensibly targeted against. In countries where the Jews have all but disappeared, antisemitism (as sentiment, of course, married now to practices related primarily to other targets than the Jews) continues unabated. Even more remarkable is the dissociation between the acceptance of anti-Jewish sentiments and any other national, religious or racial prejudices, with which it was thought to be closely correlated. Neither are the antisemitic feelings related today to group or individual idiosyncracies, and particularly to anxiety-generating unresolved problems, acute uncertainty etc. Bernd Martin, who explored the Austrian case of 'antisemitism without Jews' has coined the term *cultural sedimentation* to account for a relatively new phenomenon: certain (usually morbid or otherwise unprepossessing or shameful) human features or behavioural patterns have come to be defined in popular consciousness as Jewish. In the absence of practical tests of such conjunction, the negative cultural definition and the antipathy to the features to which it refers feed and reinforce each other.[30]

To many other cases of contemporary antisemitism, however, the explanation in terms of 'cultural sedimentation' does not fit. In our global village, news travels fast and wide, and culture has long become a game without frontiers. *Rather than a product of cultural sedimentation, contemporary antisemitism seems to be subject to the processes of cultural diffusion,* today much more intense than at any time in the past. Like other objects of such diffusion, antisemitism, while retaining affinity with its original form, is on the way transformed – sharpened or enriched – to adapt to the problems and needs of its new home. Of such problems and needs there is no shortage in the times of 'uneven development' of modernity with its attendant tensions and traumas. Judeophobic stereotype offers a ready-made intelligibility to the otherwise puzzling and frightening dislocations and previously unexperienced forms of suffering. For instance, in Japan it has become in recent years increasingly popular as a universal key to the understanding of unanticipated obstacles in the path of economic expansion; the activity of world Jewry is proposed as the explanation of events so diverse as the over-valuation of the yen and the alleged threat of fall-out in the case of another Czernobyl-style nuclear mishap followed by another Soviet cover-up.[31]

One variety of antisemitic stereotype that travels easily is described in length by Norman Cohn as the image of the Jews as an international conspiracy set on ruining all local powers, decomposing all local cultures and traditions, and uniting the world under Jewish domination. This is, to be sure, the most vituperative and potentially lethal form of antisemitism; it was under the auspices of this stereotype that extermination of the Jews was attempted by the Nazis. It seems that in the contemporary world the multi-faceted imagery of Jewry, once drawing inspiration from multiple dimensions of 'Jewish incongruity', tends to be tapered down to just one fairly straightforward attribute: that *of a supra-national elite, of invisible power behind all visible powers, of a hidden manager of allegedly spontaneous and uncontrollable, but usually unfortunate and baffling turns of fate.*

The now dominant form of antisemitism is a product of theory, not of elementary experience; it is supported by the process of teaching and learning, not by intellectually unprocessed responses to the context of daily interaction. At the beginning of this century by far the most widespread variant of antisemitism in the affluent countries of Western Europe was one aimed at impoverished and strikingly alien masses of Jewish immigrants; it arose from the unmediated experience of the native lower classes, which were alone in touch with the strange and bizarre foreigners and which responded to their disconcerting and destabilizing presence with mistrust and suspicion. Their feelings were seldom shared by the elites, who had no direct experience of interaction with Yiddish-speaking newcomers and for whom the immigrants were not essentially distinct from the rest of the unruly, culturally depressed and potentially dangerous lower classes. As long as it remained unprocessed by a theory which only middle-class or upper-class intellectuals could offer, the elemental heterophobia of the masses stayed (to paraphrase the famous adage of Lenin) at the level of 'trade-union consciousness'; it could hardly be lifted from there as long as reference was made only to the low-level experience of intercourse with the Jewish poor. It could be generalized into a platform for mass unrest simply by adding up individual anxieties and presenting private troubles as shared problems (as it has been in the case of Mosley's British Movement, aimed above all against London's East End, or the present-day British National Front, aimed at the likes of Leicester and Notting Hill, and the French, targeted at Marseilles). It could advance as far as the demand to 'send the aliens back where they came from'. Yet there was no road leading from such heterophobia or even boundary-drawing anxiety of the masses, in a way a 'private affair' of the lower classes, to sophisticated antisemitic theories of universal ambitions, like this of a deadly race or the 'world conspiracy'. To capture popular imagination, such theories much refer to facts normally inaccessible and unknown to the masses and certainly not located within the realm of their daily and unmediated experience.

Our previous analysis has brought us, however, to the conclusion that the true role of the sophisticated, theoretical forms of antisemitism lay not so much in its capacity to foment the antagonist practices of the masses, as in its unique link with the social-engineering designs and ambitions of the modern state (or, more precisely, the extreme and radical variants of such ambitions). On the evidence of the present trends towards withdrawal of the Western state from direct management of many areas of previously controlled social life, and towards a pluralism-generating, market-led structure of social life, it seems unlikely that a racist form of antisemitism may be again used by a Western state as an instrument of a large-scale social-engineering project. For a *foreseeable* future, to be more precise; the post-modern, consumer-oriented and market-centred condition of most Western societies seems to be founded on a brittle basis of an exceptional economic superiority, which for the time being secures an inordinately large share of world resources but which is not bound to last forever. One can assume that situations calling for a direct take-over of social management by the state may well happen in some not too distant future – and then the well-entrenched and well-tested racist perspective may again come handy. In the meantime, the non-racist, less dramatic versions of Judeophobia may be on numerous less radical occasions deployed as means of political propaganda and mobilization.

With the Jews moving today massively towards the upper-middle classes, and hence out of reach of the direct experience of the masses, group antagonisms arising from freshly fomented concerns with boundary-drawing and boundary-maintenance tend to focus today in most Western countries on immigrant workers. There are political forces eager to capitalize on such concerns. They often use a language developed by modern racism to argue in favour of segregation and physical separation: a slogan successfully used by the Nazis on their road to power as a means of gaining the support of the combative enmity of the masses for their own racist intentions. In all countries that attracted in the time of post-war economic reconstruction large numbers of immigrant workers, the popular press and the populistically-inclined politicians supply innumerable examples of the new uses to which racist language is currently put. Gérard Fuchs, as well as Pierre Jouve and Ali Magoudi,[32] have recently published large collections and convincing analyses of these uses. One can read of *Le Figaro* magazine of 26 October 1985 dedicated to the question 'Will we still be French in thirty years?' or of prime minister Jacques Chirac speaking in one breath of his government's determination to fight with great firmness for the strengthening of personal security and of the identity of the French national community. The British reader, to be sure, has no need to look to French authors in the search for quasi-racist, segregationist language in the service of the mobilization of popular heterophobia and boundary fears.

However abominable they are, and however spacious is the reservoir of potential violence they contain, heterophobia and boundary-contest anxieties do not result – directly or indirectly – in genocide. *Confusing heterophobia with racism and the Holocaust-like organized crime is misleading and also potentially harmful, as it diverts scrutiny from the genuine causes of the disaster, which are rooted in some aspects of modern mentality and modern social organization*, rather than in timeless reactions to the strangers or even in less universal, yet fairly ubiquitous identity conflicts. In the initiation and perpetuation of the

Holocaust, traditional heterophobia played but an auxiliary role. The truly indispensable factors lay elsewhere, and bore at the utmost a merely historical relation to more familiar forms of group resentment. The *possibility* of the Holocaust was rooted in certain universal features of modern civilization: its *implementation* on the other hand, was connected with a specific and not at all universal relationship between state and society. The next chapter will be devoted to a more detailed survey of these connections.

4

The Uniqueness and Normality of the Holocaust

Up until then, the evil – since some name must be given to this amazing conjunction of circumstances, unexpected only in appearance – had infiltrated gradually, in silence, in seemingly harmless stages ... Nonetheless, on looking back and analysing things in retrospect, it seemed obvious that the accumulation of signs was not the mere result of happenstance, but rather, possessed, so to speak, its own dynamics, as yet still secret, like an underground stream that swell and broadens before suddenly and impetuously surfacing; one needed only to hark back to the time when the first ominous signs appeared and draw a graph, outline a clinical picture, of its irresistible rise.

Juan Goytisolo, *Landscapes After The Battle*

'Wouldn't you be happier if I had been able to show you that all the perpetrators were crazy?' asks the great historian of the Holocaust, Raul Hilberg. Yet this is precisely what he is *unable* to show. The truth he does show brings no comfort. It is unlikely to make anybody happy. 'They were educated men of their time. That is the crux of the question whenever we ponder the meaning of Western Civilization after Auschwitz. Our evolution has outpaced our understanding; we can no longer assume that we have a full grasp of the workings of our social institutions, bureaucratic structures, or technology.'[1]

This is certainly bad news for philosophers, sociologists, theologians and all the other learned men and women who are professionally concerned with understanding and explaining. Hilberg's conclusions mean that they have not done their job well; they cannot explain what has happened and why, and they cannot help us to understand it. This charge is bad enough as far as the scientists go (it is bound to make the scholars restless, and may even send them, as they say, back to the drawing board), but in itself it is not a cause for public alarm. There have been, after all, many other important events in the past that we feel we do not fully understand. Sometimes this makes us angry; most of the time, however, we do not feel particularly perturbed. After all – so we console ourselves – these past events are matters of *academic interest*.

But are they? It is not the Holocaust which we find difficult to grasp in all its monstrosity. *It is our Western Civilization which the occurence of the Holocaust has made all but incomprehensible* – and this at a time when we thought we had come to terms with it and seen through its innermost drives and even through its prospects, and at a time of its world-wide, unprecedented cultural expansion. If Hilberg is right, and our most crucial social institutions elude our mental and practical grasp, then it is not just the professional academics who ought to be worried. True, the Holocaust occurred almost half a century ago. True, its immediate results are fast receding into the past. The generation that experienced it at first hand has almost died out. But – and this is an awesome, sinister 'but' – these once-familiar features of our civilization, which the Holocaust had made mysterious again, are still very much part of our life. They have not gone away. Neither has, therefore, the *possibility* of the Holocaust.

We shrug off such a possibility. We pooh-pooh the few obsessed people riled by our balance of mind. We have a special, derisive name for them – 'prophets of doom'. It comes easy to dismiss their anguished warnings. Are we not vigilant already? Do we not condemn violence, immorality, cruelty? Do we not muster all our ingenuity and considerable, constantly growing resources to fight them? And besides, is there anything at all in our life that points to the sheer possibility of a catastrophe? Life is getting better and more comfortable. On the whole, our institutions seem to cope. Against the enemy, we are well protected, and our friends surely won't do anything nasty. Granted, we hear from time to time of atrocities that some not particularly civilized, and for this reason spiritually far-away people, visit upon their equally barbaric neighbours. Ewe massacre a million Ibos, having first called them vermin, criminals, money-grabbers and subhumans without culture;[2]

Iraqis poison-gas their Kurdish citizens without even bothering to call them names; Tamils massacre Singhalese; Ethiopians exterminate Eritreans; Ugandans exterminate themselves (or was it the other way round?). It is all sad, of course, but what can it possibly have to do with us? If it proves anything at all, it certainly proves how bad it is to be unlike us, and how good it is to be safe and sound behind the shield of our superior civilization.

Just how untoward our complacency may prove in the end becomes apparent once we recall that still in 1941 the Holocaust was not expected; that, given the extant knowledge of the 'facts of the case', it was not expectable; and that, when it finally came to pass one year later, it met with universal incredulity. People refused to believe the facts they stared at. Not that they were obtuse or ill-willed. It was just that nothing they had known before had prepared them to believe. For all they had known and believed, the mass murder for which they did not even have a name yet was, purely and simply, unimaginable. In 1988, it is unimaginable again. In 1988, however, we know what we did not know in 1941; that also *the unimaginable ought to be imagined*.

The problem

There are two reasons for which the Holocaust, unlike many other topics of academic study, cannot be seen as a matter of solely academic interest; and for which the problem of the Holocaust cannot be reduced to the subject-matter of historical research and philosophical contemplation.

The first reason is that the Holocaust, even if it is plausible that, 'as a central historical event – not unlike the French Revolution, the discovery of America, or the discovery of the wheel – it has changed the course of subsequent history,'[3] has most certainly changed little, if anything, in the course of the subsequent history of our collective consciousness and self-understanding. It made little visible impact on our image of the meaning and historical tendency of modern civilization. It left the social sciences in general, and sociology in particular, virtually unmoved and intact, except for the still marginal regions of specialist research, and some dark and ominous warnings of the morbid proclivities of modernity. Both exceptions are consistently kept at a distance from the canon of sociological practice. For these reasons, our understanding of the factors and mechanisms that once made the Holocaust possible has not significantly advanced. And with the understanding not much improved over that of half a century ago, we could be once more unprepared to notice and decode the warning signs – were they now, as they had been then, blatantly displayed all around.

The second reason is that whatever happened to the 'course of history', nothing much happened to those products of history which in all probability contained the potentiality of the Holocaust – or at least we cannot be sure that it did. For all we know (or, rather, for all we do not know) they may still be with us, waiting for their chance. We can only suspect that the conditions that once before gave birth to the Holocaust have not been radically transformed. If there was something in our social order which made the Holocaust possible in 1941, we cannot be sure that it has been eliminated since then. A growing number of renowned and respected scholars warns us that we had better not be complacent.

> The ideology and system which gave rise to [Auschwitz] remains intact. This means that the nation-state itself is out of control and capable of triggering acts of social cannibalism on an undreamed-of scale. If not checked, it can consume an entire civilization in fire. It cannot carry a humanitarian mission; its trespasses cannot be checked by legal and moral codes, it has no conscience. (Henry L. Feingold)[4]

> Many features of contemporary 'civilized' society encourage the easy resort to genocidal holocausts ...
> The sovereign territorial state claims, as an integral part of its sovereignty, the right to commit genocide, or engage in genocidal massacres, against people under its rule, and ... the UN, for all practical purposes, defends this right. (Leo Kuper)[5]

> Within certain limits set by political and military power considerations, the modern state may do anything it wishes to those under its control. There is no moral-ethical limit which the state cannot transcend if it wishes to do so, because there is no moral-ethical power higher than the state. In matters of ethics and morality, the situation of the individual in the modern state is in principle roughly equivalent to the situation of the prisoner in Auschwitz: either act in accord with the prevailing standards of conduct enforced by those in authority, or risk whatever consequences they may wish to impose ...
> Existence now is more and more recognizably in accord with the

principles that governed life and death in Auschwitz. (George M. Kren and Leon Rapoport)[6]

Overwhelmed by the emotions which even a perfunctory reading of the Holocaust records cannot but arouse, some of the quoted authors are prone to exaggerate. Some of their statements sound incredible – and certainly unduly alarmist. They may be even counterproductive; if everything we know is like Auschwitz, then one can live with Auschwitz, and in many a case live reasonably well. If the principles that ruled over life and death of Auschwitz inmates were like these that rule our own, then what has all this outcry and lamentation been about? Truly, one would be well advised to avoid the temptation to deploy the inhuman imagery of the Holocaust in the service of a partisan stance towards larger or smaller, but on the whole routine and daily human conflicts. Mass destruction was the extreme form of antagonism and oppression, yet not all cases of oppression, communal hatred and injustice are 'like' the Holocaust. Overt, and hence superficial similarity is a poor guide to causal analysis. Contrary to what Kren and Rappoport suggest, having to choose between conformity and bearing the consequences of disobedience does not necessarily mean living in Auschwitz, and the principles preached and practised by most contemporary states do not suffice to make their citizens into Holocaust victims.

The real cause for concern, one that cannot be easily argued away, nor dismissed as a natural yet misleading outcome of post-Holocaust trauma, lies elsewhere. It can be gleaned from two related facts.

First, ideational processes that by their own inner logic may lead to genocidal projects, and the technical resources that permit implementation of such projects, not only have been proved fully compatible with modern civilization, but have been conditioned, created and supplied by it. The Holocaust did not just, mysteriously, avoid clash with the social norms and institutions of modernity. It was these norms and institutions that made the Holocaust feasible. Without modern civilization and its most central essential achievements, there would be no Holocaust.

Second, all those intricate networks of checks and balances, barriers and hurdles which the civilizing process has erected and which, as we hope and trust, would defend us from violence and constrain all over ambitious and unscrupulous powers, have been proven ineffective. When it came to mass murder, the victims found themselves alone. Not only had they been fooled by an apparently peaceful and humane, legalistic and orderly society – their sense of security became a most powerful factor of their downfall.

To put it bluntly, there are reasons to be worried because we know now that *we live in a type of society that made the Holocaust possible, and that contained nothing which could stop the Holocaust from happening*. For these reasons alone it is necessary to study the lessons of the Holocaust. Much more is involved in such a study than the tribute to the memory of murdered millions, settling the account with the murderers and healing the still-festering moral wounds of the passive and silent witnesses.

Obviously, the study itself, even a most diligent study, is not a sufficient guarantee against the return of mass murderes and numb bystanders. Yet without such a study, we would not even know how likely or improbable such a return may be.

Genocide extraordinary

Mass murder is not a modern invention. History is fraught with communal and sectarian enmities, always mutually damaging and potentially destructive, often erupting into overt violence, sometimes leading to massacre, and in some cases resulting in extermination of whole populations and cultures. On the face of it, this fact denies the uniqueness of the Holocaust. In particular, it seems to deny the intimate link between the Holocaust and modernity, the 'elective affinity' between the Holocaust and modern civilization. It suggests instead that murderous communal hatred has always been with us and will probably never go away; and that the only significance of modernity in this respect is that, contrary to its promise and to the widespread expectations, it did not file smooth the admittedly rough edges of human coexistence and thus has not put a definite end to man's inhumanity to man. Modernity has not delivered on its promise. Modernity has failed. But modernity bears no responsibility for the episode of the Holocaust – as genocide accompanied human history from the start.

This is not, however, the lesson contained in the experience of the Holocaust. No doubt the Holocaust was another episode in the long series of attempted mass murders and the not much shorter series of accomplished ones. It also bore features that it did not share with any of the past cases of genocide. It is these features which deserve special attention. They had a distinct modern flavour. Their presence suggests that modernity contributed to the Holocaust more directly than through its own weakness and ineptitude. It suggests that the role of modern civilization in the incidence and the perpetration of the Holocaust was active, not passive. It suggests that the Holocaust was as much a product, as it was a failure, of modern civilization. Like everything else done in the modern – rational, planned, scientifically informed, expert, efficiently managed, co-ordinated – way, the Holocaust left behind and put to shame all its alleged pre-modern equivalents, exposing them as primitive, wasteful and ineffective by comparison. Like everything else in our modern society, the Holocaust was an accomplishment in every respect superior, if measured by the standards that this society has preached and institutionalized. It towers high above the past genocidal episodes in the same way as the modern industrial plant towers above the craftsman's cottage workshop, or the modern industrial farm, with its tractors, combines and pesticides, towers above the peasant farmstead with its horse, hoe and hand-weeding.

On 9 November 1938 an event took place in Germany which went down in history under the name of *Kristallnacht*. Jewish businesses, seats of worship, and homes were attacked by an unruly, though officially encouraged and surreptitiously controlled, mob; they were broken down, set on fire, vandalized. About one hundred persons lost their lives. *Kristallnacht* was the only large-scale pogrom that occured on the streets of German towns throughout the duration of the Holocaust. It was also the one episode of the Holocaust that followed the established, centuries-old tradition of anti-Jewish mob violence. It did not differ much from past pogroms; it hardly stood out from the long line of crowd violence stretching from ancient time, through the Middle Ages and up to the almost contemporary, but still largely pre-modern, Russia, Poland or Rumania. Were the Nazis treatment of the Jews composed only of *Kristallnächte* and suchlike events, it would hardly add anything but an extra paragraph, a chapter at best, to the multi-volume chronicle of emotions running amok, of lynching mobs, of soldier looting and raping their way through the conquered towns. This was not, however, to be.

This was not to be for a simple reason: one could neither conceive of, nor make, mass murder on the Holocaust scale of no matter how many *Kristallnächte*.

Consider the numbers. The German state annihilated approximately six million Jews. At the rate of 100 per day this would have required nearly 200 years. Mob violence rests on the wrong psychological basis, on violent emotion. People can be manipulated into fury, but fury cannot be maintained for 200 years. Emotions, and their biological basis, have a natural time course; lust, even blood lust, is eventually sated. Further, emotions are notoriously fickle, can be turned. A lynch mob is unreliable, it can sometimes be moved by sympathy – say by a child's suffering. To eradicate a 'race' it is essential to kill the children.

Thorough, comprehensive, exhaustive murder required the replacement of the mob with a bureaucracy, the replacement of shared rage with obedience to authority. The requisite bureaucracy would be effective whether manned by extreme or tepid anti-Semites, considerably broadening the pool of potential recruits; it would govern the actions of its members not by arousing passions but by organizing routines; it would only make distinctions it was designed to make, not those its members might be moved to make, say, between children and adults, scholar and thief, innocent and guilty; it would be responsive to the will of the ultimate authority through a hierarchy of responsibility – whatever that will might be.[7]

Rage and fury are pitiably primitive and inefficient as tools of mass annihilation. They normally peter out before the job is done. One cannot build grand designs on them. Certainly not such designs as reach beyond momentary effects like a wave of terror, the breakdown of an old order, clearing the ground for a new rule. Ghengis Khan and Peter the Hermit did not need modern technology and modern, scientific methods of management and co-ordination. Stalin or Hitler did. It is the adventurers and dilletantes like Ghengis Khan and Peter the Hermit that our modern, rational society has discredited and, arguably, put paid to. It is the practitioners of cool, thorough and systematic genocide like Stalin and Hitler for whom the modern, rational society paved the way.

Most conspicuously, the modern cases of genocide stand out for their sheer scale. On no other occasion but during Hitler's and Stalin's rule were so many people murdered in such a short time. This is not, however, the only novelty, perhaps not even a primary one – merely a by-product of other, more seminal features. Contemporary mass murder is distinguished by a virtual absence of all spontaneity on the one hand, and the prominence of rational, carefully calculated design on the other. It is marked by an almost complete elimination of contingency and chance, and independence from group emotions and personal motives.

It is set apart by merely sham or marginal – disguising or decorative – role of ideological mobilization. But first and foremost, it stands out by its purpose.

Murderous motives in general, and motives for mass murder in particular, have been many and varied. They range from pure, cold-blooded calculation of competitive gain, to equally pure, disinterested hatred or heterophobia. Most communal strifes and genocidal campaigns against aborigines lie comfortably within this range. If accompanied by an ideology, the latter does not go much further than a simple 'us or them' vision of the world, and a precept 'There is no room for both of us', or 'The only good injun is a dead injun'. The adversary is expected to follow mirror-image principles only if allowed to. Most genocidal ideologies rest on a devious symmetry of assumed intentions and actions.

Truly modern genocide is different. *Modern genocide is genocide with a purpose.* Getting rid of the adversary is not an end in itself. It is a means to an end: a necessity that stems from the ultimate objective, a step that one has to take if one wants ever to reach the end of the road. *The end itself is a grand vision of a better, and radically different, society.* Modern genocide is an element of social engineering, meant to bring about a social order conforming to the design of the perfect society.

To the initiators and the managers of modern genocide, society is a subject of planning and conscious design. One can and should do more about the society than change one or several of its many details, improve it here or there, cure some of its troublesome ailments. One can and should set oneself goals more ambitious and radical: one can and should remake the society, force it to conform to an overall, scientifically conceived plan. One can create a society that is objectively better than the one 'merely existing' – that is, existing without conscious intervention. Invariably, there is an aesthetic dimension to the design: the ideal world about to be built conforms to the standards of superior beauty. Once built, it will be richly satisfying, like a perfect work of art; it will be a world which, in Alberti's immortal words, no adding, diminishing or altering could improve.

This is a gardener's vision, projected upon a world-size screen. The thoughts, feelings, dreams and drives of the designers of the perfect world are familiar to every gardener worth his name, though perhaps on a somewhat smaller scale. Some gardeners hate the weeds that spoil their design – that ugliness in the midst of beauty, litter in the midst of serene order. Some others are quite unemotional about them: just a problem to be solved, an extra job to be done. Not that it makes a difference to the weeds; both gardeners exterminate them. If asked or given a chance to pause and ponder, both would agree; weeds must die not so much because of what they are, as because of what the beautiful, orderly garden ought to be.

Modern culture is a garden culture. It defines itself as the design for an ideal life and a perfect arrangement of human conditions. If constructs its own identity out of distrust of nature. In fact, it defines itself and nature, and the distinction between them, through its endemic distrust of spontaneity and its longing for a better, and necessarily artificial, order. Apart from the overall plan, the artificial *order* of the garden needs tools and raw materials. It also needs defence – against the unrelenting danger of what is, obviously, a disorder. The order, first conceived of as a design, determines what is a tool, what is a raw material, what is useless, what is irrelevant, what is harmful, what is a weed or a pest. It classifies all elements of the universe by their relation to itself. This relation is the only meaning it grants them and tolerates – and the only justification of the gardener's actions, as differentiated as the relations themselves. From the point of view of the design all actions are instrumental, while all the objects of action are either facilities or hindrances.

Modern genocide, like modern culture in general, is a gardener's job. It is just one of the many chores that people who treat society as a garden need to undertake. If garden design defines its weeds, there are weeds wherever there is a garden. And weeds are to be exterminated. Weeding out is a creative, not a destructive activity. It does not differ in kind from other activities which combine in the construction and sustenance of the perfect garden. All visions of society-as-garden define parts of the social habitat as human weeds. Like all other weeds, they must be segregated, contained, prevented from spreading, removed and kept outside the society boundaries; if all these means prove insufficient, they must be killed.

Stalin's and Hitler's victims were not killed in order to capture and colonize the territory they occupied. Often they were killed in a dull, mechanical fashion with no human emotions – hatred included – to enliven it. They were killed because they did not fit, for one reason or another, the scheme of a perfect society. Their killing was not the work of destruction, but creation. They were eliminated, so that an objectively better human world – more efficient, more moral, more beautiful – could be established. A Communist world. Or a racially pure, Aryan world. In both cases, a harmonious world, conflict-free, docile in the hands of their rulers, orderly, controlled. People tainted with ineradicable blight of their past or origin could not be fitted into such unblemished, healthy and shining world. Like weeds, their nature could not be changed. They could not be improved or re-educated. They had to be eliminated for reasons of genetic or ideational heredity – of a natural mechanism, resilient and immune to cultural processing.

The two most notorious and extreme cases of modern genocide did not betray the spirit of modernity. They did not deviously depart from the main track of the civilizing process. They were the most consistent, uninhibited expressions of that spirit. They attempted to reach the most ambitious aims of the civilizing process most other processes stop short of, not necessarily for the lack of good will. They showed what the rationalizing, designing, controlling dreams and efforts of modern civilization are able to accomplish if not mitigated, curbed or counteracted.

These dreams and efforts have been with us for a long time. They spawned the vast and powerful arsenal of technology and managerial skills. They gave birth to institutions which serve the sole purpose of instrumentalizing human behaviour to such an extent that any aim may be pursued with efficiency and vigour, with or without ideological dedication or moral approval on the part of the pursuers. They legitimize the rulers' monopoly on ends and the confinement of the ruled to the role of means. They define most actions as means, and means as subordination – to the ultimate end, to those who set it, to supreme will, to supra-individual knowledge.

Emphatically, this does not mean that we all live daily according to Auschwitz principles. From the fact that the Holocaust is modern, it does not follow that modernity is a Holocaust. The Holocaust is a by-product of the modern drive to a fully designed, fully controlled world, once the drive is getting out of control and running wild. Most of the time, modernity is prevented from doing so. Its ambitions clash with the pluralism of the human world; they stop short of their fulfilment for the lack of an absolute power absolute enough and a monopolistic agency monopolistic enough to be able to disregard, shrug off, or overwhelm all autonomous, and thus countervailing and mitigating, forces.

Peculiarity of modern genocide

When the modernist dream is embraced by an absolute power able to monopolize modern vehicles of rational action, and when that power attains freedom from effective social control, genocide follows. A modern genocide – like the Holocaust. The short circuit (one almost wishes to say: a chance encounter) between an ideologically obsessed power elite and the tremendous facilities of rational, systemic action developed by modern society, may happen relatively seldom. Once it does happen, however, certain aspects of modernity are revealed which under different circumstances are less visible and hence may be easily 'theorized away'.

Modern Holocaust is unique in a double sense. *It is unique among other historic cases of genocide because it is modern. And it stands unique against the quotidianity of modern society because it brings together some ordinary factors of modernity which normally are kept apart.* In this second sense of its uniqueness, only the combination of factors in unusual and rare, not the factors that are combined. Separately, each factor is common and normal. And the knowledge of saltpetre, sulphur or charcoal is not complete unless one knows and remembers that, if mixed, they turn into gunpowder.

The simultaneous uniqueness and normality of the Holocaust has found excellent expression in the summary of Sarah Gordon's findings:

> systematic extermination, as opposed to sporadic pogroms, could be carried out only by extremely powerful government, and probably could have succeeded only under the cover of wartime conditions. It was only the advent of Hitler and his radical anti-Semitic followers and their subsequent centralization of power that made the extermination of European Jewry possible ...
>
> the process of organized exclusion and murder required cooperation by huge sections of the military and bureaucracy, as well as acquiescence among the German people, whether or not they approved of Nazi persecution and extermination.[8]

Gordon names several factors which had to come together to produce the Holocaust; radical (and, as we remember from the last chapter, modern: racist and exterminatory) antisemitism of the Nazi type; transformation of that antisemitism into the practical policy of a powerful, centralized state; that state being in command of a huge, efficient bureaucratic apparatus; 'state of emergency' – an extraordinary, wartime condition, which allowed that government and the bureaucracy it controlled to get away with things which could, possibly, face more serious obstacles in time of peace; and the non-interference, the passive acceptance of those things by the population at large. Two among those factors (one can argue that the two can be reduced to one: with Nazis in power, war was virtually inevitable) could be seen as coincidental – not necessary attributes of a modern society, though always its possibility. The remaining factors, however, are fully 'normal'. They are constantly present in every modern society, and their presence has been made both possible and inescapable by those processes which are properly associated with the rise and entrenchment of modern civilization.

In the preceding chapter I have tried to unravel the connection between radical, exterminatory antisemitism, and the socio-political and cultural transformations usually referred to as the development of modern society. In the last chapter of the book I shall attempt to analyse those social mechanisms, also set in motion under contemporary conditions, that silence or neutralize moral inhibitions and, more generally, make people refrain from resistance against evil. Here I intend to focus on one only, yet arguably the most crucial among the constituent factors of the Holocaust: the typically modern, technological-bureaucratic patterns of action and the mentality they institutionalize, generate, sustain and reproduce.

There are two antithetical ways in which one can approach the explanation of the Holocaust. One can consider the horrors of mass murder as evidence of the fragility of civilization, or one can see them as evidence of its awesome potential. One can argue that, with criminals in control, civilized rules of behaviour may be suspended, and thus the eternal beast always hiding just beneath the skin of the socially drilled being may break free. Alternatively, one can argue that, once armed with the sophisticated technical and conceptual products of modern civilization, men can do things their nature would otherwise prevent them from doing. To put it differently; one can, following the Hobbesian tradition, conclude that the inhuman pre-social state has not yet been fully eradicated, all civilizing efforts notwithstanding. Or one can, on the contrary, insist that the civilizing process has succeeded in substituting artificial and flexible patterns of human conduct for natural drives, and hence made possible a scale of inhumanity and destruction which had remained inconceivable as long as natural predispositions guided human action. I propose to opt for the second approach, and substantiate it in the following discussion.

The fact that most people (including many a social theorist) instinctively choose the first, rather than the second, approach, is a testimony to the remarkable success of the etiological myth which, in one variant or another, Western civilization has deployed over the years to legitimize its spatial hegemony by projecting it as temporal superiority. Western civilization has articulated its struggle for domination in terms of the holy battle of humanity against barbarism, reason against ignorance, objectivity against prejudice, progress against degeneration, truth against superstition, science against magic, rationality against passion. It has interpreted the history of its ascendance as the gradual yet relentless substitution of human mastery over nature for the mastery of nature over man. It has presented its own accomplishment as, first and foremost, a decisive advance in human freedom of action, creative potential and security. It has identified freedom and security with its own type of social order: Western, modern society is defined as *civilized* society, and a civilized society in turn is understood as a state from which most of the natural ugliness and morbidity, as well as most of the immanent human propensity to cruelty and violence, have been eliminated or at least suppressed. The popular image of civilized society is, more than anything else, that of the absence of violence; of a gentle, polite, soft society.

Perhaps the most salient symbolic expression of this master-image of civilization is the sanctity of the human body: the care which is taken not to invade that most private of spaces, to avoid bodily contact, to abide by the culturally prescribed bodily distance; and the trained disgust and repulsion we feel whenever we see or hear of that sacred space being trespassed on. Modern civilization can afford the fiction of the sanctity and autonomy of the human body thanks to the efficient mechanisms of self-control it has developed, and on the whole successfully reproduced in the process of individual education. Once effective, the reproduced mechanisms of self-control dispose of the need of subsequent external interference with the body. On the other hand, privacy of the body underlines personal responsibility for its behaviour, and thus adds powerful sanctions to the bodily drill. (In recent years the severity of sanctions, keenly exploited by the consumer market, have finally produced the tendency to interiorize demand for the drill; development of individual self-control tends to be itself self-controlled, and pursued in a DIY fashion.) Cultural prohibition against coming into too close a contact with another body serves therefore as an effective safeguard against diffuse, contingent influences which may, if allowed, counteract the centrally administered pattern of social order. Non-violence of the daily and diffuse human intercourse is an indispensable condition, and a constant output, of the centralization of coercion.

All in all, the overall non-violent character of modern civilization is an illusion. More exactly, it is an integral part of its self-apology and self-apotheosis; in short, of its legitimizing myth. It is not true that our civilization exterminates violence due to the inhuman, degrading or immoral character of the latter. If modernity

> is indeed antithetical to the wild passions of barbarism, it is not at all antithetical to efficient, dispassionate destruction, slaughter, and torture ... As the quality of thinking grows more rational, the quantity of destruction increases. In our time, for example, terrorism and torture are no longer instruments of passions; they have become instruments of political rationality.[9]

What in fact has happened in the course of the civilizing process, is the redeployment of violence, and the re-distribution of access to violence. Like so many other things which we have been trained to abhor and detest, violence has been taken out of sight, rather than forced out of existence. It has become invisible, that is, from the vantage point of narrowly circumscribed and privatized personal experience. It has been enclosed instead in segregated and isolated territories, on the whole inaccessible to ordinary members of society; or evicted to the 'twilight areas', off-limits for a large majority (and the majority which counts) of society's members; or exported to distant places which on the whole are irrelevant for the life-business of civilized humans (one can always cancel holiday bookings).

The ultimate consequence of all this is the concentration of violence. Once centralized and free from competition, means of coercion would be capable of reaching unheard of results even if not technically perfected. Their concentration, however, triggers and boosts the escalation of technical improvements, and thus the effects of concentration are further magnified. As Anthony Giddens repeatedly emphasized (see, above all, his *Contemporary Critique of Historical Materialism* (1981), and *The Constitution of Society* (1984), the removal of violence from the daily life of civilized societies has always been intimately associated with a thoroughgoing militarization of inter-societal exchange and inner-societal production of order; standing armies and police forces brought together technically superior weapons and superior technology of bureaucratic management. For the last two centuries, the number of people who have suffered violent death as the result of such militarization has been steadily growing to reach a volume unheard of before.

The Holocaust absorbed an enormous volume of means of coercion.

Having harnessed them in the service of a single purpose, it also added stimulus to their further specialization and technical perfection. More, however, than the sheer quantity of tools of destruction, and even their technical quality, what mattered was the way in which they were deployed. Their formidable effectiveness, relied mostly on the subjection of their use to purely bureaucractic, technical considerations (which made their use all but totally immune to the countervailing pressures, such as they might have been submitted to if the means of violence were controlled by dispersed and unco-ordinated agents and deployed in a diffuse way). Violence has been turned into a technique. Like all techniques, it is free from emotions and purely rational. 'It is, in fact, entirely reasonable, if "reason" means instrumental reason, to apply American military force, B-52's, napalm, and all the rest to "communist-dominated" Viet-Nam (clearly an "undesirable object"), as the "operator" to transform it into a "desirable object".'[10]

Effects of the hierarchical and functional divisions of labour

Use of violence is most efficient and cost-effective when the means are subjected to solely instrumental-rational criteria, and thus dissociated from moral evaluation of the ends. As I pointed out in the first chapter, such dissociation is an operation all bureaucracies are good at. One may even say that it provides the essence of bureaucratic structure and process, and with it the secret of that tremendous growth of moblizing and co-ordinating potential, and of the rationality and efficiency of action, which modern civilization has achieved thanks to the development of bureaucratic administration. The dissociation is by and large and outcome of two parallel processes, which are both central to the bureaucratic model of action. The first is the *meticulous functional division of labour* (as additional to, and distinct in its consequences, from linear graduation of power and subordination); the second is the *substitution of technical for a moral responsibility*.

All division of labour (also such division as results from the mere hierarchy of command) creates a distance between most of the contributors to the final outcome of collective activity, and the outcome itself. Before the last links in the bureaucratic chain of power (the direct executors) confront their task, most of the preparatory operations which brought about that confrontation have been already performed by persons who had no personal experience, and sometimes not the knowledge either, of the task in question. Unlike in a pre-modern unit of work, in which all steps of the hierarchy share in the same occupational skills, and the practical knowledge of working operations actually grows towards the top of the ladder (the master knows the same as his journeyman or apprentice, only more and better), persons occupying successive rungs of modern bureaucracy differ sharply in the kind of expertise and professional training their jobs require. They may be able to put themselves imaginatively into their subordinates' position; this may even help in maintaining 'good human relations' inside the office – but it is not the condition of proper performance of the task, nor of the effectiveness of the bureaucracy as a whole. In fact, most bureaucracies do not treat seriously the romantic recipe that requires every bureaucrat, and particularly those who occupy the top, to 'start from the bottom' so that on the way to the summit they should acquire, and memorize, the experience of the entire slope. Mindful of the multiplicity of skills which the managerial jobs of various magnitudes demand, most bureaucracies practise instead separate avenues of recruitment for different levels of the hierarchy. Perhaps it is true that each soldier carries a marshal's baton in his knapsack, but few marshals, and few colonels or captains for that matter, keep soldiers' bayonets in their briefcases.

What such practical and mental distance from the final product means is that most functionaries of the bureaucratic hierarchy may give commands without full knowledge of their effects. In many cases they would find it difficult to visualize those effects. Usually, they only have an abstract, detached awareness of them; the kind of knowledge which is best expressed in statistics, which measure the results without passing any judgement, and certainly not moral ones. In their files and their minds the results are at best diagramatically represented as curves or sectors of a circle; ideally, they would appear as a column of numbers. Graphically or numerically represented, the final outcomes of their commands are devoid of substance. The graphs measure the *progress* of work, they say nothing about the nature of the operation or its objects. The graphs make tasks of widely different character mutually exchangeable; only the quantifiable success or failure matter, and seen from that point of view, the tasks do not differ.

All these effects of distance created by the hierarchical division of labour are radically magnified once the division becomes functional. Now it is not just the lack of direct, personal experience of the actual execution of the task to which successive command contribute their share, but also the lack of similarity between the task at hand and the task of the office as a whole (one is not a miniature version, or an icon, of the other), which distances the contributor from the job performed by the bureaucracy of which he is a part. The psychological impact of such distantiation is profound and far-reaching. It is one thing to give a command to load bombs on the plane, but quite different to take care of regular steel supply in a bomb factory. In the first case, the command-giver may have no vivid, visual impression of the devastation the bomb is about to cause. In the second case, however, the supply manager does not, if he chooses to, have to think about the use to which bombs are put at all. Even in abstract, purely notional knowledge of the final outcome is redundant, and certainly irrelevant as far as the success of his own part of the operation goes. In a functional division of labour, everything one does is in principle *multifinal*; that is, it can be combined and integrated into more than one meaning-determining totality. By itself, the function is devoid of meaning, and the meaning which will be eventually bestowed on it is in no way pre-empted by the actions of its perpetrators. It will be 'the others' (in most cases anonymous and out of reach) who will some time, somewhere, decide that meaning. 'Would workers in the chemical plants that produced napalm accept responsibility for burned babies?' ask Kren and Rappoport. 'Would such workers even be aware that others might reasonably think they were responsible?'[11] Of course they wouldn't. And there is no bureaucratic reason why they should. The splitting of the baby-burning process in minute functional tasks and then separating the tasks from each other have made such awareness irrelevant – and exceedingly difficulty to achieve. Remember as well that it is chemical plants that produce napalm, not any of their individual workers ...

The second process responsible for distantiation is closely related to the first. The substitution of technical for moral responsibility would not be conceivable without the meticulous functional dissection and separation of tasks. At least it would not be conceivable to the same extent. The substitution takes place, to a degree, already within the purely linear graduation of control. Each person within the hierarchy of command is accountable to his immediate superior, and thus is naturally interested in his opinion and his approval of the work. However much this approval matter to him, he is still, though only theoretically, aware of what the ultimate outcome of his work is bound to be. And so there is at least an abstract chance of one awareness being measured against the other; benevolence of superiors being confronted with repulsiveness of the effects. And whenever comparison is feasible, so is the choice.

Within a purely linear division of command, technical responsibility remains, at least in theory, vulnerable, It may still be called to justify itself in moral terms and to compete with moral conscience. A functionary may, for instance, decide that by giving a particular command his superior overstepped his terms of reference, as he moved from the domain of purely technical interest to that charged with ethical significance (shooting soldiers is OK; shooting babies is a different matter); and that the duty to obey an authoritative command does not extend so far as to justify what the functionary considers as morally unacceptable deeds. All these theoretical possibilities disappear, however, or are considerably weakened, once the linear hierarchy of command is supplemented, or replaced, by functional division and separation of tasks. The triumph of technical responsibility is then complete, unconditional, and for all practical purposes, unassailable.

Technical responsibility differs from moral responsibility in that it forgets that the action is a means to something other than itself. As outer connections of action are effectively removed from the field of vision, the bureaucrat's own act becomes an end in itself. It can be judged only by its intrinsic criteria of propriety and success. Hand-in-hand with the vaunted relative autonomy of the official conditioned by his functional specialization, comes his remoteness from the overall effects of divided yet co-ordinated labour of the organization as a whole. Once isolated from their distant consequences, most functionally specialized acts either pass moral test easily, or are morally indifferent. When unencumbered by moral worries, the act can be judged on unambiguously rational grounds. What matters then is whether the act has been performed according to the best available technological know-how, and whether its output has been cost-effective. Criteria are clear-cut and easy to operate.

For our topic, two effects of such context of bureaucratic action are most important. First is the fact that the skills, expert knowledge, inventiveness and dedication of actors, complete with their personal motives that prompted them to deploy these qualities in full, can be fully mobilized and put to the service of the overall bureaucratic purpose even if (or perhaps because) the actors retain relative functional autonomy towards this purpose and even if this purpose does not agree with the actors' own moral philosophy. To put it bluntly, *the result is the irrelevance of moral standards for the technical success of the bureaucratic operation.* The instinct of workmanship, which according to Thorstein Veblen is present in every actor, focuses fully on proper performance of the job in hand. The practical devotion to the task may be further enhanced by the actor's craven character and severity of his superiors, or by the actor's interest in promotion, the actor's ambition or disinterested curiosity, or by many other personal circumstances, motives, or character features – but, on the whole, workmanship will suffice even in their absence. By and large, the actors want to excel; whatever they do, they want to do well. Once, thanks to the complex functional differentiation within bureaucracy, they have been distantiated from the ultimate outcomes of the operation to which they contribute, their moral concerns can concentrate fully on the good performance of the job at hand. Morality boils down to the commandment to be a good, efficient and diligent expert and worker.

Dehumanization of bureaucratic objects

Another, equally important effect of bureaucratic context of action is *dehumanization of the objects of bureaucratic operation*; the possibility to express these objects in purely technical, ethically neutral terms.

We associate dehumanization with horrifying pictures of the inmates of concentration camps – humiliated by reducing their action to the most basic level of primitive survival, by preventing them from deploying cultural (both bodily and behavioural) symbols of human dignity, by depriving them even of recognizably human likeness. As Peter Marsh put it, 'Standing by the fence of Auschwitz, looking at these emaciated skeletons with shrunken skin and hollowed eyes – who could believe that these were really people?'[12] These pictures, however, represent only an extreme manifestation of a tendency which may be discovered in all bureaucracies, however benign and innocuous the tasks in which they are currently engaged. I suggest that the discussion of the dehumanizing tendency, rather than being focused on its most sensational and vile, but fortunately uncommon, manifestations, ought to concentrate on the more universal, and for this reason potentially more dangerous, manifestations.

Dehumanization starts at the point when, thanks to the distantiation, the objects at which the bureaucratic operation is aimed can, and are, reduced to a set of quantitative measures. For railway managers, the only meaningful articulation of their object is in terms of tonnes per kilometre. They do not deal with humans, sheep, or barbed wire; they only deal with the cargo, and this means an entity consisting entirely of measurements and devoid of quality. For most bureaucrats, even such a category as cargo would mean too strict a quality-bound restriction. They deal only with the financial effects of their actions. Their object is money. Money is the sole object that appears on both input and output ends, and *pecunia*, as the ancients shrewdly observed, definitely *non olet*. As they grow, bureaucratic companies seldom allow themselves to be confined to one qualitatively distinct area of activity. They spread sideways, guided in their movements by a sort of *lucrotropism* – a sort of gravitational pulling force of the highest returns on their capital. As we remember, the whole operation of the Holocaust was managed by the Economic Administration Section of the *Reichsicherheithauptamt*. We know that this one assignment, exceptionally, was not intended as a strategem or a camouflage.

Reduced, like all other objects of bureaucratic management, to pure, quality-free measurements, human objects lose their distinctiveness. They are already dehumanized – in the sense that the language in which things that happen to them (or are done to them) are narrated, safeguards its referents from ethical evaluation. In fact, this language is unfit for normative-moral statements. It is only humans that may be objects of ethical propositions. (True, moral statements do extend sometimes to other, non-human living beings; but they may do so only by expanding from their original anthropomorphic foothold.) Humans lose this capacity once they are reduced to ciphers.

Dehumanization is inextricably related to the most essential, rationalizing tendency of modern bureaucracy. As all bureaucracies affect in some measure some human objects, the adverse impact of dehumanization is much more common than the habit to identify it almost totally with its genocidal effects would suggest. Soldiers are told to shoot *targets*, which *fall* when they are *hit*. Employees of big companies are encouraged to destroy *competition*. Officers of welfare agencies operate *discretionary awards* at one time, *personal credits* at another. Their objects are *supplementary benefit recipients*. It is difficult to perceive and remember the humans behind all such technical terms. The point is that as far as the bureaucratic goals go, they are better not perceived and not remembered.

Once effectively dehumanized, and hence cancelled as potential subjects of moral demands, human objects of bureaucratic task-performance are viewed with ethical indifference, which soon turns into disapprobation and censure when their resistance, or lack of co-operation, slows down the smooth flow of bureaucratic routine.

Dehumanized objects cannot possibly possess a 'cause', much less a 'just' one; they have no 'interests' to be considered, indeed no claim to subjectivity. Human objects become therefore a 'nuisance factor'. Their obstreperousness further strengthens the self-esteem and the bonds of comradeship that unite the functionaries. The latter see themselves now as companions in a difficult struggle, calling for courage, self-sacrifice and selfless dedication to the cause. It is not the objects of bureaucratic action, but its subjects who suffer and deserve compassion and moral praise. They may justly derive pride and assurance of their own dignity from crushing the recalcitrance of their victims – much as they are proud of overriding any other obstacle. Dehumanization of the objects and positive moral self-evaluation reinforce each other. The functionaries may faithfully serve any goal while their moral conscience remains unimpaired.

The overall conclusion is that the bureaucratic mode of action, as it has been developed in the course of the modernizing process, contains all the technical elements which proved necessary in the execution of genocidal tasks. This mode can be put to the service of a genocidal objective without major revision of its structure, mechanisms and behavioural norms.

Moreover, contrary to widespread opinion, bureaucracy is not merely a tool, which can be used with equal facility at one time for cruel and morally contemptible, at another for deeply humane purposes. Even if it does move in any direction in which it is pushed, bureaucracy is more like a loaded dice. It has a logic and a momentum of its own. It renders some solutions more, and other solutions less, probable. Given an initial push (being confronted with a purpose), it will – like the brooms of the sorcerer's apprentice – easily move beyond all thresholds at which many of those who gave it the push would have stopped, were they still in control of the process they triggered. Bureaucracy is programmed to seek the optimal solution. It is programmed to measure the optimum in such terms as would not distinguish between one human object and another, or between human and inhuman objects. What matters is the efficiency and lowering of costs of their processing.

The role of bureaucracy in the Holocaust

It so happened in Germany half a century ago that bureaucracy was given the task of making Germany *judenrein* – clean of Jews.

Bureaucracy started from what bureaucracies start with: the formulation of a precise definition of the object, then registering those who fitted the definition and opening a file for each. It proceeded to segregate those in the files from the rest of the population, to which the received brief did not apply. Finally, it moved to evicting the segregated category from the land of the Aryans which was to be cleansed – by nudging it to emigrate first, and deporting it to non-German territories once such territories found themselves under German control. By that time bureaucracy developed wonderful cleansing skills, not to be wasted and left to rust. *Bureaucracy which acquitted itself so well of the task of cleansing Germany made more ambitious tasks feasible, and their choice well-nigh natural.* With such a superb cleaning facility, why stop at the *Heimat* of the Aryans? Why refrain from cleaning the whole of their empire? True, as the empire was now ecumenical, it had no 'outside' left where the dumping ground for the Jewish litter could be disposed of. Only one direction of deportation remained; upward, in smoke.

For many years now historians of the Holocaust have been split into the 'intentionalist' and the 'functionalist' camps. The first insist that killing the Jews was from the start Hitler's firm decision, waiting only for opportune conditions to emerge. The second credit Hitler with only a general idea of 'finding a solution' to the 'Jewish problem': clear only as far as the vision of 'clean Germany' goes, but vague and muddled as to the practical steps to be taken to bring that vision closer. Historical scholarship ever more convincingly supports the functionalist view. Whatever the ultimate outcome of the debate, however, there is hardly any doubt that the space extending between the idea and its execution was filled wall-to-wall with bureaucratic action. Neither is there any doubt that however vivid was Hitler's imagination, it would have accomplished little if it had not been taken over, and translated into routine process of problem-solving, by a huge and rational bureaucratic apparatus. Finally, and perhaps most importantly, the bureaucratic mode of action left its indelible impression of the Holocaust process. Its fingerprints are all over the Holocaust history, for everyone to see. True, bureaucracy did not hatch the fear of racial contamination and the obsession with racial hygiene. For that it needed visionaries, as bureaucracy picks up where visionaries stop. But bureaucracy made the Holocaust. And it made it in its own image.

Hilberg has suggested that the moment the first German official had written the first rule of Jewish exclusion, the fate of the European Jews was sealed. There is a most profound and terrifying truth in this comment. What bureaucracy needed was the definition of its task. Rational and efficient as it was, it could be trusted to see the task to its end.

Bureaucracy contributed to the perpetuation of the Holocaust not only through its inherent capacities and skills, but also through its immanent ailments. The tendency of all bureaucracies to lose sight of the original goal and to concentrate on the means instead – the means which turn into the ends – has been widely noted, analysed and described. The Nazi bureaucracy did not escape its impact. Once set in motion, the machinery of murder developed its own impetus: the more it excelled in cleansing the territories it controlled of the Jews, the more actively it sought new lands where it could exercise its newly acquired skills. With the approaching military defeat of Germany, the original purpose of the *Endlösung* was becoming increasingly unreal. What kept the murdering machine going then was solely its own routine and impetus. The skills of mass murder had to be used simply because they were there. The experts created the objects for their own expertise. We remember the experts of Jewish Desks in Berlin introducing every new petty restriction on German Jews who had long before all but disappeared from German soil; we remember the SS commanders who forbade the *Wehrmacht* generals from keeping alive the Jewish craftsmen they badly needed for military operations. But nowhere was the morbid tendency of substituting the means for the ends more visible than in the uncanny and macabre episode of the murder of Romanian and Hungarian Jews, perpetrated with the Eastern Front just a few miles away, and at an enormous cost to the war effort: priceless rail carriages and engines, troops and administrative resources were diverted from military tasks in order to cleanse distant parts of Europe for the German habitat which was never to be.

Bureaucracy is intrinsically *capable* of genocidal action. To *engage* in such an action, it needs an encounter with another invention of modernity: a bold design of a better, more reasonable and rational social order – say a racially uniform, or a classless society – and above all the capacity of drawing such designs and determination to make them efficacious. Genocide follows when two common and abundant inventions of modern times meet. It is only their meeting which has been, thus far, uncommon and rare.

Bankruptcy of modern safeguards

Physical violence and its threat

> is no longer a perpetual insecurity that it brings into the life of the individual, but a peculiar form of security ... a continuous, uniform pressure is exerted on individual life by the physical violence stored behind the scenes of everyday life, a pressure totally familiar and hardly perceived, conduct and drive economy having been adjusted from earliest youth to this social structure.[13]

In these words, Norbert Elias restated the familiar self-definition of civilized society. Elimination of violence from daily life is the main assertion around which that definition revolves. As we have seen, the apparent elimination is in fact merely an eviction, leading to the reassembly of resources and disposition of centres of violence in new locations within the social system. According to Elias, the two developments are closely interdependent. The area of daily life is comparatively free from violence precisely because somewhere in the wings physical violence is stored – in quantities that put it effectively out of the control of ordinary members of society and endow it with irresistible power to suppress unauthorized outbursts of violence. Daily manners mellowed mainly because people are now threatened with violence in case they are violent – with violence they cannot match or reasonably hope to repel. The disappearance of violence from the horizon of daily life is thus one more manifestation of the centralizing and monopolizing tendencies of modern power; violence is absent from individual intercourse because it is now controlled by forces definitely outside the individual reach. But the forces are not outside *everybody's* reach. Thus the much vaunted mellowing of manners (which Elias, following the etiological myth of the West, celebrates with such a relish), and the cosy security of daily life that follows have their price. A price which we, dwellers in the house of modernity, may be called to pay at any time. Or made to pay, without being called first.

Pacification of daily life means at the same time its defencelessness. By agreeing, or being forced to renounce the use of physical force in their reciprocal relations, members of modern society disarm themselves in front of the unknown and normally invisible, yet potentially sinister and always formidable managers of coercion. Their weakness is worrying not so much because of the high probability that the managers of coercion will indeed take advantage of it and hurry to turn the means of violence they control against the disarmed society, as for the simple fact that whether such advantage will or will not be taken, does not in principle depend on what ordinary men and women do. By themselves, the members of modern society cannot prevent the use of massive coercion from happening. Mellowing of manners goes hand-in-hand with a radical shift in control over violence.

Awareness of the constant threat which the characteristically modern imbalance of power contains would make life unbearable, were it not for our trust in safeguards which we believe have been built into the fabric of modern, civilized society. Most of the time we have no reason to think that the trust is misguided. Only on a few dramatic occasions a doubt is cast on the reliability of the safeguards. Perhaps the main significance of the Holocaust lies in its having been one of the most redoubtable of such occasions to date. *In the years leading to the Final Solution the most trusted of the safeguards had been put to a test. They all failed – one by one, and all together.*

Perhaps the most spectacular was the failure of science – as a body of ideas, and as a network of institutions of enlightenment and training. The deadly potential of the most revered principles and accomplishments of modern science has been exposed. The emancipation of reason from emotions, of rationality from normative pressures, of effectiveness from ethics have been the battle-cries of science since its inception. Once implemented, however, they made science, and the formidable technological applications it spawned, into docile instruments in the hands of unscrupulous power. The dark and ignoble role which science played in the perpetuation of the Holocaust was both direct and indirect.

Indirectly (though centrally to its general social function), science cleared the way to genocide through sapping the authority, and questioning the binding force, of all normative thinking, particularly that of religion and ethics. Science looks back at its history as the long and victorious struggle of reason over superstition and irrationality. In as far as religion and ethics could not rationally legitimize the demands they made on human behaviour, they stood condemned and found their authority denied. As values and norms had been proclaimed immanently and irreparably subjective, instrumentality was left as the only field where the search for excellence was feasible. Science wanted to be value-free and took pride in being such. By institutional pressure and by ridicule, it silenced the preachers of morality. In the process, it made itself morally blind and speechless. It dismantled all the barriers that could stop it from co-operating, with enthusiasm and abandon, in designing the most effective and rapid methods of mass sterilization or mass killing; or from conceiving of the concentration camps' slavery as a unique and wonderful opportunity to conduct medical research for the advancement of scholarship and – of course – of mankind.

Science (or this time, rather the scientists) helped the Holocaust perpetrators directly as well. Modern science is a gigantic and complex institution. Research costs dear, as it requires huge buildings, expensive equipment and large teams of highly paid experts. Thus science depends on a constant flow of money and non-monetary resources, which only equally large institutions are able to offer and to guarantee. Science is not, however, mercantile, nor are the scientists avaricious. Science is about truth, and scientists are about pursuing it. Scientists are overwhelmed with curiosity and excited by the unknown. If measured by all other earthly concerns, including monetary, curiosity is disinterested. It is only the value of knowledge and truth which scientists preach and search. It is just a coincidence, and preferably a minor irritant, that curiosity cannot be sated, and the truth found, without ever-growing funds, ever-more costly laboratories, ever-larger salary bills. What scientists want is merely to be allowed to go where their thirst for knowledge prompts them.

A government who stretches its helpful hand and offers just that can count on the scientists' gratitude and co-operation. Most scientists would be prepared in exchange to surrender quite a long list of lesser precepts. They would be prepared, for instance, to make do with the sudden disappearance of some of their colleagues with the wrong shape of nose or biographical entry. If they object at all, it will be that taking all these colleagues away in one swoop may put the research schedule in jeopardy. (This is not a slur nor a squib; this is what the protests of German academics, medics and engineers, if recorded at all, boiled down to. Less still was heard from their Soviet equivalents during the purges.) With relish, German scientists boarded the train drawn by the Nazi locomotive towards the brave, new, racially purified and German-dominated world. Research projects grew more ambitious by the day, and research institutes grew more populous and resourceful by the hour. Little else mattered.

In his fascinating new study of the contribution of biology and medical science to the designing and implementing of Nazi racial policy Robert Proctor puts paid to the popular myth of science under Nazism as, first and foremost, the victim of persecution and an object of intense indoctrination from above (a myth dating at least from Joseph

Needham's influential *The Nazi Attack on International Science*, published in 1941). In the light of Proctor's meticulous research, the widespread opinion sorely underestimates the degree to which political initiatives (indeed, some of the most gruesome among them) were generated by the scientific community itself, rather than imposed from outside on reluctant yet craven boffins, and the extent to which racial policy itself was initiated and managed by the recognized scientists with academically impeccable credentials. If there was coercion, 'it often took the form of one part of the scientific community coercing another'. On the whole, 'many of the social and intellectual foundations [for racial programmes] were laid down long before the rise of Hitler to power', and biomedical scientists 'played an active, even leading role in the initiation, administration, and execution of the Nazi racial pro- grammes'.[14] That the biomedical scientists in question were by no standards a lunatic or fanatical fringe of the profession is shown by Proctor's painstaking study of the composition of the editorial boards of 147 medical journals published in Nazi Germany. After Hitler's rise to power, the boards remained either unchanged or they replaced only a small minority of their members (in all probability, the change is accounted for by the removal of Jewish scholars).[15]

At best, the cult of rationality, institutionalized as modern science, proved impotent to prevent the state from turning into organized crime; at worst, it proved instrumental in bringing the transformation about. Its rivals, however, did not earn a higher score either. In their silence German academics had plenty of companions. Most conspicuously, they were joined by the Churches – all of them. Silence in the face of the organized inhumanity was the only item on which the Churches, so often at loggerheads, found themselves in agreement. None of them attempted to reclaim its flouted authority. None of the Churches (as distinct from single, and mostly isolated churchmen) acknowledged its responsibility for deeds perpetrated in a country it claimed as its domain, and by people in its pastoral charge. (Hitler never left the Catholic Church; neither was he excommunicated.) None upheld its right to pass moral judgements on its flock and impose penitence on the wayward.

Most pertinently, the culturally trained revulsion against violence proved a poor safeguard against organized coercion; while civilized manners showed an astounding ability to cohabit, peacefully and harmoniously, with mass murder. The protracted, and often painful, civilizing process failed to erect a single foolproof barrier against the genocide. Those mechanisms needed the civilized code of behaviour to co-ordinate criminal actions in such a way that they seldom clashed with the self-righteousness of the perpetrators. Among the bystanders, the civilized disgust of inhumanity did not prove strong enough to encourage an active resistance to it. Most bystanders reacted as civilized norms advise and prompt us to react to things unsightly and barbaric; they turned their eyes the other way. The few who stood up against cruelty did not have norms or social sanctions to support them and reassure. They were loners, who in justification of their fight against evil could only quote one of their distinguished ancestors: 'Ich kann nicht anders.'

In the face of an unscupulous team saddling the powerful machine of the modern state with its monopoly of physical violence and coercion, the most vaunted accomplishments of modern civilization failed as safeguards against barbarism. *Civilization proved incapable of guaranteeing moral use of the awesome powers it brought into being.*

Conclusions

If we ask now what the original sin was which allowed this to happen, the collapse (or non-emergence) of democracy seems to be the most convincing answer. In the absence of traditional authority, the only checks and balances capable of keeping the body politic away from extremities can be supplied by political democracy. The latter is not, however, quick to arrive, and it is slower still to take root once the hold of the old authority and system of control had been broken – particularly if the breaking was done in a hurry. Such situations of interregnum and instability tend to occur during and after deep-reaching revolutions, which succeed in paralysing old seats of social power without as yet replacing them with new ones – and create for this reason a state of affairs in which *political and military forces are neither counterbalanced nor restrained by resourceful and influential social ones.*

Such situations emerged, arguably, in pre-modern times as well – in the wake of bloody conquests or protracted internecine strifes which led on occasion to well-nigh complete self-annihilation of established elites. The expectable consequences of such situations were, however, different. A general collapse of the larger social order normally followed. War destruction seldom reached as low as the grass-root, communal networks of social control; communally regulated local islands of social order were now exposed to erratic acts of violence and pillage, but they had themselves to fall back upon once the social organization above the local level disintegrated. In most cases, even the most profound blows to traditional authorities in pre-modern societies differed from modern unheavals in two crucial aspects; first, they left the primeval, communal controls of order intact or at least still viable; and second, they weakened, rather than strengthened the possibility of organized action on a supra-communal level, as the social organization of the higher order fell apart and whatever exchange was left between localities was once again subjected to a free play of unco-ordinated forces.

Under modern conditions, on the contrary, upheavals of a similar kind occur, on the whole, after communal mechanisms of social regulation have all but disappeared and local communities ceased to be self-sufficient and self-reliant. Instead of an instinctive reflex of 'falling back' upon one's own resources, the void tends to be filled by new, but again supra-communal, forces, which seek to deploy the state monopoly of coercion to impose a new order on the societal scale. Instead of collapsing, political power becomes therefore virtually the only force behind the emerging order. In its drive it is neither stopped nor restrained by economic and social forces, seriously undermined by the destruction or paralysis of old authorities.

This is, of course, a theoretical model, seldom implemented in full in historical practice. Its use consists however in drawing attention to those social dislocations that seem to make the surfacing of genocidal tendencies more likely. Dislocations may differ in form and intensity, but they are united by the general effect of *the pronounced supremacy of political over economic and social power, of the state over the society.* They went perhaps deepest and farthest in the case of the Russian Revolution and the subsequent prolonged monopoly of the state as the only factor of social integration and order-reproduction. Yet also in Germany they went farther and deeper than it is popularly believed. Arriving after the brief Weimar interlude, the Nazi rule undertook and completed the revolution that the Weimar Republic – that uneasy interplay of old and new (but immature) elites which only at the surface resembled political democracy – was, for various reasons, incapable of administering. Old elites were considerably weakened or pushed aside. One by one, the forms of articulation of economic and social forces were dissembled and replaced with new, centrally supervised forms emanating from, and legitimized by, the state. All classes were profoundly affected, but the most radical blow was delivered to the classes that can carry non-political power only collectively, i.e. to the non-proprietary classes, and to the working class above all. Etatization or disbanding of all autonomous labour institutions coupled with the subjection of local government to almost total central control, left the popular masses virtually powerless and, for all practical purposes, excluded from the political process. Resistance of social forces was prevented additionally by the surrounding of state activity with an impenetrable wall of secrecy – indeed, the state conspiracy of silence against the very population it ruled. The overall and ultimate effect was the replacement of traditional authorities not by the new vibrant forces of self-governing citizenship, but by an almost total monopoly of the political state, with social powers prevented from self-articulation, and thus from forming a structural foundation of political democracy.

Modern conditions made possible the emergence of a resourceful state, capable of replacing the whole network of social and economic controls by political command and administration. More importantly still, modern conditions provide substance for that command and administration. Modernity, as we remember, is an age of artificial order and of grand societal designs, the era of planners, visionaries, and – more generally – 'gardeners' who treat society as a virgin plot of land to be expertly designed and then cultivated and doctored to keep to the designed form.

There is no limit to ambition and self-confidence. Indeed, through the spectacles of modern power 'mankind' seems so omnipotent and its individual members so 'incomplete', inept and submissive, and so much in need of improvement, that treating people as plants to be trimmed (if necessary, uprooted) or cattle to be bred does not look fanciful or morally odious. One of the earliest and principal ideologists of German National Socialism, R. W. Darré, took the practices of animal husbandry as the pattern of 'population policy' to be implemented by the future *volkish* government:

He who leaves the plants in a garden to themselves will soon find to his surprise that the garden is overgrown by weeds and that even the basic character of the plants has changed. If therefore the garden is to remain the breeding ground for the plants, if, in other words, it is to lift itself above the harsh rule of natural forces, then the forming will of a gardener is necessary, a gardener who, by providing suitable conditions for growing, or by keeping harmful influences away, or by both together, carefully tends what needs tending, and ruthlessly eliminates the weeds which would deprive the better plants of nutrition, air, light, and sun ... Thus we are facing the realization that questions of breeding are not trivial for political thought, but that they have to be at the centre of all considerations, and that their answers must follow from the spiritual, from the ideological attitude of a people. We must even assert that a people can only reach spiritual and moral equilibrium if a well-conceived breeding plan stands at the very *centre* of its culture ...[16]

Darré spelled out in unambiguous and radical terms the 'reality-improving' ambitions which form the essence of the modern stance and which only the resources of modern power allow us to entertain seriously.

Periods of deep social dislocations are times when this most remarkable feature of modernity comes into its own. Indeed, at no other time does society seem to be so formless – 'unfinished', indefinite and pliable – literally waiting for a vision and a skilful and resourceful designer to give it a form. At no other time does society seem so devoid of forces and tendencies of its own, and hence incapable of resisting the hand of the gardener, and ready to be squeezed into any form he chooses. *The combination of malleability and helplessness constitutes an attraction which few self-confident adventurous visionaries could resist. It also constitutes a situation in which they cannot be resisted.*

The carriers of the grand design at the helm of modern state bureaucracy, emancipated from the constraints of non-political (economic, social, cultural) powers; this is the recipe for genocide. Genocide arrives as an integral part of the process through which the grand design is implemented. *The design gives it the legitimation; state bureaucracy gives it the vehicle; and the paralysis of society gives it the 'road clear' sign.*

The conditions propitious to the perpetration of genocide are thus special, yet not at all exceptional. Rare, but not unique. Not being an immanent attribute of modern society, they are not an alien phenomenon either. As far as modernity goes, genocide is neither abnormal nor a case of malfunction. It demonstrates what the rationalizing, engineering tendency of modernity is capable of if not checked and mitigated, if the pluralism of social powers is indeed eroded – as the modern ideal of purposefully designed, fully controlled, conflict-free, orderly and harmonious society would have it. Any impoverishment of grass-root ability to articulate interests and self-govern, every assault on social and cultural pluralism and the opportunities of its political expression, every attempt to fence off the untramelled freedom of the state by a wall of political secrecy, each step towards the weakening of the social foundations of political democracy make a social disaster on a Holocaust scale just a little bit more feasible. Criminal designs need social vehicles to be effective. But so does the vigilance of those who want to prevent their implementation.

Thus far the vehicles for vigilance seem in short supply, while there is no shortage of institutions that seem capable of serving criminal designs or – worse still – incapable of preventing an ordinary task-oriented activity from acquiring a criminal dimension. Joseph Weizenbaum, one of the most acute observers and analysts of the social impact of information technology (admittedly a recent development, not available at the time of the Nazi Holocaust), suggests that the capacity for genocidal action has been, if anything, increased:

> Germany implemented the 'final solution' of its 'Jewish Problem' as a textbook exercise in instrumental reasoning. Humanity briefly shuddered when it could no longer avert its gaze from what had happened, when the photographs taken by the killers themselves began to circulate, and when the pitiful survivors re-emerged into the light. But in the end, it made no difference. The same logic, the same cold and ruthless application of calculating reason, slaughtered at least as many people during the next twenty years as had fallen victim to the technicians of the thousand-year Reich. We have learned nothing. Civilization is as imperilled today as it was then.[17]

And the reasons why instrumental rationality, and the human networks developed to serve it, remain morally blind now as they were then, are virtually unchanged. In 1966, more than twenty years after the gruesome discovery of the Nazi crime, a group of distinguished scholars designed the scientifically elegant and exemplary rational project of the *electronic battlefield* for the use of the generals of the Vietnam war. 'These men were able to give the counsel they gave because they were operating at an enormous psychological distance from the people who would be maimed and killed by the weapons systems that would result from the idea they communicated to their sponsors.'[18]

Thanks to rapidly advancing new information technology, which more than any technology that preceded it has succeeded in obliterating the humanity of its human objects ('People, things, events are "programmed", one speaks of "inputs" and "outputs", of feedback loops, variables, percentages, processes, and so on, until eventually all contact with concrete situations is abstracted away. Then only graphs, data sets, printouts are left'[19]) – the psychological distance grows unstoppably and on an unprecedented pace. So does the autonomy of purely technological progress from any deliberately chosen and discursively agreed human purposes. Today more than at any other time, available technological means undermine their own applications and subordinate the evaluation of the latter to their own criteria of efficiency and effectiveness. By the same token, the authority of political and moral evaluation of action has been reduced to a minor consideration – if not discredited and rendered irrelevant. Action can hardly need any other justification than the recognition that the available technology has made it feasible. Jacques Ellul has warned that, having emancipated itself from the constraint of discursively-set social tasks, technology

> never advances toward anything but *because* it is pushed from behind. The technician does not know why he is working, and generally he does not care. He works *because* he has instruments allowing him to perform a certain task, to succeed in a new operation ... There is no call towards a goal; there is constraint by an engine placed in the back and not tolerating any halt to the machine.[20]

There seems to be less hope than before that the civilized guarantees against inhumanity can be relied upon to control the application of human instrumental-rational potential, once the calculation of efficiency has been awarded supreme authority in deciding political purposes.

5

Soliciting the Co-operation of the Victims

It is the interaction *of perpetrators and victims that is 'fate'.*

Raul Hilberg

The memorable verdict of Hannah Arendt – that were it not for the deeds of the Jewish collaborators, and for the zeal of the *Judenräte*, the number of victims would have been considerably reduced – would seem not to be able to bear closer scrutiny. Arendt's harsh verdict can hardly stand up to the fact that in spite of the wide range of attitudes taken by the leaders of persecuted communities – from Czerniakow's suicide through Rumkowski's and Gens's active and conscious co-operation with the Nazi supervisors and up to the Bialystok case of the *Judenräte*'s semi-official assistance to the armed resistance – the final effect was much the same: almost total annihilation of communities and their leaders. One can also point out that about one-third of all Jews murdered by the Nazis were killed without recourse to any direct or indirect assistance of the Jewish councils or committees (the war against Russia was officially declared by Hitler a war of annihilation, and the notorious *Einsatzgruppen* which followed the victorious *Wehrmacht* in its early sweep through the Soviet lands did not bother with establishing ghettos or electing *Judenräte*). On a continuum of opinions on the impact of Jewish co-operation on the destruction of the European Jews, the view expressed by Isaiah Trunk, in conclusion of the most thorough and comprehensive investigation of the extant records of the *Judenräte*, occupies the opposite pole to Arendt's. According to this view, 'Jewish participation or non-participation in the deportations had no substantial influence – one way or the other – on the final outcome of the Holocaust in Eastern Europe.' To substantiate his conclusion, Trunk points to the numerous cases where refusal to particular *Judenrät* officials to obey SS commands led either to their replacement by more obedient persons or even to the by-passing of the Jewish intermediate link altogether by the SS, who performed the 'selection' themselves (though in most cases with some help from the Jewish police). To be sure, *individual* cases of disobedience remained ineffective precisely because in so many other cases the Nazis *could* count on Jewish co-operation and hence on perpetrating the murderous operation with the deployment of only residual force of their own. One would not know how much more effective the disobedience could have been were it universally expected.

It seems, however, likely that, were the co-operation not forthcoming, or not available on such a large scale, the complex operation of the mass murder would confront the administrators with managerial, technical and financial problems of an entirely different magnitude. As I mentioned in the first chapter, the leaders of the doomed communities performed most of the preliminary bureaucratic work the operation required (supplying the Nazis with the records and keeping the files on their prospective victims), supervised the productive and distributive activities needed to keep the victims alive until the time when the gas chambers were ready to receive them, policed the captive population so that law-and-order tasks did not stretch the ingenuity or resources of the captors, secured the smooth flow of the annihilation process by appointing the objects of its successive stages, delivered the selected objects to the sites from which they could be collected with a minimum of fuss, and mobilized the financial resources needed to pay for the last journey. *Without* all this substantial and diverse help, the Holocaust would probably have taken place anyway – but it would have gone down in history as a different, and perhaps somewhat less frightening, episode; as just another of the many cases of massive coercion and violence visited upon a disempowered population by blood-thirsty conquerors guided by vengeance or communal hatred. *With* all this, on the other hand, the Holocaust confronts the historian and the sociologist with an entirely new challenge. It serves as a window through which one can catch a glimpse of such processes as have been brought into being by the thoroughly modern art of rational action; of the new potency and new horizons of modern power, which become possible once such processes have been deployed in the service of its objectives. As far as this formidable aspect of the Holocaust is concerned, the proper frame of reference and comparison seems to be provided by the 'normal' exercise of power in the running of modern society, rather than by the blood-soaked history of spectacular genocidal violence.

Indeed, the routine of genocide on the whole excludes that co-operation of the victims which was so prominent in the course of the Holocaust. 'Ordinary' genocide is rarely, if at all, aimed at the total annihilation of the group; the purpose of the violence (if the violence is purposeful and planned) is to destroy the marked category (a nation, a tribe, a religious sect) as a viable communmity capable of self-perpetuation and defence of its own self-identity. If this is the case, the objective of the genocide is met once (1) the volume of violence has been large enough to undermine the will and resilience of the sufferers, and to terrorize them into surrender to the superior power and into the acceptance of the order it imposed; and (2) the marked group has been deprived of resources necessary for the continuation of the struggle. With these two conditions fulfilled, the victims are at the mercy of their tormentors. They may be forced into protracted slavery, or offered a place in the new order on the terms set by the victors – but which sequel is chosen depends fully on the conquerors' whim. Whichever option has been selected, the perpetrators of the genocide benefit. They extend and solidify their power, and eradicate the roots of the opposition.

Among the resources of resistance that must be destroyed to make the violence effective (resources whose destruction, arguably, is the central point of the genocide and ultimately the measure of its effectiveness), by far the most crucial position is occupied by the traditional elites of the doomed community. The most seminal effect of the genocide is the 'beheading' of the enemy. It is hoped that the marked group, once deprived of leadership and centres of authority, will lose it cohesiveness and the ability to sustain its own identity, and consequently its defensive potential. The inner structure of the group will collapse, thereby dissipating it into a collection of individuals who may be then picked one by one and incorporated within the new structure administered by the victors, or forcibly re-assembled into a subjugated, segregated category, ruled and policed directly by the managers of the new order. The traditional elites of the doomed community constitute therefore the prime target of the genocide, as long as the latter is aimed indeed at the destruction of the marked people as a community, as a cohesive, autonomous entity. Following Hitler's vision of Eastern Europe as a vast

Lebensraum for the expanding German race, and its current inhabitants as the future slave labour serving the needs of the new masters, the German occupying forces proceeded to extinguish systematically all vestiges of the native political structure and cultural autonomy. They hunted, incarcerated and attempted to destroy physically all active elements of the conquered Slav nations, and to prevent the reproduction of national elites by disbanding all but the most elementary educational institutions and prohibiting all but morally corrupting local cultural initiative. By so doing, however, they ruled out the opportunity to enlist the co-operation of the enslaved nations in the pursuit of Hitler's grand vision (if they ever entertained such a possibility), except perhaps for the auxiliary services of marginal criminal elements. With local elites marked for destruction, the conquerors were left to their own resources and had to calculate the actions of the vanguished nations among their costs, not assets.

Enslavement of the Jews was never Nazi purpose. Even if mass murder was not pondered as the ultimate end from the start, the state of affairs the Nazis wished to create was one of total *Entfernung* – an effective removal of the Jews from the life-world of the German race. Hitler and his followers had no use for the services the Jews could offer, even in the role of slave labour. The completeness of the sought solution – whether in the form of emigration, forcible eviction, or physical annihilation – made all 'special treatment' of Jewish elites unecessary; the latter were destined to share the lot of their brethren, and whatever plight was to be prepared for the Jews as a whole was seen as exceptionless, applying in the same measure and form to all members of the race. Perhaps an anticipated effect of such a 'totalization' of the Jewish problem was the survival of Jewish communal structure, autonomy and self-government long after similar factors of communal existence came under a frontal assault in all occupied Slav lands. This survival meant first and foremost that Jewish traditional elites retained their adminstrative and spiritual leadership throughout the duration of the Holocaust; if anything, that leadership was further reinforced and made well-nigh uncontestable following the physical segregation of the Jews and the fencing off of the ghettos.

The method used to establish Jewish elites in their new role of the *Judenräte* did vary – from Nazi insistence on holding elections in some of the larger ghettos in the east and in the well rooted Jewish communities in the west, all the way to the appointment of the *Präses* from among a group of venerable elders rounded up in the local market square. And yet there is ample evidence that the Nazi supervisors of the 'Jewish quarters' were keen to sustain and enhance the authority of appointed Jewish leaders; they needed the prestige of the 'Jewish Councils' to obtain the supineness of the Jewish masses. In his famous *Schnellbrief*, dispatched from Berlin on 21 September 1939 to all German *Kommandanten* in newly-occupied Polish towns, Heydrich emphasized that the Councils of Jewish Elders were to be composed of 'the remaining influential personalities and rabbis' – and then spelled out a long list of vital tasks for which the Councils were to bear sole responsibility and hence assume control and authority. One may surmise that the Nazi insistence on doing everything in the ghetto with Jewish hands had as one of its perverse causes the wish to make the power of Jewish leadership all the more visible and convincing. The Jewish population was virtually exempt (in Germany gradually; in the conquered territories abruptly) from the jurisdiction of normal administrative authorities, and thrust fully and without qualification into the hands of their co-religionist leaders, who in turn received their orders from, and reported to, a German institution similarly exempt from the 'normal' power structure. The legal-theoretical principles of the ghetto's bizarre mixture of self-government with isolation were spelled out and codified in 1940 by Hermann Erich Seifert:

> The individual Jew does not exist for the German authorities in the occupied territory. There are in principle no negotiations with an individual Jew ... but exclusively with the Jewish Ältestenräte ... With the help of their Ältenstenräte the Jews can arrange fully for themselves their internal affairs, including the affairs of their religious communities, but on the other hand they have to execute in full responsibility the tasks and requirements of the German administration. The members of the Ältestenrat, in most cases the richest and most distinguished, are personally responsible for this execution. No doubt this Ältestenrat is remotely reminiscent of the Kahals of which the [Tsarist] Russian Jew-policy made use, but with one great difference: Jewish rights were given and defended by Kahals; Jewish duties are received and distributed by the Ältestenräte in the Gouvernment General ... There is no discussion of or argument against the German order.[1]

Downwards, Jewish leadership exercised a formally unlimited power over the captive population; upwards, it was at the mercy of a criminal organization free from all control exercised by the constitutional organs of the state. Jewish elites played therefore a crucial mediating role in the incapacitation of the Jews; quite untypically for a genocide, the total subjection of a population to an unconstrained will of their captors was achieved not through destruction, but by reinforcing the communal structure and the integrative role played by native elites.

Paradoxically, therefore, the situation of the Jews during the preliminary stages of the Final Solution was more akin to that experienced by a subordinate group within a normal power structure, than by the victims of an 'ordinary' genocidal operation. To some remarkable extent, *the Jews were part of that social arrangement which was to destroy them.* They provided a vital link in the chain of co-ordinated actions; their own actions were an indispendable part of the total operation and a crucial condition of its success. 'Ordinary' genocide splits the actors unambiguously into the murderers and the murdered; for the latter, resistance is the only rational response. In the Holocaust, divisions were less clear. Incorporated in the overall power structure, given an extended set of tasks and functions within it, the doomed population had apparently a range of options to choose from. Co-operation with their sworn enemies and future killers was not without its own measure of rationality. *The Jews could therefore play into the hands of their oppressors, facilitate their task, bring closer their own perdition, while guided in their action by the rationally interpreted purpose of survival.*

Because of this paradox, the Holocaust records offer a unique insight into the general principles of bureaucratically administered oppression. The Holocaust was, of course, an extreme case of a phenomenon which normally appears in a much milder form and is rarely aimed at the total annihilation of the oppressed. Yet precisely because of its extremity, the Holocaust revealed aspects of the bureaucratic oppression which otherwise might have remained unnoticed. In their general form, these aspects have a much wider application; indeed, they must be taken account of it the way power operates in modern society is to be fully understood. Most prominent among these aspects is *the ability of modern, rational, bureaucratically organized power to induce actions functionally indispensable to its purposes while jarringly at odds with the vital interests of the actors.*

'Sealing off' the victims

Such an ability is not universal; in order to possess it, bureaucracy must fulfil further conditions in addition to its own, inner hierarchy of command and principles of co-ordinated action. Bureaucracy has to be, above all, fully specialized, and possess an unconditional monopoly in the specialized function it performs. In simpler terms this means that whatever bureaucracy is to do to its targeted objects must be explicitly aimed at no one else and hence is unlikely to affect the situation of other categories; and that the targeted objects must remain within the competence of this one specialized bureaucracy, and no other institution. The first condition results in the improbability of all outside interference with the bureaucratic process; unaffected groups are unlikely to rush to the rescue of the targeted category, as the problems faced by the two sides cannot easily find a common denominator and inspire an integrated, united action. Once the second condition is met, the targeted category knows or soon finds out that any appeals to authoritative and resourceful centres, other than the bureaucracy in whose administration they have been thrust, are vain or ineffective; in some cases such appeals may be construed as a breach of the rules (which only their own bureaucracy is entitled to define), and hence invite consequences more sinister still than dutiful compliance with the bureaucratic ruling. Between them, the two conditions leave the targeted category alone with 'its own' bureaucracy as the only frame of reference for rational decision-making. In other words, the bureaucracy that conducts a 'targeted' policy and retains the exclusive right to conduct it, is fully competent to set the parameters for its victims' behaviour and thus able to enlist the victims' own rational motives among the resources it can deploy in the pursuit of its task. Before the bureaucratically organized power may count on the co-operation of the selfsame category that is to be destroyed or hurt, that category must be effectively 'sealed off': either removed physically from the context of the daily life and concerns of other groups, or separated psychologically by overtly and unambiguously discriminating definitions and the emphasis on the targeted category's uniqueness.

In a speech delivered in April 1935, Rabbi Joachim Prinz of Berlin summed up the experience of the 'sealed-off' category: 'The ghetto is the "world". Outside is the ghetto. On the marketplace, in the street, in the public tavern, everywhere is ghetto. And it has a sign. That sign is; neighbourless. Perhaps this has never before happened in the world, and no one knows how long it can be borne; life without a neighbour ...'[2] By 1935, the future victims of the Holocaust already knew that they were alone. They could not count on the solidarity of others. The suffering they were living through was theirs alone. People physically so close were spiritually infinitely remote: they did not share in their experience. And the experience of the suffering is not easy to communicate. The Jews on whose behalf Rabbi Prinz spoke knew that the officials of the 'Jewish desks' were in sole command of the game; they set the rules, they changed them at will and decided the stakes. Their actions were, therefore, the only solid facts to focus on and to calculate in one's own action. Withdrawal of the outside world cut down the boundaries of the 'situation'; it had to be defined now solely in terms of the persecutors' power, from which there was no appeal. 'The physical removal of the Jews went largely unremarked, because the Germans had long since removed them from their hearts and minds.'[3] Spiritual isolation was first. It has been achieved through a variety of means.

The most obvious means was a straightforward appeal to popular antisemitism and a fomenting of the antisemitic feelings of the people thus far indifferent to or unaware of a special 'Jewish problem'. This the Nazi propaganda did, and did skilfully, with no expense or effort spared. The Jews had been charged with odious crimes, baneful intentions and loathsome hereditary vices. Above all, in keeping with the hygienic sensitivity of modern civilization, fears and phobias normally aroused by vermin and bacteria were stirred, and the modern man's obsession with health and sanitation appealed to. Jewishness was represented as a contagious disease; its carriers as an updated version of Typhoid Mary. Intercourse with the Jews was pregnant with danger. The socio-psychological mechanisms used to produce the reaction of revulsion and disgust to, say, the sight of raw flesh or the smell of human urine – so convincingly described by Norbert Elias in his account of the civilizing process – were deployed to render the very presence of the Jews nauseating and repellent.

There were, however, limits to the effectiveness of the antisemitic gospel. Many people proved immune to the propaganda of hatred or, more generally, to the irrational interpretation of the world that propaganda demanded that they should accept. Many more still, while conceding with little protest the official definition of Jewishness, refused to apply it to the individual Jews they knew. Were the antisemitic propaganda the only means of 'sealing off' the Jews from communal life, it would be likely to fail – resulting at best in the splitting of the population into the camp of rabid Jew-haters and a perhaps less well integrated, and more poorly organized, yet reasonably effective mass of non-collaborators and active defenders of the 'unduly victimized'. It certainly would not suffice to remove the Jews 'from the hearts and minds' of the Germans radically enough to render the subsequent physical destruction of the Jews unopposed and unresented.

The impact of the antisemitic propaganda was, however, supported and considerably reinforced by the care taken to aim all anti-Jewish measures closely on the target, so that each successive act, even if ineffective in its declared purpose, deepened the gulf between the Jews and the rest, and further underlined the message; however atrocious are the things happening to the Jews, they definitely have no adverse influence on the plight of the rest of the population, and therefore are of no concern for anybody but the Jews. We know now from the thoroughly researched historical evidence how much of the energy of the top Nazi bureaucrats and the experts they hired went into designing the proper definition of the Jews – apparently a legalistic subtlety, looking ridiculously out of place against the background of brutal and unscrupulous violence. In fact, the search for a legally perfect definition was more than the last vestige of the *Jurisprudenzkultur* the Nazi could not quite get rid of, or a homage paid to the not-yet fully forgotten tradition of the *Rechtsstaat*. Precise definition of the Jew was necessary for reassuring the witnessess to the victimization that what they saw or suspected would not happen to them, and hence that their interests were not under threat. To achieve this effect, one needed such a definition as one would be able to use to decide exactly who was and who was not a Jew; to eliminate all possibility of unclear, intermediate, mixed, equivocal cases allowing for contradictory interpretation. However absurd in their substance and ostensibly functional relevance, the notorious Nuremberg Laws served this purpose splendidly.[4] They left no no-man's-land between the Jews and the non-Jews. It created a category of people earmarked for *Sonderbehandlung* and ultimately for annihilation. Yet it also created, in one fell swoop, a much wider category of safe and clean citizens of the Reich; the German of pure blood. The same purpose was served, with varying degree of success, by marking the Jewish shops (and thereby emphasizing the propriety and security of the unmarked ones), or by forcing the leftovers of German Jewry to adorn their dress with yellow badges. In effect, 'remarkable as it may sound, the Jewish Question was of not more than minimal interest to the vast majority of Germans'. When the *Reich* moved to the East and the time of the *Aussiedlung* arrived, most people 'probably thought little and asked less about what was happening to the Jews in the East. The Jews were out of sight and out of mind for most ... The road to Auschwitz was built by hate, but paved with indifference.'[5]

The process of separation was accompanied by a deafening silence of all established and organized elites of German society – all those who could, theoretically, raise their voices against the impending disaster and make them heard. One can surmise that part of the reason was a broad sympathy with the master plan of the *Entfernung* of a nation and a culture seen for various reasons as foreign and undesirable. This was not, however, the whole reason, and perhaps not even its most fateful part. The capture of state power by the Nazis did not change the rules of professional conduct; the latter remained loyal as it had been since before the dawn of the modern era, to the principle of the moral neutrality of reason and the pursuit of rationality, which brooks no compromise with factors unrelated to the technical success of the enterprise. German universities, like their counterparts in other modern countries, carefully cultivated the ideal of science as an emphatically value-free activity; they bestowed upon their wards the right and the duty to serve the 'interests of knowledge' and to brush aside other interests with which the welfare of scientific pursuits might clash. Once one remembers this, then the silence, and even the keen co-operation of German scientific institutions in the implementation of Nazi tasks, loses much of its shocking power. The American Franklin H. Littell insists that the less they are amazing, the more that silence and that co-operation are (or at least ought to be) worrying:

> The credibility crisis of the modern university arises from the fact that the death camps were not planned and built, and their operational scheme devised by illiterates, by ignorant and unschooled savages. The killing centres were, like their inventors, products of what had been for generations one of the best university systems in the world ...
>
> Our graduates work without serious internal conflict for social democratic Chile or fascist Chile, for the Greek junta or the Greek republic, for Franco Spain or republican Spain, for Russia, for China, for the Kuwaitis or the Israelis, for America, England, Indonesia or Pakistan ... This summarises, if harshly, the historical role of trained technicians, those who have been 'educated' to skills in the moral and ethical and religious indifference of the modern university ...

He then proceeds to complain that for many years it was easier in his country to discuss the Nazi abuse and misuse of science than the services offered by American universities to 'Dow Chemical, Minneapolis,

Honeywell, or Boeing Aircraft ... or to ITT in the re-establishment of fascism in Chile.'[6]

What truly mattered to German scientific (and more generally, intellectual) elites, and to the best and most distinguished individuals among them was the preservation of their integrity as scholars and spokesmen of Reason. And that task did not include (and did exclude in case of conflict) concern with the ethical meaning of their activity. As Alan Beyerchen found out, in the spring and summer of 1933 the luminaries of German science, people like Planck, Sommerfeld, Heisenberg, or von Laue, all 'counselled patience and restraint in dealing with the government, especially regarding dismissals and emigration. The primary goal was to preserve the professional autonomy of their discipline by avoiding confrontation and waiting for orderly life and procedures to resume.'[7] They all wanted to defend and to save what mattered to them – and save it they did, as soon as they showed a readiness to forget about what mattered less. Showing such readiness came easy, as the 'orderly life' which did resume after the vagaries of the Nazi honeymoon was not very different from what these professors were used to and valued dearly. (It was just that some of their old colleagues were missing, and there was a new salute to make when entering the class full of uniformed students.) Their professional services were in high demand and praised, funds for ambitious and scientifically exciting projects were forthcoming, and for that no price seemed too high. Heisenberg went to Himmler for reassurance that he and his colleagues (that is, except those who went missing) would be allowed to do what they wanted and cherished. Himmler advised him to make a careful distinction between scientific findings and the political conduct of the physicists. This must have been a music to Heisenberg's ears: was it not what he was trained to do from the start? He 'therefore pulled his punches, actively promoting the Nazi cause, especially abroad, and during the hostilities, diligently directing one of the two teams engaged in designing atomic explosives, stimulated, no doubt, as the inveterate scientific animal that he was, by the desire to "see" and to succeed.'[8]

'The story of the withdrawal of power from the intellectuals is always the story of voluntary relinquishment', – wrote Joachim C. Fest, – 'and if resistance is called for, it is merely resistance to the temptation to suicide.'[9] As it were, the intellectual victims-turned-courtiers of the Nazi type of 'orderly life' found few reasons for suicide, and plenty for voluntary, sometimes enthusiastic, surrender.

The remarkable thing about the surrender is that it is difficult to say where it starts and virtually impossible to foresee where is it likely to end. During the *Kristallnacht* pogrom the wife of the eminent orientalist professor Kahle had been found helping her Jewish friend to sweep up her ruined shop; her husband was subjected to boycott and other tender mercies which forced him to resign.

> The intervening months were a period of quarantine during which a total of three people – out of the Professor's entire social and professional circle – called on him under cover of darkness. He received one other communication from the outside world: a letter from a group of colleagues expressing regret that he had forfeited an honourable exit from the University through his wife's lack of instinct.[10]

Another remarkable thing about the surrender is that however painful it might have felt at the beginning, it tends to travel from shame to pride. Those who surrender become accomplices of the crime, and deal appropriately with the cognitive dissonance the complicity generates. People who watched with disdain and disgust the antisemitic inanities of Nazi propaganda and kept silent 'only for the sake of saving the greater values' a few years later found themselves rejoicing in the blessed cleanliness of universities and purity of German science. Their own, rational antisemitism

> grew stronger as the persecution of the Jews grew worse. The explanation is plain, if depressing: when people know even with half their minds that a great injustice is being done, and lack the generosity and the courage to protest, they automatically throw the blame on to the victims as the simplest way of easing their own consciences.[11]

One way or the other, the loneliness of the Jews of Germany became complete. They lived now in a world without neighbours. For all that mattered to their fate, the other Germans could have not existed. The Jewish world contained the Nazi power as the only other agent; however the Jews defined their situation, that situation was reduced to one factor only; the actions their Nazi persecutors deemed useful to undertake. As rational beings, the Jews had to adjust their own conduct to the anticipated Nazi responses. As rational beings, they had to assume that there was a logical link between actions and reactions, and hence also such actions as were more reasonable and advisable than others. As rational beings, they had to be guided by the same behavioural principles as those promoted by their bureaucratic gaolers: efficiency, higher gain, less expense. Since the Nazis had the undivided and uncontested command of the rules and the stakes of the game, they could deploy that Jewish rationality as a resource in the pursuit of their own goals. They could arrange the rules and the stakes in such a fashion that each rational step would deepen the helplessness of their prospective victims and bring them an inch or two nearer to their ultimate destruction.

The 'save what you can' game

The game in which the Jews were forced by the Nazis to participate was one of death and survival, and thus rational action in their case could be only aimed at, and measured by, the increase of the chances of escaping destruction, or of limiting the scale of destruction. The world of values was reduced to one – remaining alive (or was at least overshadowed by it). That much is now clear, but it was not necessarily clear to the victims at the time, and certainly not at the early stages of the 'twisted road to Auschwitz'. We already know that the Nazis themselves, including their leaders, did not start their war against the Jews with a clear notion of its ultimate outcome; the war started with a modest objective of *Entfernung*, of setting the Jews apart from the German race, and in the long run making Germany *judenrein*; it was in the course, and under the impact, of the bureaucratic pursuit of that objective that at some later stage the physical destruction of the Jews became both 'rational' as a 'solution', and technologically feasible. Yet even when Hitler's fateful decision to murder the Russian Jews opened new horizons and previously unconsidered options in front of the zealous 'Jewish experts', keeping the nature of the Final Solution secret was an integral and crucial part of the Nazi design. Carrying the victims to the gas chambers was called 'resettlement' and the identity of the annihilation camps was dissolved in the vague idea of 'the East'. When ghetto spokesmen called on the SS commanders to find out whether the stubborn rumours of the impending killings were true, the Germans would flatly deny the truth. The secret was kept until, literally, the last moment. One crime for which the Jewish members of *Sonderkommando* servicing the gas chambers and crematoria were punished with immediate death was to tell the newcomers alighting from the cattle trucks that the building they saw from the platform was not a communal bath. The reason was not, of course, to spare the victims agony and anguish, but to make them enter the gas chamber voluntarily and with no resistance.

At all stages of the Holocaust, therefore, the victims were *confronted with a choice* (at least subjectively – even when objectively the choice did not exist any more, having been pre-empted by the secret decision of physical destruction). They could not choose between good and bad situations, but they could at least choose between greater and lesser evil. Most importantly, they could divert some blows from themselves by stressing, and manifesting, their entitlement to an exemption or to a special treatment. In other words, they *had something to save.* To make their victims' behaviour predictable and hence manipulable and controllable, the Nazis had to induce them to act in the 'rational mode'; to achieve that effect, they had to make the victims believe that there was indeed something to save, and that there were clear rules as to how one should go about saving it. To believe that, the victims had to be convinced that the treatment of the group as a whole would not be uniform, that the lot of individual members would be diversified, and in each case dependent on individual merit. The victims had to think, in other words, that their conduct did matter; and that their plight could be at least in part influenced by what they were about to do.

The sheer existence of bureaucratically defined categories of varying degrees of rights and deprivations prompted frantic efforts to obtain a 're-classification', to prove that one 'deserves' to be assigned to a better category. In no case was this effect more visible than in that of the *Mischlinge* – a 'third race' created by the German legislation, and located awkwardly between disfranchised 'full Jews' and blameless members of the German *Volk.* 'Because of these discriminations, pressure for exceptional treatment was applied to colleagues, superiors, friends and relatives. Consequently, in 1935 a procedure was instituted for the reclassification of a Mischling into a higher category ... The procedure was known as *Befreiung* (liberation).' Knowledge that the efforts are not necessarily vain, that the verdict of the blood can be successfully appealed against and quashed, added zeal to the pressure. One could – and many did – obtain an *echte* ('genuine') liberation on proving one's merit (the highest court in Germany ruled that 'conduct was not enough; the attitude disclosed by the conduct was decisive'). One could even, like a Ministerialrat (and a *Mischling*) Killy, a man with a distinguished contribution to the destruction of the Jews, received the certificate of *Befreiung* as a Christmas gift delivered by a special courier straight under the family Christmas tree.[12]

The diabolical aspect of this setting was that the beliefs and convictions it sanctioned, and the actions it encouraged, supplied legitimacy to the Nazi masterplan and made it digestible to most, the victims included. While fighting for petty privileges, exempted statuses or simply the stay of execution which the overall design of destruction provided for, the victims and those who tried to help them tacitly accepted the premises of the design. Arguing, for example, that this or that person has a right to be exempt from the professional bar on the ground of his past merits, one admitted in practice that without such special merit, the professional bar was uncontestable.

> What was morally so disastrous in the acceptance of these privileged categories was that everyone who demanded to have an 'exception' made in his case implicitly recognized the rule, but this point, apparently, was never grasped by these 'good men', Jewish and Gentile, who busied themselves about all those 'special cases' for which preferential treatment could be asked ... Even after the end of the war, Kasztner [a leader of the Hungarian Jews who negotiated with the Nazis an exemption of some of his wards from death camps] was proud of his success in saving 'prominent Jews', a category officially introduced by the Nazis in 1942, as though in his view, too, it went without saying that a famous Jew had more right to stay alive than an ordinary one.[13]

The opportunities to add authority to the rule through fighting for exemptions (and in the end reinforcing the rule by deploying it as an entitlement to seek individual privileges) were ample and varied. They had been offered, though in changing forms, at all stages of the Holocaust. In the case of German Jewry such opportunities were particularly profuse and elaborate. The Jews who fought on the German side in the Great War, who were wounded in battle, who had been decorated for bravery, were proclaimed a special case and for a protracted period kept free from most restrictions applied to their less meritorious brethren. This benevolent ruling took attention away from the much more sweeping rule from which it provided an exception. Whoever saw in the ruling a personal chance could claim the benefits only while simultaneously accepting the assumption that warranted both the general rule and the exceptions: that 'normal' Jews, Jews 'as such', did not deserve the ordinary rights offered by German citizenship. The flood of closely argued applications, letters of recommendation, interventions in support of distinguished personalities, friends or business associates, the vehement search for documents and testimonies which the ruling triggered contributed in no small a measure to the quiet reconciliation to the new state of affairs created by the anti-Jewish legislation. The righteous among the Gentiles did their best to secure privileges for people they knew, liked or respected, stressing in their letters to the authorities that _this particular_ person does not deserve harsh treatment because of his _unique_ service to the German nation. Clergymen were busy defending the _converted_ Jews – Christians of Jewish origin. On the way, the principle that one needs to be a _special kind_ of Jew to protest discrimination and persecution was tacitly accepted, or at any rate accommodated.

On the whole, there was no shortage of persons and groups who all too eagerly embraced the idea of their own exclusive quality and right to a more benevolent treatment. One of the most conspicuous examples was the notorious and ubiquitous split between the 'established' and the 'immigrant' Jews in occupied Western Europe. The split had its precedent in the long-standing enmity of the well-settled and partly assimilated Jewish communities toward their uncouth, ignorant, Yiddish-speaking East-European brethren, whose troublesome obtrusiveness they saw as a threat to their own, hard-earned respectability. (Old and rich Jewish families in Britain would not mind paying for the return fares of the poor and illiterate Jewish masses who fled the Russian pogroms at the turn of the century; in Germany, the 'more German than the Germans' Jews of the old stock, 'hoped to get rid of the antipathy . . . by divesting it against the poor and yet unassimilated immigrant brethren'.)[14] The long tradition of superior, disdainful stance toward the Jews of the _shtetl_ prevented the leaders of the Jewish communities in the West from perceiving in the fate of the Eastern Jews a pattern of their own future; no commonality of fate, and hence no solidary strategy could conceivably be engendered by histories and cultures so diverse. When the information of mass murder in Poland had been broadcast all over Holland by the BBC, David Cohen, the President of the Jewish Council, flatly denied its relevance to the prospects of Dutch Jewry:

> The fact that the Germans had perpetrated atrocities against Polish Jews was no reason for thinking that they would behave in the same way toward Dutch Jews, firstly because the Germans had always held Polish Jews in disrepute, and secondly because in the Netherlands, unlike Poland, they had to sit up and take notice of public opinion.[15]

This self-contented view was not just the matter of fanciful, fairy-tale conception of the world, with potentially suicidal consequences for its holders. World-views tend to determine actions, and the conduct of organized Jewish communities convinced of their own superiority greatly reduced the chance of a unified Jewish reaction to Nazi policy and facilitated the 'destruction by stages'. Even if the spokesmen of the established Jewish community felt compassion for the immigrant Jews rounded up, incarcerated and deported in front of their eyes, they appealed to community members to keep calm and refrain from resistance for the sake of 'higher values'. According to Jacques Adler's study, the strategy of French Jewry, spelled out as early as September 1940, in response to the differential treatment proclaimed by the German occupying forces, left no doubt about the hierarchy of preferences: 'As its first priority that strategy strove to ensure the continued existence of French Judaism – and that objective did not include the foreign Jews.' It assumed that 'the immigrant Jews represented a liability' in regard to the survival of the French Jews. The Jewish establishment assented to the Vichy resolution that the price for protecting the French Jews was dumping the immigrants over to the Germans: 'There is no doubt that French Judasim agreed with Vichy that these foreign Jews were socially and politically undesirable.'[16]

Rejection of solidarity in the name of personal or group privileges (which always, albeit indirectly, meant consent to the principle that not all members of the marked category deserve to survive, and that differential treatment should follow the duly assessed 'objective' quality) was prominent not only in the inter-communal relations. Inside each community, differential treatment was hoped and fought for, with the *Judenräte* normally cast in the role of survival brokers. Preoccupied with the 'save what you can' strategy, the future victims lost from sight, if only temporarily, the awesome identity of imminent fate. This gave the Nazis a chance to achieve their purpose with greatly reduced costs and a minimum of trouble. In Hilberg's words,

> The Germans were notably successful in deporting Jews by stages, because those who remained behind would reason that it was necessary to sacrifice the few in order to save the many. The operation of this psychology may be observed in the Vienna Jewish community, which concluded a deportation 'agreement' with the Gestapo, with the 'understanding' that six categories of Jews would not be deported. Again, the Warsaw ghetto Jews argued in favour

of co-operation and against resistance on the grounds that the Germans would deport sixty thousand Jews but not hundreds of thousands. The bisection phenomenon occured also in Salonika, where the Jewish leadership co-operated with the German deportation agencies upon the assurance that only 'Communist' elements from the poor sections would be deported, while the 'middle-class' would be left alone. The fatal arithmetic was also applied in Vilna, where Judenrat chief Gens declared: 'With a hundred victims I save a thousand people. With a thousand I save ten thousand.'[17]

Life under oppression was so structured that – from the vantage point of day-to-day existence – the chances of survival seemed indeed distributed unevenly; moreover, they seemed manipulable. Resources in personal or group command could be used to turn public inequality to private advantage. As Helen Fein indicated,

> The threat of collective death was not anticipated because the social organization of political economy of the ghetto created differential death chances every day. The chance of each to survive depended on his or her place in the class order, and the whole class order arose from imposed scarcity and political terror, rewarding those most able to serve the Nazis directly or indirectly ... The system of controls also obscured recognition of a common enemy, by displacing anger against the conquerors onto the *Judenrat* and perpetuating the belief that it was a war of all against all rather than that of them against us.[18]

The individualization of survival strategies led to a universal scramble for roles and positions deemed to be favourable or privileged, and to widespread efforts to ingratiate oneself in the eyes of the oppressors – invariably at the other victims' expense. Anxiety and aggression generated on the way were discharged by using the *Judenräte* as lightning rods; yet at each stage of the destruction *Judenräte* could count on a certain constituency which, having benefited from the successive turn of policy, would gladly cast its support behind the hapless community officials, and thus offer legitimation and authority to the current move. At each stage of the destruction – except the final one – there were individuals and groups eager to save what could be saved, to defend what could be defended, to exempt what could be exempted; and thus – although only obliquely – to co-operate.

Individual rationality in the service of collective destruction

Inhuman oppression of the Nazi type leaves admittedly little room for manoeuvre; many of the options people are trained or educated to choose under normal conditions are excluded or beyond their grasp. Under exceptional conditions, conduct is by definition exceptional; but it is exceptional in its overt form and its tangible consequences, not necessarily in the principles of choice and the motives which guide it. Throughout their journey to the final destruction most people, most of the time, were not completely devoid of choice. And where there is choice, there is a chance to behave rationally. And behave rationally most people did. While in full command of the means of coercion, the Nazis saw to it that *rationality meant co-operation*; that everything the Jews did to serve their own interest brought the Nazi objective somewhat nearer to full success.

Co-operation is perhaps too vague and too inclusive a notion. It may be callous and unjust to consider mere refraining from an open rebellion (and following the established routine instead) as an act of co-operation. All responsibilities of the future Jewish Councils spelled out in Heydrich's *Schnellbrief* were concerned with the services the Jewish leaders were obliged to render to the German authorities; Heydrich did not concern himself with other functions *Judenräte* might think useful or necessary to undertake. He presumably counted on such functions to be undertaken on the councils' own initiative, out of the rational consideration of the needs of a community crowded together in a narrow space and faced with a necessity to secure its coexistence and means of survival. If there was such a wager, it proved to be well chosen. Jewish Councils did not need German instructions to take care of the religious, educational, cultural and welfare needs of the Jews. By so doing, they already willy-nilly accepted the role of the lower rung of the German administrative hierarchy. Their activity, which took all the problems related to the daily life of the Jews off German hands, was already a co-operation – of sorts. In this however, the role of Jewish communal authorities, notwithstanding the extremity of the oppressive regime, was not essentially different from the roles normally played by the leaderships of oppressed minorities in making the continuation of repression (indeed, the sheer reproduction of the oppressive regime) feasible. It was not essentially different either from the traditional forms of Jewish self-government (particularly in Poland and some other parts of Eastern Europe) and the closely guarded autonomy of the *kehila*.

At the start of German occupation, and before the *Judenräte* became an official link in German administrative structure, the pre-war *kehila* elders undertook on their own initiative the task of representing Jewish interests in elaborating a *modus vivendi* with new authorities. By habit and training, they tried to employ the old and tested methods of writing petitions and complaints, obtaining hearing for their grievances, negotiating – and bribing. They did not oppose the German decision to concentrate the Jews in the ghettos. Fencing Jews off from the rest of the population seemed a good protection against harassment and pogroms. It also seemed a welcome means to enhance Jewish self-management and preserve a Jewish way of life in a hostile and threatening environment. It seemed, in other words, that confinement in the ghettos served – under the circumstances – Jewish interests, and that consent to confinement was a rational attitude to take by all those with Jewish interests close to their hearts.

At the same time, however, the acceptance of ghetto enclosures meant playing into Nazi hands. In the long run, ghettos were to disclose their role as instruments of concentration – that necessary preliminary stage on the road to deportation and destruction. In the meantime, however, ghettos meant also that one German officer could exercise complete supervision over tens of thousands of Jews – with the help of the Jews themselves, who supplied clerical and manual labour, the communal infrastructure of daily life and the organs responsible for the maintenance of law and order. In this sense, all Jewish self-management meant *objectively* co-operation. And the co-operation element in the *Judenräte* activity was destined to swell in time at the expense of all other functions. Rational decisions taken yesterday in the name of the defence of Jewish interests modified the context of action in such a way that rational decision-making has become that much more difficult today; and that rational choices were bound to turn downright impossible tomorrow.

Isaiah Trunk's definitive study of *Judenräte* leaves no doubt as to the frantic and desperate struggle of the Jewish Councils to find rational solutions to ever more mind-boggling and severe problems. It was not their fault that, in the face of German superior force and the total elimination of moral inhibitions attained by the bureaucratic machinery of the anti-Jewish war, there was no solution within the range of their options that did not serve German objectives. German bureaucratic machinery was put in the service of a goal incomprehensible in its irrationality. The goal was the annihilation of the Jews; all of them, old and young, invalid and able-bodied, economic liabilities and potential economic assets. There was no way, therefore, in which Jews could ingratiate themselves with the German bureaucracy of destruction, make themselves useful or for whatever other reason desirable or at least tolerable. The war, in other words, was lost for the Jews before it had started. And yet at each phase of that war decisions were to be made, steps were to be undertaken, purposes were to be rationally pursued. Each day there was an occasion, and a demand, for rational conduct. It was because the ultimate objective of the Holocaust operation defied all rational calculation that its success could be built out of the rational actions of its prospective victims. Long before the Holocaust was conceived, K., the resourceful yet hapless land-surveyor of Kafka's *The Castle*, went through the same experience. He failed in his lonely strife against the Castle – not because he acted irrationally, but because, on the contrary, he went out of his way to deploy reason in his intercourse with a power which (as he wrongly assumed) would respond rationally to rational overtures, but in fact did not.

One of the most heart-rending episodes in the brief and gory history of the ghettos was the rescue-through-work campaign undertaken on the initiative of Jewish Councils in some of the biggest East-European ghettos. Pre-war East-European antisemitism accused the Jews of economic parasitism; traders and middlemen all, they were unproductive to boot, and as a whole made a group the rest of the population would be better off without. When the German invaders made the dispensability of the Jews into their declared programme, it made more sense than ever to seek the reversal of their intention by supplying tangible proof of Jewish usefulness. Circumstances seemed particularly propitious for such a strategy, as the Germans, with their resources stretched to the limits by the war, were surely bound to welcome any extra economic asset or productive force they could lay their hands on. One can hardly charge Chaim Rumkowski, the *Präses* of the Lódź ghetto and by far the most pious apostle of the industrial faith, with making an irrational response to the German threat. He had surely underestimated the Germans' murderous irrationality, and over-estimated their inherent business-like rationality (or, more generally, the grip of the values and principles ostensibly guiding the world organized form the point of view of efficiency). It is however difficult to see what else could he do even if he knew of his error. He had to behave as if the adversaries were indeed rationally acting agents; there was no way one could decide one's own course of action without making such an assumption. In the valley of the blind, the one-eyed man was king. In the rational world of modern bureaucracy, the irrational adventurer is the dictator.

And so, in a way, Rumkowski did behave according to the only form of rationality open to him, however deceitful and treacherous. 'On innumerable occasions, in all his public utterances both before and during the "resettlements", he untiringly repeated that the physical existence of the ghetto depended solely on labour useful to the Germans and that under no circumstances, even the most tragic ones, should the ghetto give up this justification for its continuation.'[19] Rumkowski of Lódź, Ephraim Barash of Bialystok, Gens of Vilna and many others spoke often and with conviction of the impact of their diligent work on the predispositions of their German masters. It seems that they did believe that once the productivity and profitability of Jewish labour was demonstrated, German commissions and subsidies would replace deportations and random murder; or so, at least, they talked or forced themselves into believing. On the way, they made no mean contribution to the German war effort. *They worked to postpone the final defeat of the selfsame sinister force that swore their destruction.* Before the twisted road wound up in Auschwitz, many bridges on the River Kwai were built by skilful and keen Jewish hands.

The less ideologically committed functionaries of German bureaucracy were indeed impressed. For purely pragmatic reasons, to be sure. That the Jews were humans with a lasting place in the scheme of things did not seem to cross their minds, but they certainly accepted that exploiting Jewish industrial zeal made more economic (and military) sense than killing off of such a devoted and disciplined labour force. There is evidence that some military commanders in the East were particularly eager to postpone the murder once they found out that most of the local artisans, with skills indispensable to keep the military machine going, were Jews. Their half-hearted attempts to defend slave Jewish labour against the machine-guns of the *Einsatzgruppen* were promptly countermanded, once discovered, by the supreme authorities who knew that rational considerations were admissible only if, and in as much as, they brought closer the irrational objective. The resolution of the Ministry of Occupied Eastern Territories left no room for argument: 'As a matter of principle, no economic factors were to be taken into consideration in the solution of the Jewish question. Should any problems arise in the future, advice was to be requested from the Higher SS and Police Leader.'[20] By and large, 'useful' labour initiated by the Jewish Council did not seem to rescue anybody (though it did prolong the life of some). Encomiums lavished by Rumkowski or Barash on skilful and enthusiastic, and hence 'irreplaceable' Jewish workers, could not change the sombre fact that those workers were Jews. Even when the workers lubricated the German war machine, they remained Jews first, and 'useful' later. Mostly too late.

The true test of rationality came when the *Judenräte* had been instructed to take charge of 'resettlement'. Having mobilized all their operative force to fight the constantly growing Russian pressure, the Nazis could ill afford servicing the Final Solution with their own uniformed men. This time they accepted that they did need Jewish labour. The *Judenräte* had been made responsible for all the jobs the preparation of murder demanded. They had to supply detailed lists of ghetto residents destined for deportation. They had to select them first. They had to deliver them to the rail carriages later. In case of resistance or hiding, the Jewish police had to trace and locate the obstinate and force them to comply. Ideally, the Nazis themselves would limit their own role to that of detached observers.

Were the Jews to be murdered wholesale, in one swoop, the choice (or, rather, the absence of choice) would be clear and unambiguous for all. An appeal to general resistance, however little hope it promised, would be the obvious response – with 'marching like sheep to the slaughter' as its only alternative. From the German point of view, such clarity would considerably increase the cost of the operation. The Germans would not be able to harness the rational drives of the victims in the service of their own destruction. Simply, the victims would not co-operate. Deploying the rationality of the victims was a much more rational solution. And so whenever possible, the Nazis tried to avoid total deportations. They seemed to prefer to do the job in instalments.

In towns where liquidation of the Jews was accomplished in instalments, the Germans reassured them after each subsequent 'action' that it was the last one ... All this intentional fraudulence and cheating in cold blood during the Final Solution process was used by the Germans in order to soothe the panic-stricken Jews, reduce their alertness, and entirely disorient them so that to the very last minute, they had no inkling of what 'resettlement' really meant. The instinct of self-preservation, which prompts people to resist the thought of imminent destruction and to cling to even a spark of hope, here played into the hands of the executioners.[21]

In many small towns in the Western territories of the USSR, soon turned by the invading German Army into hell's backyard, complex stratagems were unnecessary. As Hitler instructed his troops, the war against the USSR was unlike any other war – everything was allowed and no rules applied. The Wehrmacht, and particularly the *Einsatzgruppen*, acted as if the only rule still obeyed was *kill as you kill can*. The Jews were herded into the nearest woods or ravine and cut down by machine-gun fire. There was no shortage of enthusiastic Ukrainian auxiliaries, and no squeamishness among seasoned soldiers of the 'war unlike any other war'. Only in a few places where the Jewish population was particularly numerous, or the need of Jewish craftsmen particularly acute, did they take trouble to establish Councils and institute a Jewish police – which on the previously captured Polish territories they did as a rule. Wherever the ghettos were established, Jewish co-operation in their own destruction was wanted, and, on the whole, obtained.

At a relatively early stage the Councils knew – or at least could know, unless they tried hard not to – what was the true purpose of the 'selections' they were commanded to make. Quite a few members of the Councils flatly refused to co-operate. Some committed suicide, others joined voluntarily the transports heading to the death camps, often having first to deceive the Germans who still needed Jewish councillors alive. Most, however, went along with the successive 'last actions'. These were not short of convincing, rational explanations of their conduct. With Jewish tradition prohibiting the bargaining for survival of some at the expense of others[22], the explanations could be drawn only from the folklore of the modern, rational age and wrapped in the vocabulary of modern technology. Of the greatest use was, expectedly, the game of numbers: the life of a greater number is better than the life of a smaller one, to kill less is less odious than to kill more. *To sacrifice some, in order to save many* – this was the most frequent and recurring refrain in the recorded apologias of the *Judenräte* leaders. In a curious twist of mind, condemning to death was conceived of as the noble and morally commendable defence of life. 'We do not decide who is to die; we only decide who is to live.' It was not enough to play God; many *Judenräte* leaders wished to be remembered as benevolent, protective gods. And so having sent thousands of the elderly, sick, and children, to their deaths, Rumkowski declared on 4 September 1942; 'We were not ... motivated by the thought of how many would be lost, but by the consideration of how many it would be possible to save.'[23] Others dipped into the rich metaphorics of modern medicine and dressed themselves as life-saving surgeons: 'One needs to cut off a limb to save the body;' or 'if one needs to amputate a poisoned arm to save a life, it is done.'

All this said, and the passing of death sentences presented as a praiseworthy achievement of modern rational mind combined with warm Jewish heart, one question continued to nag even the most self-apologetic collaborators: providing that cutting of the limbs is unavoidable, should it be I to perform the surgery? And, more hauntingly still; providing that some must perish so that others may live, who am I to decide who ought to be sacrificed, and for whom?

There is evidence that questions like these did torment many of the Jewish councillors and leaders, even those (particularly those) who did not refuse to serve and did not seek to escape through suicide. The dignified departure of Warsaw's Cherniakov is widely known; yet the list of suicides was long, and the number of Jewish councillors who drew the line which their moral standards did not allow them to cross was large and still remains uncounted. Here are just a few, random examples. Before committing suicide, the *Präses* of the Równe *Judenräte*, Dr Bergman, told the Germans that he could deliver for 'resettlement' only himself and his family. Motel Chajkin of Kosów Poleski scornfully rejected the *Stadtkommissar's* offer to save him. David Liberman of Luków threw in the face of the German supervisor money collected for an unsuccessful bribe – which he had first torn into shreds, shouting 'Here is your payment for our trip, you bloody tyrant!' He was shot on the spot. Faced with the Nazi demand to select a contingent of Jews for the 'work in Russia', the entire Jewish Council of Bereza Kartuska committed suicide at the meeting of 1 September 1942.

As to the others, cowardly enough or bold enough to live, they badly needed an answer; an excuse, a justification, a moral or rational argument. In most recorded cases, they settled for the latter, apparently the most acceptable to the rest and the most convincing. After each successive 'action' the likes of Gens and Rumkowski felt the need to call general meetings of the remaining ghetto prisoners in order to explain why they decided 'to do it ourselves'. (In the case of Gens, 'doing it' meant delivering 400 elders and children of Oszmiana to the place of execution, and having them killed by the Jewish policemen.) The stunned audience was then treated to a display of rational mind; calculation of numbers. 'If we left the job to the Germans, many more would have died.' Or, more personally still; 'Did I refuse to be in command, the Germans would have put in my place a much more cruel and sinister man, with unimaginable consequences.' Rationally calculated 'gain' was then re-forged into a moral obligation. 'Yes, it is my duty to foul my hands', decided Gens, the self-appointed God of Vilna Jews, the killer who died convinced that he was the Saviour.

The 'save what you can' strategy was pursued until the last Jew lay buried in a Ukrainian ditch or went up in smoke through a Treblinka chimney. It was pursued by people armed with logic and well trained in the art of rational thinking. The strategy itself was a triumph and an ultimate accolade of rationality. There was always something or somebody to save, and so there was always an occasion to be rational. Logical and rational Jewish councillors argued themselves into doing the murderers' job. Their logic and their rationality was a part of the murderers' plan. It was deployed each time the murder squads were too thin or the murder weapons were not immediately available. Logic and rationality were always available, and so a good supply of efficient co-operation was always there, waiting and ready to fill the gap. It was as if the ancient wisdom should have been rephrased. It appeared that when God wanted to destroy someone, He did not make him mad. He made him rational.

As we know well today, the 'save what you can' strategy, rational as it might have been, did not help the victims. But then it was not a strategy of the victims in the first place. It was an addendum, an extension, of the strategy of destruction, worked out and administered by forces bent on annihilation. Those who embraced the 'save what you can' strategy had been first marked as the victims. Those who had marked them as victims created a situation in which things needed to be saved in order to exist, and thus the calculation of 'loss avoidance', 'costs of survival', 'lesser evil', was set in operation. In such a situation the rationality of the victims had become the weapon of their murderers. But then the *rationality of the ruled is always the weapon of the rulers.*

We know today that all these theoretical truths notwithstanding, the oppressors encountered surprisingly little difficulty in soliciting the rationally motivated complicity of their victims.

Rationality of self-preservation

The success of the oppressors depended on inducing the rational calculation of the victims to outlive the possibility of reaching the objective it was meant originally to serve; on enabling the people – at least some people, and for some time – to act rationally in an admittedly irrational setting. This in turn depended on cutting out enclaves of normality from the total context; and cutting a process, which ultimately led to perdition, into such stages as, whenever contemplated separately, allowed for a choice guided by rational criteria of survival. All single acts which in the end combined into the *Endlösung* were rational from the point of view of the administrators of the Holocaust; most of them were also rational from the point of view of the victims.

For this effect to be achieved, the appearance had to be created that selective survival was a feasible target at most times, and hence the conduct dictated by the interest in self-preservation was both rational and sensible. Once self-preservation had been chosen as the supreme criterion of action, its price could be gradually yet relentlessly increased – until all other considerations have been devalued, all moral or religious inhibitions broken, all scruples disavowed and disallowed. In the tormented admission of the notorious Resvö Kasztner, 'In the beginning, relatively unimportant things were asked of [the Jewish Council], replaceable things of material value like personal possessions, money, and apartments. Later, however, the personal freedom of the human beings was demanded. Finally, the Nazis asked for the life itself.'[24] The inherent moral indifference of the principles of rationality was thereby pushed to the extreme and exploited in full. The potential, always present in actors trained to pursue rational gain, but dormant as long as not exposed to extreme test, here came into its own. In a dazzling flash, the rationality of self-preservation was revealed as the enemy of moral duty.

According to an eyewitness testimony, on Easter Day of 1942 the *Amtskomissar* of Sokoly commanded the local *Judenrät* to deliver all able-bodied men of the town. When at the appointed time the *Präses* reported the failure of his efforts,

The *Amtkomissar* went wild, cutting him off and slapping his head and face. He snapped open his pocket watch and screamed: '*Im Verlaufe einer halben Stunde sollen alle hier versammelt sein! Sonst wird der Judenrät bald erschossen!*' This sent a new shock through the *Judenrat*. Suddenly, they were changed men. All twelve of them along with their aides and assistants rushed through the streets of the *shtetl*, going from house to house and dragging everyone out, big and small. No one could stop them. Then they lined everyone up in rows. If any 'malingerers' didn't show up, they said, that Asmodeus would execute the whole

Judenrat! In fifteen minutes, the street was jammed with people, and the *Judenrat* marched them off in double file.[25]

Scenes like this repeated themselves with awesome regularity throughout the vast expanses of Nazi-ruled Europe. Jewish councillors and Jewish policemen were faced with a simple choice; to die or to let others die. Many chose to postpone their own death and the death of their relatives and friends. Playing God was made easier by self-interest.

It is impossible to say how many of those who chose 'to foul their hands' did hope to survive. Life-and-death choice puts the instinct of self-preservation to the extreme test. It is unfair and misleading to judge human behaviour under conditions of such choice against the standards of much less consequential and dramatic decisions made in ordinary life, where conflicts between self-interest and responsibility for others are often sharp, but hardly ever ultimate, or calling for irreversible choices. Most ordinary conflicts, besides, are faced singly, in an environment in which most other people do not need to make choices of comparable moral intensity – and hence the visibility of moral standards remains strong. Such an environment was effectively destroyed in ghettos in the course of the staged destruction. Whatever remained of the authority of moral obligations over rational self-interest was 'phased out' in the passage through successive circles of hell. The normal procedure of every bureaucracy – making obedience more certain and easier to obtain through devaluation or defusion of all contravening pressures, including the moral ones – here was pushed to the extreme and revealed its full potential. Co-operation of the victims with the designs of their persecutors was made easier by the moral corruption of the victims. By facing them with choices in which the 'fittest', who survived, could only emerge from the test with soiled hands, the designers made sure that with the passage of time the ghetto population would turn more and more into a company of accomplices to murder, and with it moral insensitivity and callousness would grow – to the detriment, and possibly extinction, of all brakes that normally constrain the pressure of the naked instinct of self-preservation.

Marek Edelman, one of the leaders and the few surviving fighters of the Warsaw ghetto uprising, recorded immediately after the end of the war his reminiscences of 'ghetto society':

Complete separation, embargo on the outside press and cutting off of all communication with the outside world had also their special purpose and effect on the Jewish population. Everything which happened on the other side of the walls became gradually ever more distant, blurred, alien. What counted instead was what happened today, in the immediate vicinity; these were the most important affairs, on which all the attention of the average ghetto resident was concentrated. To remain alive has become the sole important matter. This 'life' everybody interprets in his own way, depending on conditions and the resources one commands. Comfortable for people wealthy before the war, ostentatious and exuberant for degenerated gestapo collaborators or demoralized smugglers, life means famine for the uncounted mass of labourers and unemployed, existing on watery soup from charity kitchen and on ration bread. To such 'life' everybody clings obsessively in his own way. People with money see the purpose of life in daily comforts and pleasures, which they seek in the noisy and constantly crowded cafes, night clubs, dancing halls. People who have nothing, chase the elusive 'happiness' hidden in a mouldy potato found in a refuse bin or in a piece of bread thrust into the begging hand by a passer-by; they want to forget hunger, if only for a fleeting moment ... But hunger grows by the day, it spills out from overcrowded flats onto the streets, it stings the eye with the sight of monstrously swollen bodies, ulcerated and festering limbs wrapped in filthy rags, covered with sores and wounds left by frostbites and undernourishment. Hunger speaks through the lips of begging children and destitute elders ... Poverty is so overwhelming, that people die of famine in the streets. Everyday, at 4–5 am, undertakers collect dozens of corpses, covered with newspapers held in place with a stone. Some fall down in the streets, others die indoors, but the family strips them naked (to sell the dress) and throws them on the pavement, so that the Jewish Council may pay for the funeral. One after another, horse carts pass the streets, filled to the brim with naked corpses ... At the same time, typhus rages in the ghetto ... every hospital ward takes in 150 infected; two, sometimes three, are put in one bed, but still many lie on the floor. On the dying, people look impatiently; room is needed for others ... Five hundred corpses are packed into each graveditch, and yet hundreds lie unburied and the graveyard exudes sickly, nauseating odour ... Into this tragic condition of Jewish life the Germans try to inject an appearance of order and authority. From the first day, power is officially exercised by the Jewish Council. To keep order, a uniformed Jewish police has been established ... These institutions, meant to give the ghetto life some veneer of normality, have in fact become sources of far reaching corruption and demoralization.[26]

In the ghetto, distance between classes was the distance between life and death. Simply remaining alive meant closing one's eyes to other people's destitution and agony. The poor died first, and in droves. So did the unresourceful, meek, naive, honest, unpushing. From its first day, with masses of people cramped in a space fit to accommodate no more than a third of their number, with food rations calculated to yield bodily decay and spiritual decrepitude, with sources of income virtually non-existent, epidemics rampant and medicines scarce, life in the ghetto had become a zero-sum game with self-preservation as the most coveted prize; as the only prize which truly counted. Seldom was the price of compassion so high. Seldom was the mere concern with self-survival so close to moral corruption.

Class distinctions, atrocious and horrifying when access to bread and shelter was at stake, acquired murderous quality once the struggle began for the stay of execution. By that time, the poor were too enfeebled and emasculated to resist, or in any other form defend their lives. 'During ghetto-clearing operations, many Jewish families were unable to fight, unable to petition, unable to flee, and also unable to move to the concentration point to get it over with. They waited for the raiding parties in their homes, frozen and helpless.'[27] The rich and the not-so-destitute tried to outbid each other in (mostly vain) attempts to obtain the few exit passes which the Nazis as a rule took care to throw to the panic-stricken mob. Few remembered that one victim's success could not mean but the perdition of another. Fortunes were offered, and accepted, for the magic number-plates which acquitted the holder from the current 'action'; influential protectors were feverishly sought and bribed. Wladyslaw Szlengel, the unforgettable bard of the Warsaw ghetto, left the tormented description of the 'action' which took place on 19 January 1943:

> Telephones under siege. Help! Help! Help! Mobilizing the dignitaries of the Gestapo. Calling the railway camp: did they bring the trains? Is Mr. Szmerling around? Sir, my ... has been taken! Mr. Skosowski! Help! Any amount! 100,000! As much as is needed! I'll give half a million for twenty people! For ten people! For one!.
> Jews have money! Jews can pull strings! Jews are powerless! ...
> We know, how they made their monstrous fortunes – and how

they now wander through the floors in search of water, how they
offer to Ukrainians their millions, how they depart taking with
them sums of money with which they could keep these hundreds
gathered at the station alive for months ...

The cattle adorned with number plates stampedes by. A few
creatures without numbers stand helplessly among the ruins ...

The Reich treasury grows.

The Jews are dying.[28]

The higher climbed the price of life, the lower tumbled the price of
betrayal. An irresistible compulsion to live pushed aside moral scruples
and, with them, human dignity. Amidst the universal scramble for
survival, the value of self-preservation was enthroned as an
uncontestable legitimation of choice. Everything that served the self-
preservation was right. With the ultimate end at stake, all means seemed
to be justified. It is true that the Nazis asked now the *Ältestenräte* to
render services incomparably more abhorrent than those which they
demanded at first. But the stakes of the game had changed as well – both
the price and the rewards of obedience went up. And so, more often than
not, the services continued to be offered. In the bargain for another day
of life, a job in the Jewish Council or Jewish police counted more than
money or diamonds.

Not that money and diamonds were disdained. Numerous accounts
recorded by the survivors tell the dismal and disheartening story of
rampant bribery and blackmail, extortion and deceit, which had become
a mark of many *Judenräte*, or at least many individuals partaking of their
awesome power to separate death from life. Huge sums of money and
family heirlooms were asked, and paid, for many a councillor's services,
be it an official privilege or a false identity card. Particularly coveted was
a room in special buildings set aside for the members of the councils and
the police and their immediate families; such buildings were allegedly
immune to SS attention and exempt for successive *Aktionen*. As the
stakes grew and the desperation deepened, every scrap of privilege could,
however, attract an exorbitant price which only the richest among the
extant members of the doomed community could afford to pay.

Such *Judenräte* behaviour reflected the general corruption of the
victimized population. The oppression which elevated the rationality of
self-preservation and systematically devalued moral considerations did
succeed in dehumanizing its victims. It acted as a self-fulfilling prophecy
of sorts. The Jews were first proclaimed immoral and unscrupulous,

selfish and greedy detractors of values, who used their ostensible cult of humanism as a convenient cover for naked self-interest; they were then forced into an inhuman condition where the definition promoted by propaganda could become true. The cameramen of Goebbels's ministry had many a field day recording the beggars dying of famine in front of luxurious restaurants.

Corruption had its logic. It proceeded by stages, and each step made the next easier to take. It started like this:

> The vice-chairman of the Siedlce Council instantly upgraded his standard of living ... The fact that all of a sudden large amounts of money came into his hands, and that other opportunities also came his way, simply turned his head. He believed that he had limitless powers and took advantage of his position, profiting by the general misery. He took a lion's share of the large sums of money and jewellery which were entrusted to him for safekeeping against a time of emergency when it would be necessary to pay off the Germans. He lived in comfort ...

And then it went on like this:

> [The chairman of the Zawiercie Council] [d]uring the 'resettlement' of August 1943, when he received news that all Jews, except a very small group of skilled workers, would be deported to Auschwitz (and it was already known what *that* meant), assembled 40 members of his own family and put their names on the list of skilled workers.

And it ended to end up like this:

> [In Skalat ghetto] *Obersturmbannführer* Müller made a deal with the representatives of the Council and the *Kommandant* of the Ghetto police, Dr. Joseph Brif, to take an active part in the 'action', solemnly proclaiming that they and their families would be saved ... After the bloody action ... a band of the SS men went to the Jewish Council where they had a good time. A banquet was waiting for them ... caterers busied themselves around the richly adorned tables and slavishly tried to satisfy their guests. Jolly laughter was heard, music played, and the guests revealed, sang, and were merry. This at a time when 2000 persons had been driven into the synagogue and nearly suffocated from lack of air, while others were kept in the meadow by the railroad tracks in the cold.[29]

It did not end like this, as a matter of fact. The train called 'self-preservation' stopped only at Treblinka railway station.

Conclusion

If they had a choice, none of the Jewish councillors or policemen would board the train of self-destruction. None would help to kill others. None would sink into the 'plague-time orgy' style of corruption. But they did not have that choice. Or, rather, the range of choices had not been set by them. Most of them – including the utterly corrupted and unscrupulous – deployed their reason and their skill of rational judgement to the choices which had been made available to them. What the experience of the Holocaust revealed in all its awesome consequences was a distinction between the rationality of the actor (a psychological phenomenon) and the rationality of the action (measured by its objective consequences for the actor). Reason is a good guide for individual behaviour only on such occasions as the two rationalities resonate and overlap. Otherwise, it turns into a suicidal weapon. It destroys its own purpose, knocking down on the way moral inhibitions – its only constraint and potential saviour.

The coincidence of the two rationalities – of the actor and of the action – does not depend on the actor. It depends on the setting of the action, which in turn depends on stakes and resources, none of them controlled by the actor. Stakes and resources are manipulated by those who truly control the situation: who are able to make some choices too costly to be frequently selected by those whom they rule, while securing frequent and massive selection of choices which bring closer their aims and reinforce their control. This capacity does not change, whether the aims of the rulers are beneficial or detrimental to the interests of the ruled. *Under sharply asymmetrical power conditions, rationality of the ruled is, to say the least, a mixed blessing.* It may work to their gain. But it may as well destroy them.

Considered as a complex purposeful operation, the Holocaust may serve as a paradigm of modern bureaucratic rationality. Almost everything was done to achieve maximum results with minimum costs and efforts. Almost everything (within the realm of the possible) was done to deploy the skills and resources of everybody involved, including those who were to become the victims of the successful operation. Almost all pressures irrelevant or adversary to the purpose of the operation were neutralized or put out of action altogether. Indeed, the story of the organization of the Holocaust could be made into a textbook of scientific management. Were not the moral and political condemnation of its purpose imposed on the world by the military defeat of its perpetrators it would have been made into a textbook. There would be no shortage of distinguished scholars vying to research and generalize its experience for the benefit of an advanced organization of human affairs.

From the point of view of its victims, the Holocaust contains different lessons. One of the most crucial among them is the jarring insufficiency of rationality as a sole measurement of organizational proficiency. This lesson is still to be absorbed in full by the social scientists. Until this is done we may go on researching and generalizing the tremendous advance in the effectiveness of human action attained thanks to the elimination of qualitative criteria, moral norms included – and all too seldom thinking through the consequences.

Originally written for the *Festschrift* in honour of Professor Bronislau Baczko.

6

The Ethics of Obedience
(Reading Milgram)

Not yet fully recovered from the shattering truth of the Holocaust, Dwight Macdonald warned in 1945, we must now fear the person who obeys the law more than the one who breaks it.

The Holocaust had dwarfed all remembered and inherited images of evil. With that, it inverted all established explanations of evil deeds. It suddenly transpired that the most horrifying evil in human memory did not result from the dissipation of order, but from an impeccable, faultless and unchallengeable rule of order. It was not the work of an obstreperous and uncontrollable mob, but of men in uniforms, obedient and disciplined, following the rules and meticulous about the spirit and the letter of their briefing. It became known very soon that these men, whenever they took their unforms off, were in no way evil. They behaved much like all of us. They had wives they loved, children they cosseted, friends they helped and comforted in case of distress. It seemed unbelievable that once in uniform the same people shot, gassed or presided over the shooting and gassing of thousands of other people, including women who were someone's beloved wives and babies who were someone's cosseted children. It also was terrifying. How could ordinary people like you and me do it? Surely in some way, let it be a small way, a tiny way, they must have been special, different, *unlike* us? Surely they must have escaped the ennobling, humanizing impact of our enlightened, civilized society? Or, alternatively, they must have been spoiled, corrupted, subjected to some vicious or unhappy combination of educational factors which resulted in a faulty, diseased personality?

Proving these suppositions wrong would have been resented not only because it would tear apart the illusion of personal security which the life in a civilized society promises. It would also have been resented for a much more pregnant reason; because it exposed the irredeemable inconclusiveness of every morally righteous self-image, and any clear conscience. From now on, all consciences were to be clean until further notice only.

The most frightening news brought about the Holocaust and by what we learned of its perpetrators was not the likelihood that 'this' could be done to us, but the idea that we could do it. Stanley Milgram, an American psychologist from Yale University, bore the brunt of this terror when he recklessly undertook an empirical test of suppositions based on emotional urge and determined to remain oblivious to the evidence; more recklessly still, he published the results in 1974. Milgram's findings were indeed unambiguous: yes, we could do it and we still may, if conditions are right.

It was not easy to live with such findings. No wonder learned opinion came down on Milgram's research in full force. Milgram's techniques were put under the microscope, pulled apart, proclaimed faulty and even disgraceful, and reproved. At any price and by any means, respectable and less respectable, the academic world tried to discredit and disown the findings which promised terror where complacency and peace of mind should better be. Few episodes in scientific history disclose more fully the reality of the allegedly value-free search for knowledge and disinterested motives of scientific curiosity. 'I'm convinced' said Milgram in reply to his critics, 'that much of the criticism, whether people know it or not, stems from the results of the experiment. If everyone had broken off at slight shock or moderate shock, ' (that is, before the following of the experimenter's orders began to mean bringing pain and suffering to the putative victims) 'this would be a very reassuring finding and who would protest?[1] Milgram was right, of course. And he still is. Years have passed since his original experiment, yet his findings, which ought to have led to a thorough revision of our views on the mechanisms of human behaviour, remain quoted in most sociological courses as an amusing, but not exceedingly illuminating, curiosity – without affecting the main body of sociological reasoning. If one cannot beat the findings, one can still marginalize them.

Old habits of thought die hard. Shortly after the war a group of scholars headed by Adorno published *The Authoritarian Personality*, a book destined to become a pattern for research and theorizing for years to come. What was particularly important about the book were not its specific propositions – virtually all were subsequently questioned and disproved – but its location of the problem, and the research strategy derived from it. This latter contribution of Adorno and his associates, immune to empirical testing while comfortingly resonant with subconscious wishes of the learned public, proved to be much more resilient. As the title of the book suggested, the authors sought the explanation of Nazi rule and ensuing atrocities in the presence of a special type of individual; personalities inclined to obedience towards the stronger, and to the unscrupulous, often cruel, high-handedness towards the weak. The triumph of the Nazis must have been an outcome of an unusual accumulation of such personalities. Why this occurred, the authors neither explained nor wished to explain. They carefully eschewed the exploration of all supra- or extra-individual factors that could produce authoritarian personalities; nor did they care about the possibility that such factors may induce authoritarian *behaviour* in people otherwise devoid of authoritarian *personality*. To Adorno and his colleagues, Nazism was cruel because Nazis were cruel; and the Nazis were cruel because cruel people tended to become Nazis. As one of the members of the group admitted several years later, '*The Authoritarian Personality* emphasized purely personality determinants of potential fascism and ethnocentrism and discounted contemporary social influences.'[2] The fashion in which Adorno and his team articulated the problem was important not so much because of the way in which the blame was apportioned, but because of the bluntness with which all the rest of mankind was absolved. Adorno's vision divided the world into born proto-Nazis and their victims. The dark and dismal knowledge that many gentle people may turn cruel if given a chance was suppressed. The suspicion that even the victims may lose a good deal of their humanity on the road to perdition, was banned – the tacit prohibition which stretched to the extremes of absurdity in the American television portrayal of the Holocaust.

It was such academic tradition and this public opinion, both deeply entrenched, heavily fortified and mutually reinforcing, that Milgram's research challenged. A particular disquiet and rage were caused by his hypothesis that cruelty is not committed by cruel individuals, but by ordinary men and women trying to acquit themselves well of their ordinary duties; and his findings, that *while cruelty correlates but poorly with the personal characteristics of its perpetrators, it correlates very strongly indeed with the relationship of authority and subordination,* with our normal, daily encountered, structure of power and obedience. The person who, with inner conviction, loathes stealing, killing, and assault, may find himself performing these acts with relative ease when commanded by authority. Behaviour that is unthinkable in an individual who is acting on his own may be executed without hesitation when carried out under orders.[3] It may be true that some individuals are prompted into cruelty by their own, unforced, thoroughly personal inclinations. Most certainly, however, personal traits do not stop them from committing cruelty when the context of interaction in which they find themselves prompts them to be cruel.

Let us remember that the only case in which traditionally, following Le Bon, we used to admit this (that is, the perpetration of indecent things by otherwise decent people) to be possible, was a situation in which normal, civilized, rational patterns of human interaction have been broken; a crowd, brought together by hatred or panic; a casual encounter of strangers, each pulled out of his ordinary context and suspended for a time in a social void; a tightly packed town square, where shouts of panic replace command and stampede instead of authority decides the direction. We used to believe that the unthinkable may only happen when people stop thinking: when the lid of rationality is taken off the cauldron of pre-social and uncivilized human passions. Milgram's findings also turn upside-down that much older image of the world, according to which humanity was fully on the side of the rational order, while inhumanity was fully confined to its occasional breakdowns.

In a nutshell, Milgram suggested and proved that *inhumanity is a matter of social relationships. As the latter are rationalized and technically perfected, so is the capacity and the efficiency of the social production of inhumanity.*

It may seem trivial. It is not. Before Milgram's experiments, few people, professionals and lay alike, anticipated what Milgram was about to discover. Virtually all ordinary middle-class males, and all competent and respected members of the psychological profession, whom Milgram asked what the results of the experiments are likely to be, were confident that 100 per cent of the subjects would refuse to co-operate as the cruelty of actions they were commanded to perform grew, and would at some fairly low point break off. In fact the proportion of people who did withdraw their consent went down in appropriate circumstances, to as little as 30 per cent. The intensity of alleged electric shocks they were prepared to apply was up to three times higher than what the learned experts, in unison with the lay public, were able to imagine.

Inhumanity as a function of social distance

Perhaps the most striking among Milgram's findings is *the inverse ratio of readiness to cruelty and proximity to its victim*. It is difficult to harm a person we touch. It is somewhat easier to afflict pain upon a person we only see at a distance. It is still easier in the case of a person we only hear. It is quite easy to be cruel towards a person we neither see nor hear.

If harming a person involves direct bodily contact, the perpetrator is denied the comfort of unnoticing the causal link between his action and the victim's suffering. The causal link is bare and obvious, and so is the responsibility for pain. When the subjects of Milgram's experiments were told to force the victims' hands on to the plate through which the electric shock was allegedly administered, only 30 per cent continued to fulfil the command till the end of the experiment. When, instead of grasping the victim's hand they were asked only to manipulate the levers of the control desk, the proportion of the obedient went up to 40 per cent. When the victims were hidden behind a wall, so that only their anguished screams were audible, the number of subjects ready to 'see it to the end' jumped to 62.5 per cent. Switching off the sounds did not push the percentage much further – only to 65 per cent. It seems we feel mostly through the eyes. The greater was the physical and psychical distance from the victim, the easier it was to be cruel. Milgram's conclusion is simple and convincing:

> Any force or event that is placed between the subject and the consequences of shocking the victim, will lead to a reduction of strain on the participant and thus lessen disobedience. In modern society others often stand between us and the final destructive act to which we contribute.[4]

Indeed, mediating the action, splitting the action between stages delineated and set apart by the hierarchy of authority, and cutting the action across through functional specialization is one of the most salient and proudly advertised achievements of our rational society. The meaning of Milgram's discovery is that, immanently and irretrievably, the process of rationalization facilitates behaviour that is inhuman and cruel in its consequences, if not in its intentions. *The more rational is the organization of action, the easier it is to cause suffering* – and remain at peace with oneself.

The reason why separation from the victim makes cruelty easier seems psychologically obvious: the perpetrator is spared the agony of witnessing the outcome of his deeds. He may even mislead himself into believing that nothing really disastrous has happened, and thus placate the pangs of conscience. But this is not the only explanation. Again, reasons are not just psychical. Like everything which truly explains human conduct, they are social.

> Placing the victim in another room not only takes him farther away from the subject, it also draws the subject and the experimenter relatively closer. There is incipient group function between the experimenter and the subject, from which the victim is excluded. In the remote condition, the victim is truly an outsider, who stands alone, physically and psychologically.[5]

Loneliness of the victim is not just a matter of his physical separation. It is a function of the togetherness of his tormentors, and his exclusion from this togetherness. Physical closeness and continuous co-operation (even over a relatively short time – no subject was experimented with for longer than one hour) tends to result in a group feeling, complete with the mutual obligations and solidarity it normally brings about. This group feeling is produced by joint action, particularly by the complementarity of individual actions – when the result is evidently achieved by shared effort. In Milgram's experiments, action united the subject with the experimenter, and simultaneously separated both of them from the victim. On no occasion was the victim granted the role of an actor, an agent, a subject. Instead, he was held permanently on the receiving end. Unambiguously, he was made into an *object*; and as the objects of action go, it does not matter much whether they are human or inanimate. Thus loneliness of the victim and the togetherness of his tormentors conditioned and validated each other.

The effect of physical and purely psychical distance is, therefore, farther enhanced by the collective nature of damaging action. One may guess that even if obvious gains in the economy and efficiency of action brought by its rational organization and management are left out of account, the sheer fact that the oppressor is a member of a group must be assigned a tremendous role in facilitating the committing of cruel acts. It may be that a considerable part of bureaucratically callous and insensitive efficiency could be ascribed to factors other than the rational design of division of labour or chain of command: to the skilful, and not necessarily deliberate or planned, deployment of natural group-formative tendency of co-operative action, a tendency always coupled with boundary-drawing and exclusion of outsiders. Through its authority over recruitment of its members and over designation of its objects, bureaucratic organization is able to control the outcome of such a tendency, and assure that it leads to an ever-more profound and unbridgeable chasm between the actors (i.e. members of the organization) and the objects of action. This makes so much easier the transformation of the actors into the persecutors, and the objects into the victims.

Complicity after one's own act

Everyone who once inadvertently stepped into a bog knows only too well that getting oneself out of the trouble was difficult mostly because every effort to get out resulted in one's sinking deeper into the mire. One can even define the swamp as a kind of ingenious system so constructed that however the objects immersed into it move, their movements always add to the 'sucking power' of the system.

Sequential actions seems to possess the same quality. The degree to which the actor finds himself bound to perpetuate the action, and opting-out difficult, tends to grow with every stage. First steps are easy and require little, if any, moral torments. The steps to follow are increasingly daunting. Finally, taking them feels unbearable. Yet the cost of withdrawal has also grown by that time. Thus the urge to break off is weak when the obstacles to withdrawal are also weak or non-existent. When the urge intensifies, the obstacles it encounters are at every stage strong enough to balance it. When the actor is overwhelmed with the desire to back out, it is normally too late for him to do so. Milgram listed *sequential action* among the main 'binding factors' (i.e. factors locking the subject in his situation). It is tempting to ascribe the strength of this particular binding factor to the *determining impact of the subject's own past actions*.

Sabini and Silver have offered a brilliant and convincing description of its mechanism.

> Subjects enter the experiment recognizing some commitments to cooperate with the experimenter; after all, they have agreed to participate, taken his money, and probably to some degree endorse the aims of the advancement of science. (Milgram's subjects were told that they would participate in a study meant to discover ways of making learning more efficient.) When the learner makes his first error, subjects are asked to shock him. The shock level is 15 volts. A 15-volt shock is entirely harmless, imperceptible. There is

no moral issue here. Of course the next shock is more powerful, but only slightly so. Indeed every shock is only slightly more powerful than the last. The quality of the subject's action changes from something entirely blameless to something unconscionable, but by degrees. Where exactly should the subject stop? At what point is the divide between these two kinds of action crossed? How is the subject to know? It is easy to see that there must be a line; it is not so easy to see where that line ought to be.

The most important factor in the process, however, seems to be the following:

> if the subject decides that giving the next shock is not permissible, then, since it is (in every case) only slightly more intense than the last one, what was the justification for administering the last shock he just gave? To deny the propriety of the step he is about to take is to undercut the propriety of the step he just took, and this undercuts the subject's own moral position. The subject is trapped by his gradual commitment to the experiment.[6]

In the course of a sequential action, the actor becomes a slave of his own past actions. This hold seems much stronger than other binding factors. It can certainly outlast the factors which at the start of the sequence seemed much more important and played a truly decisive role. In particular, the unwillingness to re-evaluate (and condemn) one's own past conduct will still remain a powerful, and ever more powerful, stimulus to plod on, long after the original commitment to 'the cause' had all but petered out. Smooth and imperceptible passages between the steps lure the actor into a trap; the trap is the impossibility of quitting without revising and rejecting the evaluation of one's own deeds as right or at least innocent. The trap is, in other words, a paradox: *one cannot get clean without blackening oneself.* To hide filth, one must forever draggle in the mud.

This paradox might be a moving factor behind the well-known phenomenon of accomplices' solidarity. Nothing binds people to each other stronger than shared responsibility for an act that they admit is criminal. Commonsensically, we explain this kind of solidarity by the natural wish to escape punishment; the game theorists' analyses of the famous 'prisoner's dilemma' also teach us that (providing no one confuses the stakes) to assume that the rest of the team will remain solidary is the most rational decision any member may make. We may wonder, however, to what extent the accomplices' solidarity is brought about and reinforced by the fact that only the members of the team which originally engaged in the sequential action are likely to conspire to defuse the paradox, and by common consent offer some credibility to the belief in the legitimacy of past action in spite of the growing evidence to the contrary. I suggest, therefore, that another 'binding factor' named by Milgram, *situational obligations,* is, to a large extent, a derivative of the first, *the paradox of sequential action.*

Technology moralized

One of the most remarkable features of the bureaucratic system of authority is, however, the shrinking probability that the moral oddity of one's action will ever be discovered, and once discovered, made into a painful moral dilemma. In a bureaucracy, moral concerns of the functionary are drawn back from focusing on the plight of the objects of action. They are forcefully shifted in another direction – the job to be done and the excellence with which it is performed. It does not matter that much how the 'targets' of action fare and feel. It does matter, however, how smartly and effectively the actor fulfils whatever he has been told to fulfil by his superiors. And on this latter question, the superiors are the most competent, natural authority. This circumstance further strengthens the grip in which the superiors hold their subordinates. In addition to giving orders and punishing for insubordination, they also pass moral judgements – the only moral judgements that count for the individual's self-appreciation.

The commentators have repeatedly stressed that the results of Milgram's experiments could be influenced by the conviction that the action was required in the interest of *science* – undoubtedly a high, rarely contested, and generally morally placed authority. What is not pointed out, however, is that more than any other authority science is allowed by public opinion to practise the otherwise ethically odious principle of the end justifying the means. Science serves as the fullest epitome of the dissociation between the ends and the means which serves as the ideal of rational organization of human conduct: it is the ends which are subject to moral evaluation, not the means. To the expressions of moral anguish, the experimenters kept replying with a bland, routine and insipid formula: 'No permanent damage to the tissue will be caused.' Most of the participants were only too glad to accept this consolation and preferred not to think through the possibilities which the formula left undiscussed (most conspicuously, the moral virtue of temporary damage to the tissue, or simply of the agony of pain). What mattered to them was the reassurance that someone 'on high' had considered what is and what is not ethically acceptable.

Inside the bureaucratic system of authority, language of morality acquires a new vocabulary. It is filled with concepts like loyalty, duty, discipline – all pointing to superiors as the supreme object of moral concern and, simultaneously, the top moral authority. They all, in fact, converge: loyalty means performance of one's duty as defined by the code of discipline. As they converge and reinforce each other, they grow in power as moral precepts, to the point where they can disable and push aside all other moral considerations – above all, ethical issues foreign to the self-reproductory preoccupations of the authority system. They appropriate, harness to the interest of bureaucracy and monopolize all the usual socio-psychical means of moral self-regulation. As Milgram puts it, 'the subordinate person feels shame or pride depending on how adequately he has performed the actions called for by authority.... Superego shifts from an evaluation of the goodness or badness of the acts to an assessment of how well or poorly one is functioning in the authority system.[7]

What follows is that contrary to a widespread interpretation, a bureaucratic system of authority does not militate against moral norms as such, and does not cast them aside as essentially irrational, affective pressures which contradict the cool rationality of a truly efficient action. Instead, it deploys them – or, rather, re-deploys them. *Bureaucracy's double feat is the moralization of technology, coupled with the denial of the moral significance of non-technical issues.* It is the technology of action, not its substance, which is subject to assessment as good or bad, proper or improper, right or wrong. The conscience of the actor tells him to perform well and prompts him to measure his own righteousness by the precision with which he obeys the organizational rules and his dedication to the task as defined by the superiors. What kept at bay the other, 'old-fashioned' conscience in the subjects of Milgram's experiments, and effectively arrested their impulse to break off, was the *substitute conscience,* put together by the experimenters out of the appeals to the 'interests of research' or the 'needs of the experiment', and the warnings about the losses which its untimely interruption would cause. In the case of Milgram's experiments, substitute conscience had been put together hastily (no individual experiment lasted more than one hour), and yet proved amazingly effective.

There is little question that the substitution of morality of technology for the morality of substance was made much easier than it otherwise could be by the shifting of balance between the subject's closeness to the targets of his action, and his closeness to the source of authority of the action. With astonishing consistency, Milgram's experiments turned evidence of the positive dependence between the effectiveness of the substitution, and the remoteness (technical more than physical) of the subject from the ultimate effects of his actions. One experiment, for instance, showed that when 'the subject was not ordered to push the trigger that shocked the victim, but merely to perform a subsidiary act ... before another subject actually delivered the shock ... 37 out of 40 adults ... continued to the highest shock level' (one marked on the control desk 'very dangerous – XX'). Milgram's own conclusion is that it is psychologically easy to ignore responsibility when one is only an intermediate link in a chain of evil action but is far from the final consequences of the action.[8] To an intermediate link in the chain of evil action, his own operations appear technical, so to speak, on both ends. The immediate effect of his action is the setting of another technical task – doing something to the electrical apparatus or to the sheet of paper on the desk. The causal link between his action and the suffering of the victim is dimmed and can be ignored with relatively little effort. Thus 'duty' and 'discipline' face no serious competitor.

Free-floating responsibility

The system of authority in Milgram's experiments was simple and contained few tiers. The subject's source of authority – the experimenter – was the topmost manager of the system, though the subject could be unaware of this (from his point of view, the experimenter himself acted as an intermediary; his power was delegated by a higher, generalized and impersonal authority of 'science' or 'research'). Simplicity of the experimental situation rebounded in the straightforwardness of the findings. It transpired that the subject vested the authority for his action with the experimenter; and the authority indeed resided in the experimenter's orders – the final authority, one that did not require authorization or endorsement by the persons located further up in the hierarchy of power. The focus, therefore, was on the subject's readiness to renounce his own responsibility for what he had done, and particularly for what he was about to do. For this readiness, the act of endowing the experimenter with the right to demand things which the subject would not do on his own initiative, even things which he rather would not do at all, was decisive. Perhaps this endowment stemmed from an assumption that by some obscure logic, unknown and unfathomable to the subject, the things the experimenter asked the subject to perform were right even if they seemed wrong to the uninitiated; perhaps no thought was given to such logic, as the will of the authorized person did not need any legitimation in the eyes of the subject: the right to command and the duty to obey were sufficient. What we do know for sure, thanks to Milgram, is that the subjects of his experiments went on committing deeds which they recognized as cruel solely because they were commanded to do so by the authority they accepted and vested with the ultimate responsibility for their actions. These studies confirm an essential fact: the decisive factor is the response to authority, rather than the response to the particular order to administer shock. Orders originating outside of authority lose all force ... It is not what subjects do but for whom they are doing it that counts.[9] Milgram's experiments revealed the mechanism of *shifting responsibility* in its pure, pristine and elementary form.

Once responsibility has been shifted away by the actor's consent to the superior's right to command, the actor is cast in an *agentic state*[10] – a condition in which he sees himself as carrying out another person's wishes. Agentic state is the opposite of the state of autonomy. (As such, it is virtually synonymous with *heteronomy*, though it conveys in addition an implication of the self-definition of the actor, and it locates the external sources of the actor's behaviour – the forces behind his *other-directedness* – precisely in a specific point of an institutionalized hierarchy.) In the agentic state, the actor is fully tuned to the situation as defined and monitored by the superior authority: this definition of the situation includes the description of the actor as the authority's agent.

The shifting of responsibility is, however, indeed an elementary act, a single unit or building block in a complex process. It is a phenomenon that takes place in the narrow space stretched between one member of the system of authority and another, an actor and his immediate superior. Because of the simplicity of their structure, Milgram's experiments could not trace further consequences of such responsibility shifting. In particular, having intentionally focused the microscope on basic cells of complex organisms, they could not posit 'organismic' questions, such as what the bureaucratic organization is likely to be once the responsibility shifting is occurring continuously, and at all levels of its hierarchy.

We may surmise that the overall effect of such a continuous and ubiquitous responsibility shifting would be a *free-floating responsibility*, a situation in which each and every member of the organization is convinced, and would say so if asked, that he has been at some else's beck and call, but the members pointed to by others as the bearers of responsibility would pass the buck to someone else again. One can say that *the organization as a whole is an instrument to obliterate responsibility*. The causal links in co-ordinated actions are masked, and the very fact of being masked is a most powerful factor of their effectiveness. Collective perpetuation of cruel acts is made all the easier by the fact that responsibility is essentially 'unpinnable', while every participant of these acts is convinced that it does reside with some 'proper authority'. This means that shirking responsibility is not just an after-the-fact stratagem used as a convenient excuse in case charges are made of the immorality, or worse still of illegitimacy, of an action; the free-floating, unanchored responsibility is the very condition of immoral or illegitimate acts taking place with obedient, or even willing participation of people normally incapable of breaking the rules of conventional morality. Free-floating responsibility means in practice that moral authority as such has been incapacitated without having been openly challenged or denied.

Pluralism of power and power of conscience

Like all experiments, Milgram's studies were conducted in an artificial, purposefully designed environment. It differed from the context of daily life in two important respects. First, the link of the subjects with the 'organization' (the research team and the university of which it was a part) was brief and *ad hoc*, and was known to be such in advance; the subjects were hired for one hour and one hour only. Second, in most experiments, the subjects were confronted with just one superior, and one who acted as a veritable epitome of single-mindedness and consistency, so that the subjects had to perceive of the powers that authorized their conduct as monolithic and totally certain as to the purpose and meaning of their action. Neither of the two conditions is frequently met in normal life. One needs to consider, therefore, whether and to what extent they might have influenced the subjects' behaviour in a way not to be expected under normal circumstances.

To start with the first of these points: the impact of authority so convincingly shown by Milgram would, if anything, have been more profound still were the subjects convinced of the permanence of their link with the organization the authority represented, or at least convinced that the chance of such permanence was real. Additional factors, absent for obvious reasons in the experiment, would then have entered the situation: factors like solidarity and a feeling of mutual duty (the 'I cannot let him down' feeling) which are likely to develop between members of a team staying together and solving shared problems over a long period of time, *diffuse reciprocity* (services offered freely to other members of the group, hoped, if only half-consciously, to be 'repaid' at some unspecified future time, or just resulting in a good disposition of a colleague or a superior which again might be of some unspecified use in the future), and most important of all, the routine (a fully habitualized behavioural sequence which renders calculation and choice redundant and hence makes the established patterns of action virtually unassailable even in the absence of further reinforcement). It seems most likely that these and similar factors will only add strength to the tendencies observed by Milgram: those tendencies stemmed from the exposure to a legitimate authority, and the factors listed above certainly add to that legitimacy, which can only increase over a span of time long enough to allow for the development of tradition and for the emergence of multifaceted informal patterns of exchange between members.

The second departure from ordinary conditions might have, however, influenced the observed reactions to authority in a way not to be expected in daily life. In the artificial conditions carefully controlled by Milgram, there was one source of authority, and one only, and no other frame of reference of an equal standing (or even, simply, another autonomous opinion) with which the subject could confront the command in order to put its validity to something like an objective test. Milgram was fully aware of the possibility of distortion that such unnaturally monolithic character of authority must carry. To reveal the extent of distortion, he added to the project a number of experiments in which the subjects were confronted with more than one experimenter, and the experimenters were instructed to disagree openly and argue about the command. The outcome was truly shattering: the slavish obedience observed in all other experiments vanished without trace. The subjects were no longer willing to engage in actions they did not like;

certainly they would not be prompted to afflict suffering even to the unknown victims. Out of twenty subjects of this additional experiment, one broke off before the staged disagreement between the two experimenters started, eighteen refused further co-operation at the first sign of disagreement, and the last one opted out just one stage after that. 'It is clear that the disagreement between the authorities completely paralyzed action.[11]

The meaning of correction is unambiguous: *the readiness to act against one's own better judgment, and against the voice of one's conscience, is not just the function of authoritative command, but the result of exposure to a single-minded, unequivocal and monopolistic source of authority.* Such readiness is most likely to appear inside an organization which brooks no opposition and tolerates no autonomy, and in which linear hierarchy of subordination knows no exception: an organization in which no two members are equal in power. (Most armies, penitentiary institutions, totalitarian parties and movements, certain sects or boarding schools come close to this ideal type.) Such an organization, however, is likely to be effective on one of the two conditions. It may tightly seal its members from the rest of society, having been granted, or having usurped, an undivided control over most, or all its members' life activities and needs (and thus approximate Goffman's model of *total institutions*), so that possible influence of competitive sources of authority is cut out. Or it may be just one of the branches of the totalitarian or quasi-totalitarian state, which transforms all its agencies into mirror reflections of each other.

As Milgram put it, it's only when you have ... an authority who ... operates in a free field without countervailing pressures other than the victim's protests that you got the purest response to authority. In real life, of course, you're conflated with a great many countervailing pressures that cancel each other out.[12] What Milgram must have meant by 'real life' was life inside a democratic society, and outside a total institution: more precisely still, life under conditions of pluralism. A most remarkable conclusion flowing from the full set of Milgram experiments is that *pluralism is the best preventive medicine against morally normal people engaging in morally abnormal actions.* The Nazis must first have destroyed the vestiges of political pluralism to set off on projects like the Holocaust, in which the expected readiness of ordinary people for immoral and inhuman actions had to be calculated among the necessary – and available – resources. In the USSR the systematic destruction of the real and putative adversaries of the system took off in earnest only after the residues of social autonomy, and hence of the political pluralism which reflected it, had been extirpated. Unless pluralism had been eliminated on the global-societal scale, organizations with criminal purposes, which need to secure an unflagging obedience of their members in the perpetration of evidently immoral acts, are burdened with the task of erecting tight artificial barriers isolating the members from the 'softening' influence of diversity of standards and opinions. *The voice of individual moral conscience is best heard in the tumult of political and social discord*

The social nature of evil

Most conclusions flowing from Milgram's experiments may be seen as variations on one central theme: cruelty correlates with certain patterns of social interaction much more closely than it does with personality features or other individual idiosyncracies of the perpetrators. Cruelty is social in its origin much more than it is characterological. Surely some individuals tend to be cruel if cast in a context which disempowers moral pressures and legitimizes inhumanity.

If any doubts on this count have been left after Milgram, they are likely to evaporate once the findings of another experiment, by Philip Zimbardo,[13] are given a close look. From that experiment, even the potentially disturbing factor of the authority of a universally revered institution (science), embodied in the person of the experimenter, has been eliminated. In Zimbardo's experiment there was no external, established authority ready to take the responsibility off the subjects' shoulders. All authority which ultimately operated in Zimbardo's experimental context was generated by the subjects themselves. The only thing Zimbardo did was to set the process off by dividing subjects between positions within a codified pattern of interaction.

In Zimbardo's experiment (planned for a fortnight, but stopped after one week for fear of irreparable damage to the body and mind of the subjects) volunteers had been divided at random into prisoners and prison guards. Both sides were given the symbolic trappings of their position. Prisoners, for example, wore tight caps which simulated shaven heads, and gowns which made them appear ridiculous. Their guards were put in uniforms and given dark glasses which hid their eyes from being looked into by the prisoners. No side was allowed to address the other by name; strict impersonality was the rule. There was long list of petty regulations invariably humiliating for the prisoners and stripping them of human dignity. This was the starting point. What followed surpassed and left far behind the designers' ingenuity. The initiative of the guards (randomly selected males of college age, carefully screened against any sign of abnormality) knew no bounds. A genuine 'schismogenetic chain', once hypothesized by Gregory Bateson, was set in motion. The construed superiority of the guards rebounded in the submissiveness of the prisoners, which in its turn tempted the guards into further displays of their powers, which were then duly reflected in more self-humiliation on the part of the prisoners ... The guards forced the prisoners to chant filthy songs, to defecate in buckets which they did not allow them to empty, to clean toilets with bare hands; the more they did it, the more they acted as if they were convinced of the non-human nature of the prisoners, and the less they felt constrained in inventing and administering measures of an ever-more appalling degree of inhumanity.

The sudden transmogrification of likeable and decent American boys into near monsters of the kind allegedly to be found only in places like Auschwitz or Treblinka is horrifying. But it is also baffling. It led some observers to surmise that in most people, if not in all of us, there lives a little SS man waiting to come out (Amitai Etzioni suggested that Milgram discovered the 'latent Eichmann' hidden in ordinary men).[14] John Steiner coined the concept of the *sleeper* to denote the normally dormant, but sometimes awakened capacity for cruelty.

> The sleeper effect refers to the latent personality characteristic of violence-prone individuals such as autocrats. tyrants, or terrorists when the appropriate lock and key relationships became established. The sleeper is then roused from the normative stage of his behaviour pattern and the dormant, violence-prone personality characteristics become activated. in some way, all persons are sleepers inasmuch as they have a violent potential that under specific conditions can be triggered.[15]

And yet, clearly and unambiguously, the orgy of cruelty that took Zimbardo and his colleagues by surprise, stemmed from a vicious social arrangement, and not from the viciousness of the participants. Were the subjects of the experiment assigned to the opposite roles, the overall result would not be different. What mattered was the existence of a polarity, and not who was allocated to its respective sides. *What did matter was that some people were given a total, exclusive and untempered power over some other people.* If there is a sleeper in each of us, he may remain asleep forever if such a situation does not occur. And then we would never have heard of the sleeper's existence.

The most poignant point, it seems, is the easiness with which most people slip into the role requiring cruelty or at least moral blindness – if only the role has been duly fortified and legitimized by superior authority. Because of the breathtaking frequency with which such 'slipping into role' occurred in all known experiments, the concept of the sleeper seems to be no more than a metaphysical prop. We do not really need it to explain the massive conversion to cruelty. However, the concept does come into its own in reference to those relatively rare cases when individuals found the strength and courage to *resist* the command of authority and refused to implement it, once they found it contrary to their own convictions. Some ordinary people, normally law-abiding, unassuming, non-rebellious and unadventurous, stood up to those in power and, oblivious to the consequences, gave priority to their own conscience – much like those few, scattered, singly acting people, who defied the omnipotent and unscrupulous power, and risked the ultimate punishment trying to save the victims of the Holocaust. One would search in vain for social, political or religious 'determinants' of their uniqueness. Their moral conscience, dormant in the absence of an occasion for militancy but now aroused, was truly their own personal attribute and possession – unlike immorality, which had to be socially produced.

Their capacity to resist evil was a 'sleeper' through most of their lives. It could have remained asleep forever, and we would not know of it then. But *this* ignorance would be good news.

7

Towards a Sociological Theory of Morality

I propose now to consider in detail the problem that emerged at the end of the last chapter: the problem of the social nature of evil – or, more precisely, of the social production of immoral behaviour. A few of its aspects (for instance, the mechanisms responsible for the production of moral indifference or, more generally, for the delegitimization of moral precepts) have been dealt with briefly in earlier chapters. Because of its central role in the perpetration of the Holocaust, no analysis of the latter can claim to be complete unless it includes a more thorough investigation of the relation between society and moral behaviour. The need for such an investigation is further reinforced by the fact that the available sociological theories of moral phenomena prove, on closer scrutiny, ill-prepared to offer a satisfactory account of the Holocaust experience. The purpose of this chapter is to spell out certain crucial lessons and conclusions from that experience which a proper sociological theory of morality, free of the present weaknesses, would have to take into account. A more ambitious prospect, toward which this chapter will take only a few preliminary steps, is the construction of a theory of morality capable of accommodating in full the new knowledge generated by the study of the Holocaust. Whatever progress in this direction we can achieve will be a fitting summary of the various analytical themes developed in this book.

In the order of things construed by sociological discourse, the status of morality is awkward and ambiguous. Little has been done to improve it, as the status of morality is seen as of little consequence for the progress of sociological discourse, and so the issues of moral behaviour and moral choice have been allocated but a marginal position in it and, accordingly, are paid only marginal attention. Most sociological narratives do without reference to morality. In this, sociological discourse follows the pattern of science in general, which in its early years had attained emancipation from religious and magical thought by designing a language that could produce complete narratives without ever deploying such notions as purpose or will. *Science is indeed a language game with a rule forbidding the use of teleological vocabulary.* Not using teleological terms is not a sufficient condition for a sentence to belong to scientific narrative, but it certainly is a necessary condition.

In as far as sociology strived to abide by the rules of scientific discourse, morality and related phenomena sat uneasily in the social universe generated, theorized and researched by the dominant sociological narratives. Sociologists therefore focused their attention on the task of dissembling the qualitative distinction of moral phenomena, or accommodating them within a class of phenomena that can be narrated without recourse to teleological language. Between them, the two tasks and the efforts they commanded led to the denial of an independent existential mode of moral norms; if acknowledged at all as a separate factor in social reality, morality has been assigned a secondary and derivative status, which in principle should render it explicable by reference to non-moral phenomena – that is, phenomena fully and unambiguously amenable to non-teleological treatment. Indeed, the very idea of the specifically sociological approach to the study of morality has become synonymical with the strategy of, so to speak, *sociological reduction*; one which proceeds on the assumption that moral phenomena in their totality can be exhaustively explained in terms of the non-moral institutions which lend them their binding force.

Society as a factory of morality

The strategy of social-causal explanation of moral norms (i.e. conceiving of morality as, in principle, deducible from social conditions; and as effected by social processes) goes back to at least Montesquieu. His suggestions that, for instance, polygyny arises either from a surplus of women or from the particularly rapid ageing of women in certain climatic conditions may be by now quoted in history books mainly to illustrate, by contrast, the progress made by social science since its inception; and yet the pattern of explanation exemplified by Montesquieu's hypotheses was to remain by and large unquestioned for a long time to come. It has become a part of rarely challenged social-scientific common sense that the very persistence of a moral norm testifies to the presence of a collective need with which it has been designed to cope; and that, consequently, all scientific study of morality should attempt to reveal such needs and to reconstruct the social mechanisms that – through the imposition of norms – secure their satisfaction.

With the acceptance of this theoretical assumption and the related interpretive strategy, what followed was mostly circular reasoning, best perhaps expressed by Kluckhohn, who insisted that the moral norm or custom would not exist were they not functional (i.e. useful for the satisfaction of needs or for the taming of otherwise destructive behavioural tendencies – like, for example, the reduction of anxiety and the channelling of inborn aggressiveness achieved by Navaho witchcraft); and that the disappearance of a need which had originated and sustained the norm would soon lead to the disappearance of the norm itself. Any failure of the moral norm to serve its assigned task (i.e. its inability to cope adequately with the original need) would have similar results. This practice of the scientific study of morality has been codified in most explicit of forms by Malinowski, who stressed the essential instrumentality of morality, its subordinate status in relation to 'essential human needs' like food, security or defence against an inclement climate.

On the face of it, Durkheim (whose treatment of moral phenomena turned into the canon of sociological wisdom, and virtually defined the meaning of the specifically sociological approach to the study of morality) rejected the call to relate norms to needs; he did, after all, sharply criticize the accepted view that moral norms found binding in a particular society must have attained their obligatory force through the process of conscious (let alone rational) analysis and choice. In apparent opposition to the ethnographic common sense of the time, Durkheim insisted that the essence of morality should be sought precisely in the obligatory force it displays, rather than in its rational correspondence to the needs the members of society seek to satisfy; a norm is a norm not because it has been selected for its fitness to the task of promoting and defending members' interests, but because the members – through learning, or through the bitter consequences of transgression – convince themselves of its forceful presence. Durkheim's criticism of the extant interpretations of moral phenomena was not, however, aimed against the principle of 'rational explanation' as such. Still less did it undermine the practice of sociological reductionism. From that point of view, Durkheim's divergence from established interpretive practice represented no more than a family disagreement. What appeared to be an expression of radical dissent boiled down, after all, to the shifting of emphasis from the individual to *social* needs; or, rather, to one supreme need, now assigned priority over all other needs, whether predicated on individuals or on groups: *the need of social integration*. Any moral system is destined to serve the continuous existence, and the preservation of the identity, of the society which supports its binding force through socialization and punitive sanctions. The persistence of society is attained and sustained by the imposition of constraints upon natural (a-social, pre-social) predilections of society members: by forcing them to act in a way that does not contradict the need to maintain societal unity.

If anything, Durkheim's revision had rendered sociological reasoning about morality more circular than ever. If the only existential foundation of morality is the will of society, and its only function is to allow the society to survive, then the very issue of substantive evaluation of specific moral systems is effectively removed from the sociological agenda. Indeed, with social integration recognized as the only frame of reference within which the evaluation can be performed, there is no way in which various moral systems can be compared and differentially evaluated. The need each system serves arises inside the society in which it is nested, and what matters is that there must be a moral system in every society, and not the substance of moral norms this or that society happens to enforce in order to maintain its unity. *En gros*, Durkheim would say, each society has a morality it needs. And the need of the society being the only substance of morality, all moral systems are equal in the sole respect in which they can be legitimately – objectively, scientifically – measured and evaluated: their utility for the satisfaction of that need.

But there was more to Durkheim's treatment of morality than a most forceful re-affirmation of the long-established view of moral norms as social products. Perhaps the most formidable of Durkheim's influences on social-scientific practice was the conception of society as, essentially, an actively moralizing force, 'Man is a moral being only because he lives in society.' 'Morality, in all its forms, is never met with except in society.' 'the individual submits to society and this submission is the condition of his liberation. For man's freedom consists in deliverance from blind, unthinking physical forces; he achieves this by opposing against them the great and intelligent force of society, under whose protection he shelters. By putting himself under the wing of society, he makes himself also, to a certain extent, dependent upon it. But this is a liberating dependence; there is no contradiction in this.' These and similar memorable phrases of Durkheim reverberate to this day in sociological practice. All morality comes from society; there is not moral life outside society; society is best understood as a morality-producing plant; society promotes morally regulated behaviour and marginalizes, suppresses or prevents immorality. The alternative to the moral grip of society is not human autonomy, but the rule of animal passions. It is because the pre-social drives of the human animal are selfish, cruel and threatening that they have to be tamed and subdued if social life is to be sustained. Take away social coercion, and humans will relapse into the barbarity from which they had been but precariously lifted by the force of society.

This deep-seated trust in social arrangements as ennobling, elevating, humanizing factors goes against the grain of Durkheim's own insistence that actions are evil because they are socially prohibited, rather than socially prohibited because they are evil. The cool and sceptical scientist in Durkheim debunks all pretentions that there is substance in evil other than its rejection by a force powerful enough to make its will into a binding rule. But the warm patriot and devout believer in the superiority and progress of civilized life cannot but feel that what has been rejected is indeed evil, and that the rejection must have been an emancipating and dignifying act.

This feeling chimes in with the self-consciousness of the form of life which, having attained and secured its material superiority, could not but convince itself of the superiority of the rules by which it lived. It was, after all, not 'society as such', an abstract theoretical category, but modern Western society that served as the pattern for the moralizing mission. Only from the crusading-proselytizing practice of the specifically modern and Western 'gardening' society[1] could the self-confidence be derived which allowed the rule-enforcement to be viewed as the process of humanization, rather than of suppression of one form of humanity by another. The same self-confidence allowed the socially unregulated (whether disregarded, unattended to, or not fully sub-ordinated) manifestations of humanity to be cast aside as instances of inhumanity or, at best, as suspect and potentially dangerous. The theoretical vision, in the end, legitimized the sovereignty of society over its members as well as its contenders.

Once this self-confidence had been re-forged into social theory, important consequences followed for the interpretation of morality. By definition, pre-social or a-social motives could not be moral. By the same token, the possibility that at least certain moral patterns may be rooted in existential factors unaffected by contingent social rules of cohabitation could not be adequately articulated, let alone seriously considered. Even less could it be conceived, without falling into contradiction, that some moral pressures exerted by the human existential mode, by the sheer fact of 'being with others', may in certain circumstances be neutralized or suppressed by countervailing social forces; that, in other words, *society – in addition, or even contrary, to its 'moralizing function' – may, at least on occasion, act as a 'morality-silencing' force.*

As long as morality is understood as a social product, and causally explained in reference to the mechanisms which, when they function properly, assure its 'constant supply' – events which offend the diffuse yet deep-seated moral feelings and defy the common conception of good and evil (proper and improper conduct) tend to be viewed as an outcome of failure or mismanagement of 'moral industry'. The factory system has served as one of the most potent metaphors out of which the theoretical model of modern society is woven, and the vision of the *social production of morality* offers a most prominent example of its influence. The occurrence of immoral conduct is interpreted as the result of an inadequate supply of moral norms, or supply of faulty norms (i.e. norms with an insufficient binding force); the latter, in its turn, is traced to the technical or managerial faults of the 'social factory of morality' – at best to the 'unanticipated consequences' of ineptly co-ordinated productive efforts, or to the interference of factors foreign to the productive system (i.e. incompleteness of control over the factors of production). Immoral behaviour is then theorized as 'deviation from the norm', which stems from the absence or weakness of 'socializing pressures', and in the last account from defectiveness or imperfection of the social mechanisms designed to exert such pressures.[2] At the level of social system, such an interpretation points to unresolved managerial problems (of which Durkheim's *anomie* is a foremost example). At lower levels, it points to shortcomings of educational institutions, weakening of the family, or the impact of unextirpated antisocial enclaves with their own counter-moral socializing pressures. In all cases, however, the appearance of immoral conduct is understood as the manifestation of pre-social or a-social drives bursting out from their socially manufactured cages, or escaping enclosure in the first place. Immoral conduct is always a return to a pre-social state, or a failure to depart from it. It is always connected with some resistance to social pressures, or at least to the 'right' social pressures (the concept which in the light of Durkheim's theoretical scheme can be only interpreted as identical with the social *norm*, that is with the *prevailing standards*, with the *average*). Morality being a social product, resistance to standards promoted by society as behavioural norms must lead to the incidence of immoral action.

This theory of morality concedes the right of society (of any society, to be sure; or, in a more liberal interpretation, of every social collectivity, not necessarily of the 'global-societal' size, but capable of supporting its joint conscience by a network of effective sanctions) to impose its own substantive version of moral behaviour; and concurs with the practice in which social authority claims the monopoly of moral judgement. It tacitly accepts the theoretical illegitimacy of all judgements that are not grounded in the exercise of such monopoly; so that for all practical intents and purposes moral behaviour becomes synonymous with social conformity and obedience to the norms observed by the majority.

The challenge of the Holocaust

The circular reasoning prompted by virtual identification of morality with social discipline makes the daily practice of sociology well-nigh immune to the 'paradigm crisis'. There are few occasions, if any, when the application of the extant paradigm may cause embarassment. Programmatic relativism built into this vision of morality provides the ultimate safety valve in case the observed norms do arouse intinctive moral revulsion. It therefore takes events of exceptional dramatic power to shatter the grip of the dominant paradigm and to start a feverish search for alternative groundings of ethical principles. Even so, the necessity of such a search is viewed with suspicion, and efforts are made to narrate the dramatic experience in a form that would allow its accommodation within the old scheme; this is normally achieved either by presenting the events as truly unique, and hence not quite relevant to the general *theory* of morality (as distinct from the *history* of morality – much like the fall of giant meteorites would not necessitate the reconstruction of evolutionary theory), or by dissolving it in a wider and familiar category of unsavoury, yet regular and normal by-products or limitations of the morality-producing system. If neither of the two expedients measures up to the magnitude of the events, a third escape route is sometimes taken: refusal to admit the evidence into the discursive universe of the discipline, and proceeding as if the event had not taken place.

All three stratagems have been deployed in the sociological reaction to the Holocaust, an event of, arguably, the most dramatic moral significance. As we have noted before, there were numerous early attempts to narrate the most horrifying of genocides as the work of a particularly dense network of morally deficient individuals released from civilized contraints by a criminal, and above all irrational, ideology. When such attempts failed, as the perpetrators of the crime had been certified sane and morally 'normal' by the most scrupulous historical research, attention focused on revamping selected old classes of deviant phenomena, or constructing new sociological categories, into which the Holocaust episode could be assigned, and thus domesticated and defused (for instance, explaining the Holocaust in terms of prejudice or ideology). Finally, by far the most popular way of dealing with the evidence of the Holocaust has so far been not to deal with it at all. The essence and historical tendency of modernity, the logic of the civilizing process, the prospects and hindrances of progressive rationalization of social life are often discussed as if the Holocaust did not happen, as if it was not true and even worth serious consideration that the Holocaust 'bears witness to the advance of civilization',[3] or that 'civilization now includes death camps and *Muselmänner* among its material and spiritual products'.[4]

And yet the Holocaust stubbornly rejects all three treatments. For a number of reasons it posits a challenge to social theory which cannot be easily dismissed, as the decision to dismiss it is not in the hands of social theorists, or at any rate in theirs alone. Political and legal responses to the Nazi crime put on the agenda the need to legitimize the verdict of immorality passed on the actions of a great number of people who faithfully followed the moral norms of their own society. Were the distinction between right and wrong or good and evil fully and solely at the disposal of the social grouping able to 'principally co-ordinate' the social space under its supervision (as the dominant sociological theory avers), there would be no legitimate ground for proffering a charge of immorality against such individuals as did not breach the rules enforced by that grouping. One would suspect that if it had not been for the defeat of Germany, this and related problems would never arise. Yet Germany was defeated, and the need to face the problem did arise.

There would be no war criminals and no right to try, condemn and execute Eichmann unless there was some justification for conceiving of disciplined behaviour, totally conforming to the moral norms in force at that time and in that place, as criminal. And there would be no way to conceive of the punishment of such behaviour as anything more than the vengeance of the victors over the vanquished (a relationship that could be reverted without impugning the principle of punishment), were there no supra- or non-societal grounds on which the condemned actions could be shown to collide not only with a retrospectively enforced legal norm, but also with moral principles which society may suspend, but not declare out of court. *In the aftermath of the Holocaust, legal practice, and thus also moral theory, faced the possibility that morality may manifest itself in insubordination towards socially upheld principles, and in an action openly defying social solidarity and consensus.* For sociological theory, the very idea of pre-social grounds of moral behaviour augurs the necessity of a radical revision of traditional interpretations of the origins of the sources of moral norms and their obligatory power. This point was argued most powerfully by Hannah Arendt:

> What we have demanded in these trials, where the defendants had committed 'legal' crimes, is that human beings be capable of telling right from wrong even when all they have to guide them is their own judgement, which, moreover, happens to be completely at odds with what they must regard as the unanimous opinion of all these around them. And this question is all the more serious as we know that the few who were 'arrogant' enough to trust only their own judgement were by no means identical with those persons who continued to abide by old values, or who were guided by a religious belief. Since the whole of respectable society had in one way or another succumbed to Hitler, the moral maxims which determine social behaviour and the religious commandments – *'Thou shalt not kill!'* – which guide conscience had virtually vanished. These few who were still able to tell right from wrong went really only by their own judgements, and they did so freely; there were no rules to be abided by, under which the particular cases with which they were confronted could be subsumed. They had to decide each instance as it arose, because no rules existed for the unprecedented.[5]

In these poignant words Hannah Arendt had articulated the question of *moral responsibility for resisting socialization.* The moot issue of the social foundations of morality had been cast aside; whatever the solution offered to that issue, the authority and binding force of the distinction between good and evil cannot be legitimized by reference to social powers which sanction and enforce it. Even if condemned by the group – by all groups, as a matter of fact – individual conduct may still be moral; an action recommended by society – even by the whole of the society in unison – may still be immoral. Resistance to behavioural rules promoted by a given society neither should, nor can, claim its authority from an alternative normative injunction of another society; for instance, from the moral lore of a past now denigrated and rejected by the new social order. The question of the societal grounds of moral authority is, in other words, morally irrelevant.

The socially enforced moral systems are communally based and promoted – and hence in a pluralist, heterogeneous world, irreparably relative. *This relativism, however, does not apply to human 'ability to tell right from wrong'.* Such an ability must be grounded in something other than the *conscience collective* of society. Every given society faces such an ability ready formed, much as it faces human biological constitution, physiological needs or psychological drives. And it does with such ability what it admits of doing with those other stubborn realities: it tries to suppress it, or harness it to its own ends, or channel it in a direction it considers useful or harmless. *The process of socialization consists in the manipulation of moral capacity* – not in its production. And the moral capacity that is manipulated entails not only certain principles which later become a passive object of social processing; it includes as well the ability to resist, escape and survive the processing, so that at the end of the day the authority and the responsibility for moral choices rests where they resided at the start: with the human person.

If this view of moral capacity is accepted, the apparently resolved and closed problems of the sociology of morality are thrown wide open again. The issue of morality must be relocated; from the problematics of socialization, education or civilization – in other words, from the realm of socially administered 'humanizing processes' – it ought to be shifted to the area of repressive, pattern-maintaining and tension-managing processes and institutions, as one of the 'problems' they are designed to handle and accommodate or transform. The moral capacity – the object, but not the product of such processes and institutions – would then have to disclose its alternative origin. Once the explanation of moral tendency as a conscious or unconscious drive towards the solution of the 'Hobbesian problem' is rejected, the factors responsible for the presence of moral capacity must be sought in the *social*, but not *societal* sphere. Moral behaviour is conceivable only in the context of coexistence, of 'being with others', that is, a social context; but it does not owe its appearance to the presence of supra-individual agencies of training and enforcement, that is, of a societal context.

Pre-societal sources of morality

The existential modality of the social (unlike the structure of the societal) has been seldom held at the focus of sociological attention. It was gladly conceded to the field of philosophical anthropology and seen as constituting, at best, the distant outer frontier of the area of sociology proper. There is no sociological consensus, therefore, as to the meaning, experiential content and behavioural consequences of the primary condition of 'being with others'. The ways in which that condition can be made sociologically relevant are yet to be fully explored in sociological practice.

The most common sociological practice does not seem to endow 'being with others' (i.e. being with other humans) with a special status or significance. The others are dissolved in the much more inclusive concepts of the context of action, the actor's situation, or, generally, the 'environment' – those vast territories where the forces which prompt the actor's choices in a particular direction, or limit the actor's freedom of choice, are located, and which contain such objectives as attract the actor's purposeful activity and hence supply motives for the action. The others are not credited with subjectivity that could set them apart from other constituents of the 'action context'. Or, rather, their unique status as human beings is acknowledged, yet hardly ever seen in practice as a circumstance which confronts the actor with a qualitatively distinct task. For all practical intents and purposes, the 'subjectivity' of the other boils down to a decreased predictability of his responses, and hence to a constraint it casts on the actor's search of complete control over the situation and efficient performance of the set task. The erratic conduct of the *human* other, as distinct from inanimate elements of the field of action, is a nuisance; and, for all we know, a temporary one. The actor's control over the situation aims at such manipulation of the context of the other's action as would enhance the probability of a specific course of conduct, and hence further reduce the position of the other within the actor's horizon to one virtually indistinguishable from the rest of the objects relevant to the success of the action. The presence of the *human* other in the field of action constitutes a *technological* challenge; reaching mastery over the other, reducing the other to the status of a calculable and manipulable factor of purposeful activity, is admittedly difficult. It may even call for special skills on the part of the actor (such as understanding, rhetoric or knowledge of psychology) which are dispensable or useless in relations with other objects in the field of action.

Within this common perspective, the significance of the other is fully exhausted by his impact on the actor's chance of reaching his purpose. The other matters in as far (and only in as far) as his fickleness and inconstancy detracts from the probability that the pursuit of the given end will be efficiently completed. The task of the actor is to secure a situation in which the other will cease to matter and may be left out of account. The task and its performance are hence subject to a technical, not a moral, evaluation. The options open to the actor in his relation to the other split into effective and ineffective, efficient and inefficient – indeed, rational and irrational – but not right and wrong, good and evil. The elementary situation of 'being with others' does not generate by itself (that is, unless forced by extrinsic pressures) any moral problematics. Whatever moral considerations may interfere with it must surely come from outside. Whatever constraints they are likely to impose upon the actor's choice would not stem from the intrinsic logic of means–ends calculation. Analytically speaking, they need to be cast squarely on the side of irrational factors. In the 'being with others' situation fully organized by the actor's objectives, morality is a foreign intrusion.

An alternative conception of the origins of morality may be sought in Sartre's famous portrayal of the *ego–alter* relationship as the essential and universal existental mode. It is far from certain, however, that it may be also found there. If a conception of morality does emerge from Sartre's analysis, it is a negative one: morality as a limit rather than a duty, a constraint rather than a stimulus. In this respect (though in this respect only) Sartrean implications for the assessment of the status of morality do not depart significantly from the previously surveyed standard sociological interpretation of the role of morality in the context of elementary action.

The radical novelty consists, of course, in singling out the human others from the rest of the actor's horizon, as units endowed with qualitatively distinct status and capacity. In Sartre, the other turns into *alter ego*, a fellow-man, a subject like myself, endowed with a subjectivity I can think of solely as a replica of the one I know from my inner experience. An abyss separates *alter ego* from all other, true or imaginable, objects of the world. *Alter ego* does what I do; he thinks, he evaluates, he makes projects, and while doing all these he looks at me as I look at him. By merely looking at me, the other becomes the limit of my freedom. He now usurps the right to define me and my ends, thereby sapping my separateness and autonomy, compromising my identity and my being-at-home in the world. The very presence of *alter ego* in this world puts me to shame and remains a constant cause of my anguish. I cannot be all I want to be. I cannot do all I want to do. My freedom fizzles out. In the presence of *alter ego* – that is, in the world – my being for myself is also, ineradicably, being for the other. When acting, I cannot but take into account that presence, and hence also those definitions, points of view, perspectives that it entails.

One is tempted to say that the inevitability of moral considerations is inherent in the Sartrean description of *ego–alter* togetherness. And yet it is far from clear what moral obligations, if any, may be determined by the togetherness so described. Alfred Schutz was fully within his rights when he interpreted the outcome of the *ego–alter* encounter, as rendered by Sartre, in the following way:

> My own possibilities are turned into probabilities beyond my control. I am no longer the master of the situation – or at least the situation has gained a dimension which escapes me. I have become a utensil with which and upon which the Other may act. I realize this experience not by way of cognition, but by a sentiment of uneasiness or discomfort, which, according to Sartre, is one of the oustanding features of the human condition.[6]

Sartrean uneasiness and discomfort bear an unmistakable family resemblance to that stultifying external constraint which common sociological perspective imputes to the presence of others. More precisely, they represent a subjective reflection of the predicament which sociology attempts to capture in that presence's impersonal, objective structure; or, better still, they stand for an emotional, pre-cognitive appurtenance of the logical-rational stance. The two renderings of existential condition are united by the resentment they imply. In both, the other is an annoyance and a burden; a challenge, at best. In one case, his presence calls for no moral norms – indeed, no other norms but the rules of rational behaviour. In another, it moulds the morality it begets

as a set of rules rather than norms (much less as inner propulsion); rules
that are *naturally* resented, as they reveal other humans as a hostile
externality of human condition, as a constraint upon freedom.

There is, however, a third description of the existential condition of
'being with others' – one that may provide a starting point for a truly
different and original sociological approach to morality, able to disclose
and articulate such aspects of modern society as the orthodox approaches
leave invisible. Emmanuel Levinas,[7] responsible for this description,
encapsulates its guiding idea in a quotation from Dostoyevsky: 'We are
all responsible for all and for all men before all, and I more than all the
others.'

To Levinas, 'being with others', that most primary and irremovable
attribute of human existence, means first and foremost *responsibility*.
'Since the other looks at me, I am responsible for him, without even
having taken on responsibilities in his regard.' My responsibility is the
one and only form in which the other exists for me; it is the mode of his
presence, of his proximity:

> the Other is not simply close to me in space, or close like a parent,
> but he approaches me essentially insofar as I feel myself – insofar
> as I am – responsible for him. It is a structure that in nowise
> resembles the intentional relation which in knowledge attaches us
> to the object – to no matter what object, be it a human object.
> Proximity does not revert to this intentionality; in particular it
> does not revert to the fact that the Other is known to me.

Most emphatically, *my responsibililty is unconditional.* It does not
depend on prior knowledge of the qualities of its object; it precedes such
knowledge. It does not depend on an interested intention stretched
towards the object; it precedes such intention. Neither knowledge nor
intention make for the proximity of the other, for the specifically human
mode of togetherness; 'The tie with the Other is knotted only as
responsibility'; and this moreover,

> whether accepted or refused, whether knowing or not knowing
> how to assume it, whether able or unable to do something concrete
> for the Other. To say: *me voici.* To do something for the Other. To
> give. To be human spirit, that's it ... I analyze the inter-human
> relationship as if, in proximity with the Other – beyond the image
> I myself make of the other man – his face, the expressive of the

Other (and the whole human body is in this sense more or less face) were what *ordains* me to serve him ... The face orders and ordains me. Its signification is an order signified. To be precise, if the face signifies an order in my regard, this is not in the manner in which an ordinary sign signifies its signified; this order is the very signifyingness of the face.

Indeed, according to Levinas, *responsibility is the essential, primary and fundamental structure of subjectivity*. Responsibility which means 'responsibility for the Other', and hence a responsibility 'for what is not my deed, or for what does not even matter to me'. This existential responsibility, the only meaning of subjectivity, of being a subject, has nothing to do with contractual obligation. It has nothing in common either with my calculation of reciprocal benefit. It does not need a sound or idle expectation of reciprocity, of 'mutuality of intentions', of the other rewarding my responsibility with his own. I am not assuming my responsibility on behest of a superior force, be it a moral code sanctioned with the threat of hell or a legal code sanctioned with the threat of prison. Because of what my responsibility is not, I do not bear it as a burden. I become responsible while I constitute myself into a subject. Becoming responsible *is* the constitution of me as a subject. Hence it is my affair, and mine only. 'Intersubjective relation is a non-symmetrical relation ... I am responsible for the Other without waiting for reciprocity, were I to die for it. Reciprocity is *his* affair.'

Responsibility being the existential mode of the human subject, *morality is the primary structure of intersubjective relation* in its most pristine form, unaffected by any non-moral factors (like interest, calculation of benefit, rational search for optimal solutions, or surrender to coercion). The substance of morality being a duty towards the other (as distinct from an obligation), and a duty which precedes all interestedness – the roots of morality reach well beneath societal arrangements, like structures of domination or culture. Societal processes start when the structure of morality (tantamount to intersubjectivity) is already there. *Morality is not a product of society. Morality is something society manipulates* – exploits, re-directs, jams.

Obversely, immoral behaviour, a conduct which forsakes or abdicates responsibility for the other, is not an effect of societal malfunctioning. It is therefore the incidence of immoral, rather than moral, behaviour which calls for the investigation of the social administration of intersubjectivity.

Social proximity and moral responsibility

Responsibility, this building block of all moral behaviour, arises out of the proximity of the other. Proximity means responsibility, and responsibility *is* proximity. Discussion of the relative priority of one or the other is admittedly gratuitous, as none is conceivable alone. Defusion of responsibility, and thus the neutralization of the moral urge which follows it, must necessarily involve (is, in fact, synonymous with) replacing proximity with a physical or spiritual separation. The alternative to proximity is social distance. The moral attribute of proximity is responsibility; the moral attribute of social distance is lack of moral relationship, or heterophobia. *Responsibility is silenced once proximity is eroded; it may eventually be replaced with resentment once the fellow human subject is transformed into an Other.* The process of transformation is one of social separation. It was such a separation which made it possible for thousands to kill, and for millions to watch the murder without protesting. It was the technological and bureaucratic achievement of modern rational society which made such a separation possible.

Hans Mommsen, one of the most distinguished German historians of the Nazi era, has recently summarized the historical significance of the Holocaust and the problems it creates for the self-awareness of modern society:

> While Western Civilization has developed the means for unimaginable mass-destruction, the training provided by modern technology and techniques of rationalization has produced a purely technocratic and bureaucratic mentality, exemplified by the group of perpetrators of the Holocaust, whether they committed murder directly themselves or prepared deportation and liquidation at the desks of the Reich Main Security Office (Reichssicherheithauptamt), at the offices of the diplomatic service, or as plenipotentiaries of the Third Reich within the occupied or satellite countries. To this extent the history of the Holocaust seems to be the *mene tekel* of the modern state.[8]

Whatever else the Nazi state has achieved, it certainly succeeded in overcoming the most formidable of obstacles to systematic, purposeful, non-emotional, cold-blooded murder of people – old and young, men and women: that 'animal pity by which all normal men are affected in the presence of physical suffering'.[9] We do not know much about the *animal* pity, but we do know that there is a way of viewing the elementary human condition which makes explicit the universality of human revulsion to murder, inhibition against inflicting suffering on another human being, and the urge to help those who suffer; indeed, of the very personal responsibility for the welfare of the other. If this view is correct, or at least plausible, then the accomplishment of the Nazi regime consisted first and foremost in neutralizing the moral impact of the specifically human existential mode. It is important to know whether this success was related to the unique features of the Nazi movement and rule, or whether it can be accounted for by reference to more common attributes of our society, which the Nazis merely skilfully deployed in the service of Hitler's purpose.

Until one or two decades ago it was common – not only among the lay public, but also among historians – to seek the explanation of the mass murder of European Jews in the long history of European antisemitism. Such an explanation required of course singling out German antisemitism as the most intense, merciless and murderous; it was after all in Germany where the monstrous plan of total annihilation of the whole race had been begotten and put in action. As we, however, remember from the second and third chapters, both the explanation and its corollary have been discredited by historical research. There was an evident dicontinuity between the traditional, pre-modern Jew-hatred and the modern exterminatory design indispensable for the perpetration of the Holocaust. As far as the function of popular feelings is concerned, the ever-growing volume of historical evidence proves beyond reasonable doubt an almost negative correlation between the ordinary and traditional, 'neighbourly', competition-based anti-Jewish sentiment, and the willingness to embrace the Nazi vision of total destruction and to partake of its implementation.

There is a growing consensus among historians of the Nazi era that *the perpetration of the Holocaust required the neutralization of ordinary Germany attitudes toward the Jews, not their mobilization*; that the 'natural' continuation of the traditional resentment towards the Jews was much more a feeling of revulsion for the 'radical actions' of the Nazi's thugs than a willingness to co-operate in mass murder; and that the SS planners of the genocide had to steer their way toward the *Endlösung* by guarding the job's independence from the sentiments of the population at large, and thus its immunity to the influence of traditional, spontaneously-formed and communally-sustained attitudes towards their victims.

The relevant and cogent findings of historical studies have been recently recapitulated by Martin Broszat: 'In those cities and towns where Jews formed a large segment of the population, the relations between the Germans and the Jews were, even in the first years of the Nazi era, for the most part relatively good and hardly hostile.'[10] Nazi attempts to stir up antisemitic feelings and to re-forge static resentment into a dynamic one (a distinction aptly coined by Müller-Claudius) – i.e. to inflame the non-Party, ideologically uncommitted population into acts of violence against the Jews or at least into an active support of SA displays of force – foundered on the popular repugnance of physical coercion, on deep-seated inhibitions against inflicting pain and physical suffering, and on stubborn human loyalty to their neighbours, to people whom one knows and has charted into one's map of the world as persons, rather than anonymous specimens of a type. The hooligan exploits of the SA men on a binge in the first months of Hitler's rule had to be called off and forcefully supressed to stave off the threat of popular alienation and rebellion; while rejoicing in his followers' anti-Jewish frippery, Hitler felt obliged to intervene personally to put a halt to all grass-root antisemitic initiative. Anti-Jewish boycott, planned to last indefinitely, was at the last minute cut to a one-day 'warning demonstration', partly because of the fear of foreign reactions, but in a large part due to the evident lack of popular enthusiasm for the venture. After the day of boycott (1 April 1933), Nazi leaders complained in their reports and briefings of the widespread apathy of all but SA and Party members, and the whole event was evaluated as a failure; conclusions were drawn as to the need of sustained propaganda in order to awaken and alert the masses to *their* role in the implementation of the anti-Jewish measures.[11] The ensuing efforts notwithstanding, the flop of the one-day boycott set the pattern for all subsequent antisemitic policies which required for their success an active participation of the population at large. As long as they stayed open, Jewish shops and surgeries continued to attract clients and patients. Frankonian and Bavarian peasants had to be forced to stop their commerce with Jewish cattle-traders. As we saw before, the *Kristallnacht*, the only officially planned and co-ordinated massive pogrom, was also found counter-productive, in as far as it was hoped to elicit commitment of the average German to antisemitic violence. Instead, most people reacted with dismay at the sight of the pavements strewn with broken glass and their elderly neighbours bundled by young thugs into prison trucks. The point that cannot be over-emphasized is that all these negative reactions to the

open display of anti-Jewish violence coincided, without any visible contradiction, with a massive and keen approval of the anti-Jewish legislation –
with its redefinition of the Jew, eviction of the Jew from the German
Volk and the ever-thickening layer of legal restrictions and
prohibitions.[12]

Julius Streicher, the pioneer of Nazi antisemitic propaganda, found
that the most daunting of tasks his paper *Der Stürmer* was set up to
perform, was to make the stereotype of the 'Jew as such' stick to the
personal images his readers held of the Jews they knew, of the Jewish
neighbours, friends or business partners. Accoring to Dennis E.
Showalter, author of a perceptive monograph of the short yet stormy
history of the paper, Streicher was not alone in his discovery: 'A major
challenge of political anti-Semitism involves overcoming the images of
the "Jew next door" – the living, breathing acquaintance or associate
whose simple existence appears to deny the validity of that negative
stereotype, the "mythological Jew".'[13] There seemed to be amazingly
little correlation between personal and abstract images; as if it was not in
the human habit to experience the logical contradiction between the two
as a cognitive dissonance, or – more generally – as a psychological
problem; as if in spite of the apparently identical referent of personal
and abstract images, they were not generally considered as notions
belonging to the same class, as representations to be compared, checked
against each other, and ultimately reconciled or rejected. Long after the
machinery of mass destruction had been set in full swing – in October
1943, to be precise – Himmler complained in front of his henchmen that
even devoted party members, who had shown no particular compunc-
tions concerning the annihilation of the Jewish race as a whole, had their
own, private, special Jews whom they wished to exempt and protect:

> 'The Jewish people is to be exterminated', says every party
> member. 'That's clear, it's part of our programme, elimination of
> the Jews, extermination, right, we'll do it'. And then they all come
> along, the eighty million good Germans, and each one has his
> decent Jew. Of course the others are swine, but this one is a
> first-class Jew.'[14]

It seems that what keeps personal images and abstract stereotypes
apart and wards off the clash that every logician would deem inevitable
is the moral saturation of the first and the morally-neutral, purely intellectual, character of the second. That proximity-cum-responsibility
context within which personal images are formed surrounds them with

a thick moral wall virtually impenetrable to 'merely abstract' arguments. Persuasive or insidious the intellectual stereotype may be, yet its zone of application stops abruptly where the sphere of personal intercourse begins. 'The other' as an *abstract category* simply does not communicate with 'the other' *I know*. The second belongs within the realm of morality, while the first is cast firmly outside. The second resides in the semantic universe of good and evil, which stubbornly refuses to be subordinated to the discourse of efficiency and rational choice.

Social suppression of moral responsibility

We know already that there was little direct link between diffuse hetero-phobia and the mass murder designed and perpetrated by the Nazis. What the accumulated historical evidence strongly suggests in additon is that mass murder on the unprecedented scale of the Holocaust was not (and in all probability could not be) an effect of awakening, release, prompting, intensification, or an outburst of dormant personal inclinations; nor was it in any other sense continuous with hostility emerging from personal face-to-face relationships, however soured or bitter those might have been on occasion. there is a clear limit to which such personally-based animosity may be stretched. In more cases than not, it would resist being pushed beyond the line drawn by that elementary responsibility for the other which is inextricably interwoven in human proximity, in 'living with others'. *The Holocaust could be accomplished only on the condition of neutralizing the impact of primeval moral drives, of isolating the machinery of murder from the sphere where such drives arise and apply, of rendering such drives marginal or altogether irrelevant to the task.*

This neutralizing, isolating and marginalizing was an achievement of the Nazi regime deploying the formidable apparatus of modern industry, transport, science, bureaucracy, technology. Without them, the Holocaust would be unthinkable; the grandiose vision of *judenrein* Europe, of the total annihilation of the Jewish race, would peter out in a multitude of bigger and smaller pogroms perpetrated by psychopaths, sadists, fanatics or other addicts of gratuitous violence; however cruel and gory, such actions would be hardly commensurable with the purpose. It was the designing of the 'solution to the Jewish problem' as a rational, bureaucratic-technical task, as something to be done to a particular category of objects by a particular set of experts and specialized organizations – in other words, as a depersonalized task not dependent on feelings and personal commitments – which proved to be, in the end, adequate to Hitler's vision. Yet the solution could not be so designed, and certainly not executed, until the future objects of bureaucratic operations, the Jews, had been removed from the horizon of German daily life, cut off from the network of personal intercourse, transformed in practice into exemplars of a category, of a stereotype – into the abstract concept of the *metaphysical Jew*. Until, that is, they had ceased to be those 'others' to whom moral responsibility normally extends, and lost the protection which such natural morality offers.

Having thoroughly analyzed the successive failures of the Nazis to arouse the popular hatred of Jews and to harness it in the service of the 'solution to the Jewish problem', Ian Kershaw comes to the conclusion that

> Where the Nazis were most successful was in the depersonalization of the Jews. The more the Jew was forced out of social life, the more he seemed to fit the stereotypes of a propaganda which intensified, paradoxically, its campaign against 'Jewry' the fewer actual Jews there were in Germany itself. Depersonalization increased the already existent widespread indifference of German popular opinion and formed a vital stage between the archaic violence and the rationalized 'assembly line' annihilation of the death camps.
>
> The 'Final Solution' would not have been possible without the progressive steps to exclude the Jews from German society which took place in full view of the public, in their legal form met with widespread approval, and resulted in the depersonalization and debasement of the figure of the Jew.[15]

As we have already noted in the third chapter, the Germans who did object to the exploits of SA hoodlums when the 'Jew next door' was their victim (even those among them who found the courage to make their revulsion manifest), accepted with indifference and often with satisfaction legal restrictions imposed on 'the Jew as such'. What would stir their moral conscience if focused on persons they knew, aroused hardly any feelings when targeted on an abstract and stereotyped category. They noted with equanimity, or failed to note, the gradual disappearance of Jews from their world of everyday life. Until, for the young German soldiers and SS men entrusted with the task of 'liquidation' of so many *Figuren*, the Jew was 'only a "museum-piece", something to look at with curiosity, a fossil wonder-animal, with the yellow star on its breast, a witness to bygone times but not belonging to the present, something one had to journey far to see.'[16] Morality did not travel that far. Morality tends to stay at home and in the present.

In Hans Mommsen's words,

> Hedrich's policy of isolating the Jewish minority socially and morally from the majority of population proceeded without major protest from the public because that part of the Jewish population who had been in close contact with their German neighbours were either not included in the growing discrimination or were step by step isolated from them. Only after cumulative discriminatory legislation had pressed Germany's Jews into the role of social pariahs, completely deprived of any regular social communication with the majority population, could deportation and extermination be put in effect without shaking the social structure of the regime.[17]

Raul Hilberg, the foremost authority on the history of the Holocaust, had the following to say about the steps leading to the gradual silencing of moral inhibitions and setting in motion the machinery of mass destruction:

> In its completed form a destruction process in a modern society will thus be structured as shown in this chart:

Definition

↓

Dismissals of employees and expropriation of business firms

↓

Concentration

↓

Exploitation of labour and starvation measures

↓

Annihilation

↓

Confiscation of personal effects

> The sequence of steps in a destruction process is thus determined. If there is an attempt to inflict maximum injury upon a group of people, it is therefore inevitable that a bureaucracy – no matter

how decentralized its apparatus or how unplanned its activities – should push its victims through these stages.[18]

The stages, Hilberg suggests, are logically determined; they form a rational sequence, a sequence conforming to the modern standards which prompt us to seek the shortest ways and the most efficient means to the end. If we now try to discover the guiding principle in this rational solution to the problem of mass destruction, we find out that *the successive stages are arranged according to the logic of eviction from the realm of moral duty* (or, to use the concept suggested by Helen Fein,[19] from the *universe of obligations*).

Definition sets the victimized group apart (all definitions mean splitting the totality into two parts – the marked and the unmarked), as a *different* category, so that whatever applies to it does *not* apply to all the rest. By the very act of being defined, the group has been targeted for *special* treatment; what is proper in relation to 'ordinary' people must not necessarily be proper in relation to it. Individual members of the group become now in addition exemplars of a type; something of the nature of the type cannot but seep into their individualized images, compromise the originally innocent proximity, limit its autonomy as the self-sustained moral universe.

Dismissals and expropriations tear apart most of the general contracts, substituting physical and spiritual distance for past proximity. The victimized group is now effectively removed from sight; it is a category one at best hears of, so that what one hears about it has no chance to be translated into the knowledge of individual destinies, and thus to be checked against personal experience.

Concentration completes this process of distantiation. The victimized group and the rest do not meet any more, their life-processes to not cross, communication grinds to a halt, whatever happens to one of the now segregated groups does not concern the other, has no meaning easy to translate into the vocabulary of human intercourse.

Exploitation and starvation perform a further, truly astonishing, feat: they disguise inhumanity as humanity. There is ample evidence of local Nazi chiefs asking their superiors for permission to kill some Jews under their jurisdiction (well before the signal was given to start mass killings) in order to spare them the agony of famine; as the food supplies were not available to sustain a mass of ghettoized population previously robbed of wealth and income, killing seemed an act of mercy – indeed, the manifestation of humanity. 'The diabolical circle of fascist policies' allowed to 'create deliberately intolerable conditions and states of emergency and then to use them to legitimize even more radical steps.'[20]

And thus the final act, annihilation, was in no way a revolutionary departure. It was, so to speak, a logical (though, remember, unanticipated at the start) outcome of the many steps taken before. None of the steps was made inevitable by the already attained state of affairs, but each step rendered rational the choice of the next stage on the road to destruction. *The further away the sequence moved from the original act of Definition, the more it was guided by purely rational-technical considerations, and the less did it have to reckon with moral inhibitions.* Indeed, it all but ceased to necessitate moral choices.

The passages between the stages had one striking feature in common. They all increased the physical and mental distance between the purported victims and the rest of the population – the perpetrators and the witnesses of the genocide alike. In this quality resided their inherent rationality from the point of view of the final destination, and their effectiveness in bringing the task of destruction to its completion. Evidently, moral inhibitions do not act at a distance. They are inextricably tied down to human proximity. Commitment of immoral acts, on the contrary, becomes easier with every inch of social distance. If Mommsen is right when he singles out as the 'anthropological dimension' of the Holocaust experience 'the danger inherent in present-day industrial society of a process of becoming accustomed to moral indifference in regard to actions not immediately related to one's own sphere of experience'[21] – then the danger he warns about must be traced to the capacity of that present-day industrial society to extend inter-human distance to a point where moral responsibility and moral inhibitions become inaudible.

Social production of distance

Being inextricably tied to human proximity, morality seems to conform to the law of optical perspective. It looms large and thick close to the eye. With the growth of distance, responsibility for the other shrivels, moral dimensions of the object blur, till both reach the vanishing point and disppear from view.

This quality of moral drive seems independent of the social order which supplies the framework of interaction. What does depend on that order is the pragmatic effectiveness of moral predispositions; their capacity to control human actions, to set limits to the harm inflicted on the other, to draw the parameters in which all intercourse tends to be contained. The significance – and danger – of moral indifference becomes particularly acute in our modern, rationalized, industrial technologically proficient society because in such a society human action can be effective at a distance, and at a distance constantly growing with the progress of science, technology and bureaucracy. In such a society, *the effects of human action reach far beyond the 'vanishing point' of moral visibility*. The visual capacity of moral drive, limited as it is by the principle of proximity, remains constant, while the distance at which human action may be effective and consequential, and thus also the number of people who may be affected by such action, grow rapidly. The sphere of interaction influenced by moral drives is dwarfed by comparison with the expanding volume of actions excepted from its interference.

The notorious success of modern civilization in substituting rational criteria of action for all other, and by the modern definition 'irrational' criteria (moral evaluations looming large among the latter), was in decisive measure conditioned by the progress in 'remote control', that is in extending the distance at which human action is able to bring effects. It is the remote, barely visible targets of action which are free from moral evaluation; and so the choice of action which affects such targets is free from limitations imposed by moral drive.

As Milgram's experiments dramatically demonstrated, the silencing of the moral urge and the suspension of moral inhibitions is achieved precisely through making the genuine (though often unknown to the actor) targets of action 'remote and barely visible', rather than through an overt anti-moral crusade, or an indoctrination aimed at substituting an alternative set of rules for the old moral system. The most obvious example of the technique which places the victims out of sight, and hence renders them inaccessible to moral assessment, are modern weapons. The progress of the latter consisted mostly in eliminating to an ever-growing extent the chance of face-to-face combat, of committing the act of killing in its human-size, commonsensical meaning; with weapons separating and distantiating, rather than confronting and bringing together the warring armies, the drill of the weapon-operators in suppressing their moral drives, or direct attacks on 'old-fashioned' morality, lose much of their former importance, as the use of weapons seems to bear merely an abstract-intellectual relation to the moral integrity of the users. In the words of Philip Caputo, war ethos 'seems to be a matter of distance and technology. You could never go wrong if you killed people at long range with sophisticated weapons.'[22] As long as one does not see the practical effects of one's action, or as long as one cannot unambiguously relate what one saw to such innocent and minuscule acts of one's own as pushing button or switching a pointer, a moral conflict is unlikely to appear, or likely to appear in muted form. One can think of the invention of artillery able to hit a target invisible to those who operate the guns as a symbolic starting point of modern warfare and the concomitant irrelevancy of moral factors: such artillery allows the destruction of the target while aiming the gun in an entirely different direction.

The accomplishment of modern weaponry can be taken as a metaphor for a much more diversified and ramified process of the social production of distance. John Lachs has located the unifying characteristics of the many manifestations of this process in the introduction, on a massive scale, of the *mediation of action*, and of the *intermediary man* – one who 'stands between me and my action, making it impossible for me to experience it directly'.

> The distance we feel from our actions is proportionate to our ignorance of them; our ignorance, in turn, is largely a measure of the length of the chain of intermediaries between ourselves and our acts ... As consciousness of the context drops out, the actions become motions without consequence. With the consequences out of view, people can be parties to the most abhorrent acts without ever raising the question of their own role and responsibility ...
>
> [It is extremely difficult] to see how our own actions, through their remote effects, contributed to causing misery. It is no cop out to think oneself blameless and condemn society. It is the natural result of large-scale mediation which inevitably leads to monstrous ignorance.[23]

Once the action has been mediated, the action's ultimate effects are located outside that relatively narrow area of intercourse inside which moral drives retain their regulating force. Obversely, acts contained within that morally pregnant area are for most of the participants or their witnesses innocuous enough not to come under moral censure. Minute division of labour, as well as the sheer length of the chain of acts that mediate between the initiative and its tangible effects, emancipates most – however decisive – constituents of the collective venture from moral significance and scrutiny. They are still subject to analysis and evaluation – but criteria are technical, not moral. 'Problems' call for better, more rational designs, not for soul-searching. The actors occupy themselves with the rational task of finding better means for the given – and partial – end, not with a moral task of the evaluation of the ultimate objective (of which they have but a vague idea, or for which they do not feel responsible).

In his detailed account of the history of invention and deployment of the infamous gas van, the initial Nazi solution to the technical task of fast, neat and cheap mass murder, Christopher R. Browning offers the following insight into the psychological world of the people involved.

> Specialists whose expertise normally had nothing to do with mass murder suddenly found themselves a minor cog in the machinery of destruction. Occupied with procuring, dispatching, maintaining, and repairing motor vehicles, their expertise and facilities were suddenly pressed into the service of mass murder when they were charged with producing gas vans ... What disturbed them was the criticism and complaints about faults in their product. The shortcomings of the gas vans were a negative reflection on their workmanship that had to be remedied. Kept fully abreast of the problems arising in the field, they strove for ingenious technical adjustments to make their product more efficient and acceptable to its operators ... Their greatest concern seemed to be that they might be deemed inadequate to their assigned task.[24]

Under the conditions of bureaucratic division of labour, 'the other' inside the circle of proximity where moral responsibility rules supreme is a workmate, whose successful coping with his own task depends on the actor's application to his part of the job; the immediate superior, whose occupational standing depends on the co-operation of his subordinates; and a person immediately down the hierarchy line, who expects his tasks to be clearly defined and made feasible. In dealing with such others, that moral responsibility which proximity tends to generate takes the form of loyalty to the organization – that abstract articulation of the network of face-to-face interactions. In the form of organizational loyalty, the actors' moral drives may be deployed for morally abject purposes, without sapping the ethical propriety of intercourse within that area of proximity which the moral drives cover. The actors may go on sincerely believing in their own integrity; indeed, their behaviour does conform to the moral standards held in the only region in which other standards remained operative. Browning investigated the personal stories of the four officials manning the notorious Jewish Desk (D III) at the German Foreign Ministry. He found two of them satisfied with their jobs, while two others preferred transfer to other tasks.

> Both were successful in eventually getting out of D III, but while they were there they performed their duties meticulously. They did not openly object to the job but worked covertly and quietly for their transfer; keeping their records clean was their top priority. Whether zealously or reluctantly, the fact remains that all four worked efficiently ... They kept the machine moving, and the most ambitious and unscrupulous among them gave it an additional push.[25]

The task-splitting and the resulting separation of moral mini-communities from the ultimate effects of the operation achieves the distance between the perpetrators and the victims of cruelty which reduces, or eliminates, the counter-pressure of moral inhibitions. The right physical and functional distance cannot be attained, however, all along the bureaucratic chain of command. Some among the perpetrators must meet the victims face-to-face, or at least must be so close to them as to be unable to avoid, or even to suppress, visualizing the effects their actions have upon time. Another method is needed to assure the right *psychological* distance even in the absence of the *physical* or the *functional* ones. Such a method is provided by a specifically modern form of authority – expertise.

The essence of expertise is the assumption that doing things properly requires certain knowledge, that such knowledge is distributed unevenly, that some persons possess more of it than others, that those who possess it ought to be in charge of doing things, and that being in charge places upon them the responsibility for how things are being done. In fact, the responsibility is seen as vested not in the experts, but in the skills they represent. The institution of expertise and the associated stance towards social action closely approximate the notorious Saint-Simon's ideal (enthusiastically endorsed by Marx) of the 'administration of things, not people'; the actors serve as mere agents of knowledge, as bearers of the 'know-how', and their personal responsibility rests entirely in representing knowledge properly, that is in doing things according to the 'state of the art', to the best of what extant knowledge can offer. For those who do not possess the know-how, responsible action means following the advice of the experts. In the process, personal responsibility dissolves in the abstract authority of technical know-how.

Browning quotes at length the memo prepared by a technical expert Willy Just in respect of the technical improvement of the gas vans. Just proposed that the company assembling the vans should shorten the loading space: the existing vans could not negotiate the difficult Russian terrain fully loaded, so too much carbon monoxide was needed to fill the remaining empty space, and the whole operation took too much time and lost considerably in its potential efficiency:

> A shorter, fully loaded truck could operate much more quickly. A shortening of the rear compartment would not disadvantageously affect the weight balance, overloading the front axle, because 'actually a correction in the weight distribution takes place automatically through the fact that the cargo in the struggle toward the back door during the operation always is preponderantly located there'. Because the connecting pipe was quickly rusted through the 'fluids', the gas should be introduced from above, not below. To facilitate cleaning, an eight- to twelve-inch hole should be made in the floor and provided with a cover opened from outside. The floor should be slightly inclined, and the cover equipped with a small sieve. Thus all 'fluids' would flow to the middle, the 'thin fluids' would exit even during operation, and 'thicker fluids' could be hosed out afterwards.[26]

All inverted commas are Browning's; Just did not seek nor use knowingly metaphors or euphemisms, his was the straightforward, down-to-earth, language of technology. As an expert in the truck construction, he was indeed trying to cope with the movement of the cargo, not with the human beings struggling for breath; with thick and thin fluids, not with human excreta and vomit. The fact that the load consisted of people about to be murdered and losing control over their bodies, did not detract from the technical challenge of the problem. This fact had anyway to be translated first into the neutral language of car-production technology before it could turn into a 'problem' to be 'resolved'. One wonders whether a retranslation was ever attempted by those who read Just's memo and undertook to implement the technical instructions it contained.

For Milgram's guinea pigs, the 'problem' was the experiment set and administered by the scientific experts. Milgram's experts saw to it that the expert-led actors should, unlike the workers of the *Sodomka* factory for whom Just's memo was destined, entertain no doubts as to the suffering their actions were causing, that there should be no chance for a

'I did not know' excuse. What Milgram's experiment has proved in the end is the power of expertise and its capacity to triumph over moral drives. Moral people can be driven into committing immoral acts even if they know (or believe) that the acts are immoral – providing that they are convinced that the experts (people who, by definition, know something they themselves do not know) have defined their actions as necessary. After all, most actions in our society are not legitimized by the discussion of their objectives, but by the advice or instruction offered by the people in the know.

Final remarks

Admittedly, this chapter stops far short of formulating an alternative sociological theory of moral behaviour. Its purpose is much more modest: to discuss some sources of moral drive other than social and some societally produced conditions under which immoral behaviour becomes possible. Even such a limited discussion, it seems, shows that the orthodox sociology of morality is in need of substantial revision. One of the orthodox assumptions that seems to have failed the test particularly badly is that moral behaviour is born of the operation of society and maintained by the operation of societal institutions, that society is essentially a humanizing, moralizing device and that, accordingly, the incidence of immoral conduct on anything more than a marginal scale may be explained only as an effect of the malfunctioning of 'normal' social arrangements. The corollary of this assumption is that immorality cannot on the whole be societally produced, and that its true causes must be sought elsewhere.

The point made in this chapter is that powerful moral drives have a pre-societal origin, while some aspects of modern societal organization cause considerable weakening of their constraining power; that, in effect, society may make the immoral conduct more, rather than less, plausible. The Western-promoted mythical image of the world without modern bureaucracy and expertise as ruled by the 'jungle law' or the 'law of the fist' bears evidence partly to the self-legitimizing need of modern bureaucracy[27] which set to destroy the competition of norms deriving from drives and proclivities it did not control,[28] and partly to the degree to which the pristine human ability to regulate reciprocal relations on the basis of moral responsibility has been by now lost and forgotten. What is therefore presented and conceived of as savagery to be tamed and suppressed may prove on a close scrutiny to be the self same moral drive that the civilizing process set out to neutralize, and then to replace with the controlling pressures emanating from the new structure of domination. Once the moral forces spontaneously generated by human proximity had been delegitimized and paralyzed, the new forces which replaced it acquired an unprecedented freedom of manoeuvre. They may generate on a massive scale a conduct which can be defined as ethically correct only by the criminals in power.

Among societal achievements in the sphere of the management of morality one needs to name: social production of distance, which either annuls or weakens the pressure of moral responsibility; substitution of technical for moral responsibility, which effectively conceals the moral significance of the action; and the technology of segregation and separation, which promotes indifference to the plight of the Other which otherwise would be subject to moral evaluation and morally motivated response. One needs also to consider that all these morality-eroding mechanisms are further strengthened by the principle of sovereignty of state powers usurping supreme ethical authority on behalf of the societies they rule. Except for diffuse and often ineffective 'world opinion', the rulers of states are on the whole unconstrained in their management of norms binding on the territory of their sovereign rule. Proofs are not lacking that the more unscrupulous their actions in that field, the more intense are the calls for their 'appeasement' which reconfirm and reinforce their monopoly and dictatorship in the field of moral judgement.

What follows is that under modern order the ancient Sophoclean conflict between moral law and the law of society shows no signs of abating. If anything, it tends to become more frequent and more profound – and the odds are shifted in favour of the morality-suppressing societal pressures. On many occasions moral behaviour means taking a stance dubbed and decreed anti-social or subversive by the powers that be *and* by public opinion (whether outspoken or merely manifested in majority action or non-action). Promotion of moral behaviour in such cases means resistance to societal authority and action aimed at the weakening of its grip. Moral duty has to count on its pristine source: the essential human responsibility for the Other.

That these problems have an urgency in addition to their academic interest, reminds us of the words of Paul Hilberg:

Remember, again, that the basic question was whether a western nation, a civilized nation, could be capable of such a thing. And then, soon after 1945, we see the query turned around totally as one begins to ask: 'Is there any western nation that is incapable of it? ... In 1941 the Holocaust was not expected and that is the very reason for our subsequent anxieties. We no longer dare to exclude the unimaginable.[29]

8

Afterthought: Rationality and Shame

There is a story from Sobibór: fourteen inmates tried to escape. In a matter of hours they were all caught and brought to the camp assembly square to confront the rest of the prisoners. There, they were told: 'In a moment you will die, of course. But before you do, each of you will choose his companion in death.' They said, 'Never!' 'If you refuse', said the commandant, quietly, 'I'll do the selection for you. Only I will choose fifty, not fourteen.' He did not have to carry out his threat.

In Lanzmann's *Shoah* a survivor of the successful escape from Treblinka remembers that when the inflow of the gas chambers' fodder slowed down, members of the *Sonderkommando* had their food rations withdrawn and, since they were no longer useful, were threatened with extermination. Their prospects of survival brightened when new Jewish populations were rounded up and loaded into trains destined for Treblinka.

Again in Lanzmann's film, a former *Sonderkommando* member, now a Tel-Aviv barber, reminisces how, while shaving the hair of the victims for German mattresses, he kept silent about the purpose of the exercise and prodded his clients to move faster towards what they were made to believe was a communal bath.

In the discussion started by the profound and moving article 'Poor Poles look at the Ghetto' by Professor Jan Błoński and conducted in 1987 on the pages of the respected Polish Catholic weekly *Tygodnik Powszechny*, Jerzy Jastrzębowski recalled a story told by an older member of his family. The family offered to hide an old friend, a Jew who looked Polish and spoke the elegant Polish of a nobleman, but refused to do the same for his three sisters, who looked Jewish and spoke with a pronounced Jewish accent. The friend refused to be saved alone. Jastrzębowski comments:

> Had the decision of my family been different, there were nine chances to one that we would be all shot. [In Nazi-occupied Poland, the punishment for hiding or helping Jews was death.] The probability that our friend and his sisters would survive in those conditions was perhaps smaller still. And yet the person telling me this family drama and repeating 'What could we do, there was nothing we could do!', did not look me in the eyes. He sensed I felt a lie, though all the facts were true.

Another contributor to the discussion, Kazimierz Dziewanowski, wrote:

> If in our country, in our presence and in front of our eyes, several millions of innocent people were killed, this was an event so horrifying, a tragedy so immense – that it is proper, human, and understandable that those who survived are haunted and cannot recover their calm ... It is impossible to prove that more could have been done, yet neither is it possible to prove that one could not do more.

Władysław Bartoszewski, during the occupation in charge of the Polish assistance to the Jews, commented: 'only he may say he has done everything he could, who paid the price of death'.

By far the most shocking among Lanzmann's messages is *the rationality of evil* (or was it the evil of rationality?). Hour after hour during that interminable agony of watching *Shoah* the terrible, humiliating truth is uncovered and paraded in its obscene nakedness: how few men with guns were needed to murder millions.

Amazing how frightened those few men with the rifles were; how conscious of the brittleness of their mastery over human cattle. Their power rested on the doomed living in a make-believe world, the world which they, the men with rifles, defined and narrated for their victims. In that world, obedience was rational; rationality was obedience. Rationality paid – at least for a time – but in that world there was no other, longer time. Each step on the road to death was carefully shaped so as to be calculable in terms of gains and losses, rewards and punishments. Fresh air and music rewarded the long, unremitting suffocation in the cattle carriage. A bath, complete with cloakrooms and barbers, towel and soap, was a welcome liberation from lice, dirt, and the stench of human sweat and excrement. Rational people will go quietly, meekly, joyously into a gas chamber, if only they are allowed to believe it is a bathroom.

Members of the *Sonderkommando* knew that to tell the bathers that the bathroom was a gas chamber was an offence punishable by instant death. The crime would not seem so abominable, and the punishment would not be so harsh, had the victims been led to their death simply by fear or suicidal resignation. But to found their order on fear alone, the SS would have needed more troops, arms and money. Rationality was more effective, easier to obtain, and cheaper. And thus to destroy them, the SS men carefully cultivated the rationality of their victims.

Interviewed recently on British TV, a high-ranking South African security chief let the cat out of the bag: the true danger of the ANC, he said, lies not in acts of sabotage and terrorism – however spectacular or costly – but in inducing the black population, or the large part of it, to disregard 'law and order'; if that happened even the best intelligence and most powerful security forces would be helpless (an expectation confirmed recently by the experience of *Intifada*). Terror remains effective as long as the balloon of rationality has not been pricked. The most sinister, cruel, bloody-minded ruler must remain a staunch preacher and defender of rationality – or perish. Addressing his subjects, he must 'speak to reason'. He must protect reason, eulogize on the virtues of the calculus of costs and effects, defend logic against passions and values which, unreasonably, do not count costs and refuse to obey logic.

By and large, all rulers can count on rationality being on their side. But the Nazi rulers, additionally, twisted the stakes of the game so that the rationality of survival would render all other motives of human action irrational. Inside the Nazi-made world, reason was the enemy of morality. Logic required consent to crime. Rational defence of one's survival called for non-resistance to the other's destruction. This rationality pitched the sufferers against each other and obliterated their joint humanity. It also made them into a threat and an enemy of all the others, not yet marked for death, and granted for the time being the role of bystanders. Graciously, the noble creed of rationality absolved both the victims and the bystanders from the charge of immorality and from guilty conscience. Having reduced human life to the calculus of self-preservation, this rationality robbed human life of humanity.

Nazi rule is long over, yet its poisonous legacy is far from dead. Our continuous inability to come to terms with the meaning of the Holocaust, our inability to call the bluff of the murderous hoax, our willingness to go on playing the game of history with the loaded dice of reason so understood that it shrugs the clamours of morality as irrelevant or loony, our consent to the authority of cost–effective calculus as an argument against ethical commandments – all these bear an eloquent evidence to the corruption the Holocaust exposed but did little, it appears, to discredit.

Two years of my early childhood were marked with my grandfather's heroic yet vain attempts to introduce me to the treasures of biblical lore. Perhaps he was not a very inspiring teacher; perhaps I was an obtuse and ungrateful pupil. The fact is, I remember next to nothing from his lessons. One story, however, carved itself into my brain deeply and haunted me for many years. This was a story of a saintly sage who met a beggar on the road while travelling with a donkey loaded with sackfuls of food. The beggar asked for something to eat. 'Wait,' said the sage, 'I must first untie the sacks.' Before he finished the unpacking, however, the long hunger took its toll and the beggar died. Then the sage started his prayer: 'Punish me, o Lord, as I failed to save the life of my fellow man!' The shock this story gave me is well-nigh the only thing I remember from the interminable list of my grandfather's homilies. It clashed with all the mental drill to which my schoolteachers subjected me at that time and ever since. The story struck me as illogical (which it was), and therefore wrong (which it was not). It took the Holocaust to convince me that the second does not necessarily follow from the first.

Even if one knows that not much more could have been done practically to save the victims of the Holocaust (at least not without additional, and probably formidable, costs), this does not mean that moral qualms can be put to sleep. Neither does it mean that a moral person's feeling of shame is unfounded (even if its irrationality in terms of self-preservation can be, indeed, easily proved). To this feeling of shame – an indispensable condition of victory over the slow-acting poison, the pernicious legacy of the Holocaust – the most scrupulous and historically accurate computations of the numbers of those who 'could' and those who 'could not' help, of those who 'could' and those who 'could not' be helped, are irrelevant.

Even the most sophisticated quantitative methods of researching 'the facts of the matter' would not advance us very far toward an objective (i.e. universally binding) solution to the issue of moral responsibility. There is no scientific method to decide whether their gentile neighbours failed to prevent the transportation of Jews to the camps because the Jews were so passive and docile, or whether the Jews so seldom escaped their guards because they had nowhere to escape to – sensing the hostility, or indifference, of the environment. Equally, there are no scientific methods to decide whether the well-off residents of the Warsaw ghetto could have done more to alleviate the lot of the poor dying in the streets of hunger and hypothermia, or whether the German Jews could have rebelled against the deportaton of the *Ostjuden*, or the Jews with French citizenship could have done something to prevent incarceration of the 'non-French Jews'. Worse still, however, *the calculation of objective possibilities and computation of costs only blurs the moral essence of the problem.*

The issue is not whether those who survived, collectively – fighters who on occasion could not but be bystanders, bystanders who on occasion could not but fear to become victims – *should* feel ashamed, or whether they *should* feel proud of themselves. The issue is that only the *liberating feeling of shame* may help to recover the moral significance of the awesome historical experience and thus help to exorcise the spectre of the Holocaust, which to this day haunts human conscience and makes us neglect vigilance at present for the sake of living in peace with the past. The choice is not between shame and pride. The choice is between the pride of morally purifying shame, and the shame of morally devastating pride. I am not sure how I would react to a stranger knocking on my door and asking me to sacrifice myself and my family to save his life. I have been spared such a choice. I am sure, however, that had I refused shelter, I would be fully able to justify to others and to myself that, counting the number of lives saved and lost, turning the stranger away was an entirely rational decision. I am also sure that I would feel that unreasonable, illogical, yet all-too-human shame. And yet I am sure, as well, that were it not for this feeling of shame, my decision to turn away the stranger would go on corrupting me till the end of my days.

The inhuman world created by a homicidal tyranny dehumanized its victims and those who passively watched the victimization by pressing both to use the logic of self-preservation as absolution for moral insensitivity and inaction. No one can be proclaimed guilty for the sheer fact of breaking down under such pressure. Yet no one can be excused from moral self-deprecation for such surrender. And only when feeling ashamed for one's weakness can one finally shatter the mental prison which has outlived its builders and its guards. The task today is to destroy that potency of tyranny to keep its victims and witnesses prisoners long after the prison had been dismantled.

Year by year the Holocaust shrinks to the size of a historical episode which, in addition, is fast receding into the past. The significance of its memory consists less and less in the need to punish the criminals, or to settle still-open accounts. The criminals who escaped trial are now old men well advanced in their senility; so are, or they soon will be, most of those who survived their crimes. Even if another murderer is discovered, pulled out of his hiding and brought to belated justice, it will be increasingly difficult to match the enormity of his crime with the sanctity of dignity of the legal process. (Witness the embarassing experience of Demianiuk's and Barbie's court cases.) There are also fewer and fewer people left who, in the times of gas chambers, were old enough to decide whether to open, or to close the door to the strangers seeking shelter. If repayment of crimes and account-settling exhausted the historical significance of the Holocaust, one could well let this horrifying episode stay where it ostensibly belongs – in the past – and leave it to the care of professional historians. The truth is, however, that the settling of accounts is just one reason to remember the Holocaust forever. And a minor reason at that – at no time has it yet been so evident as it is now, when that reason rapidly loses whatever remained of its *practical* importance.

Today, more than at any other time, the Holocaust is not a private property (if it ever was one); not of its perpetrators, to be punished for; not of its direct victims, to ask for special sympathy, favours or indulgence on account of past sufferings; and not of its witnesses, to seek redemption or certificates of innocence. *The present-day significance of the Holocaust is the lesson it contains for the whole of humanity.*

The lesson of the Holocaust is the facility with which most people, put into a situation that does not contain a good choice, or renders such a good choice very costly, argue themselves away from the issue of moral duty (or fail to argue themselves towards it), adopting instead the precepts of rational interest and self-preservation. *In a system where rationality and ethics point in opposite directions, humanity is the main loser.* Evil can do its dirty work, hoping that most people most of the time will refrain from doing rash, reckless things – and resisting evil is rash and reckless. Evil needs neither enthusiastic followers nor an applauding audience – the instinct of self-preservation will do, encouraged by the comforting thought that it is not my turn yet, thank God: by lying low, I can still escape.

And there is another lesson of the Holocaust, of no lesser importance.

If the first lesson contained a warning, the second offers hope; it is the second lesson that makes the first worth repeating.

The second lesson tells us that putting self-preservation above moral duty is in no way predetermined, inevitable and inescapable. One can be pressed to do it, but one cannot be forced to do it, and thus one cannot really shift the responsibility for doing it on to those who exerted the pressure. *It does not matter how many people chose moral duty over the rationality of self-preservation – what does matter is that some did.* Evil is not all-powerful. It can be resisted. The testimony of the few who did resist shatters the authority of the logic of self-preservation. It shows it for what it is in the end – *a choice*. One wonders how many people must defy that logic for evil to be incapacitated. Is there a magic threshold of defiance beyond which the technology of evil grinds to a halt?

Social Manipulation of Morality: Moralizing Actors, Adiaphorizing Action

The European Amalfi Prize Lecture

I believe that the great honour of the Amalfi European Prize has been given to the book called *Modernity and the Holocaust*, not to its author, and it is in the name of that book, and particularly of the message that book contained, that with gratitude and joy I accept your professional accolade. I am happy for the distinction this book has earned for several reasons.

First: this is a book which grew out of the experience that spans the until recently deep and seemingly unbridgeable divide between what we used to call 'Eastern' and 'Western' Europe. The ideas that went into the book and its message gestated as much in my home university of Warsaw as they did in the company of my colleagues in Britain, the country that – in the years of exile – offered me my second home. These ideas knew of no divide; they knew only of our common European experience, of our shared history whose unity may be belied, even temporarily suppressed, but not broken. It is our joint, all-European fate that my book is addressing.

Second: this book would never have come to be if not for my life-long friend and companion, Janina, whose *Winter in the Morning*, a book of reminiscences from the years of human infamy, opened my eyes to what we normally refuse to look upon. The writing of *Modernity and the Holocaust* became an intellectual compulsion and moral duty, once I had read Janina's summary of the sad wisdom she acquired in the inner circle of the man-made inferno; 'The cruellest thing about cruelty is that it dehumanizes its victims before it destroys them. And the hardest of struggles is to remain human in inhuman conditions.' It is Janina's bitter wisdom that I tried to enclose in the message of my book.

Third: the message itself, one about the hidden and unseemly face of our confident, affluent, brave world, and of the dangerous game this world plays with human moral impulse, seems to be resonant with ever more widely shared concerns. This, I presume, is the meaning of awarding the coveted Amalfi Prize to the book that contains that message. But also of the fact that the prestigious Amalfi Conference has been dedicated in full to the issue of morality and utility, whose divorce, as the message implies, lies at the foundation of our civilization's most spectacular successes and most terrifying crimes, and whose reunification is the one chance our world may have to come to terms with its own awesome powers. My lecture that follows is therefore more than a mere restatement of the book's message. It is a voice in a discourse which, one hopes, will stay in the focus of our shared vocation.

Virtutem doctrina paret naturane donet. For the Ancient Roman the dilemma was as acute as it is for us today. Is morality taught, or does it reside in the very modality of human existence? Does it arise out of the process of socialization, or is it 'in place' before all teaching starts? Is morality a social product? Or is it rather, as Max Scheler insisted, the other way round: the fellow-feeling, that substance of all moral behaviour, is a precondition of all social life?

All too often the question is dismissed as of no more than purely academic interest. Sometimes it is cast among idle and superfluous issues born of the indefatigable, but notoriously suspect, metaphysical curiosity. When asked explicitly by sociologists, it is assumed to have been answered conclusively long ago, by Hobbes and by Durkheim, in a manner leaving little to doubt, and since then to have been transformed into a non-question by routine sociological practice. For the sociologists at least, society is the root of everything human and everything human comes into existence through social learning. Hardly ever do we have occasion to argue the case explicitly. For all we care, the matter had been resolved before it could be discussed: its resolution had founded the language that constitutes our distinctively sociological discourse. In that language, one cannot speak of morality in any other way but in terms of socialization, teaching and learning, systemic prerequisites and societal functions. And, as Wittgenstein reminded us, we can say nothing except what can be said. The form of life sustained by the language of sociology does not contain socially un-sanctioned morality. In that language, nothing that is not socially sanctioned can be talked about as moral. And what one cannot speak of is bound to remain silent.

All discourses define their topics, keep their integrity by guarding the distinctiveness of their definitions and reproduce themselves through reiterating them. We could as it were stop at this trival observation and allow sociology to proceed with its habitual selective speech and selective numbness, were not the stakes of continuing silence too high. Just how high they are has been brought up, gradually yet relentlessly, by Auschwitz, Hiroshima and the Gulag. Or, rather, by the problem the victorious perpetrators of the Gulag and Hiroshima faced when bringing to trial, condemning and convicting the vanquished perpetrators of Auschwitz. It was Hannah Arendt, at her perceptive and irreverent best, who spelled out what these problems truly entailed:

> What we have demanded in these trials, where the defendants had committed 'legal' crimes, is that human beings be capable of telling right from wrong when all they have to guide them is their judgment, which, however, happens to be completely at odds with what they must regard as the unanimous opinion of all these around them. And this question is all the more serious as we know that the few who were 'arrogant' enough to trust only their own judgment were by no means identical with those persons who continued to abide by old values, or who were guided by a religious belief . . . These few who were still able to tell right from wrong went really only by their own judgments, and they did so freely; there were no rules to be abided by, under which the particular cases with which they were confronted could be subsumed.

And thus the question had to be asked: would any one of those now brought to trial have suffered from a guilty conscience if they had won? The most horrifying discovery that followed was that the answer must have been emphatically 'no', and that we lack arguments to show why it should be otherwise. Having decreed out of existence or out of court such distinctions between good and evil as do not bear the sanctioning stamp of society, we cannot seriously demand that individuals take moral initiatives. Neither can we burden them with responsibility for their moral choices unless the responsibility had been *de facto* pre-empted by the choices being prescribed by society. And we would not normally wish to do so (that is, to demand that individuals make their moral decisions on their own responsibility). Doing so would mean, after all, allowing for a moral responsibility that undermines the legislative power of society; and what society would resign such power of its own will, unless disabled by an overwhelming military force? Indeed, sitting in judgement on the perpetrators of Auschwitz was not an easy task for those who guarded the secrets of the Gulag and those who were secretly preparing for Hiroshima.

It is perhaps because of this difficulty that, as Harry Redner observed, 'much of life and thought as it is still carried on now is based on the assumption that Auschwitz and Hiroshima never happened, or, if they did, then only as mere vents, far away, and long ago, that need not concern us now'. The legal quandaries arising from the Nuremberg trials were resolved there and then, having been treated as local issues, specific to one extraordinary and pathological case, that were never allowed to spill over the boundaries of their carefully circumscribed parochiality, and were hastily wound up as soon as they threatened to get out of hand. No fundamental revision of our self-consciousness occurred or was contemplated. For many decades – to this very day, one may say – Arendt's remained a voice in the wilderness. Much of the fury with which Arendt's analysis was met at the time stemmed from the attempt to keep that self-consciousness watertight. Only such explanations of the Nazi crimes have been accepted as are conspicuously irrelevant to us, to our world, to our form of life. Such explanations commit the double feat of condemning the defendant while exonerating the world of his victors.

It is in vain to contest whether the resulting marginalization of the crime committed – in the full glare of social acclaim or with tacit popular approval – by people who 'were neither perverted nor sadistic', who 'were, and still are, terrifyingly normal' (Arendt), was deliberate or inadvertent, accomplished by design or by default. The fact is that the quarantine set half a century ago has never ended; if anything, the rows of barbed wire have grown thicker over the years. Auschwitz has gone down in history as a 'Jewish' or 'German' problem and as Jewish or German private property. Looming large in the centre of 'Jewish studies', it has been confined to footnotes or cursory paragraphs by the mainstream European historiography. Books on the Holocaust are reviewed under the heading of 'Jewish themes'. The impact of such habits is reinforced by the vehement opposition of the Jewish establishment to any attempt, however tentative, to 'expropriate' the injustice that the Jews and the Jews alone have suffered. Of this injustice, the Jewish state would keenly wish to be the sole guardian and, indeed, the only legitimate beneficiary. This unholy alliance effectively prevents the experience it narrates as 'uniquely Jewish' from turning into a universal problem of the modern human condition and thus into public property. Alternatively, Auschwitz is cast as an event explicable only in terms of the extraordinary convolutions of German history, of inner conflicts of German culture, blunders of German philo-

sophy or the bafflingly authoritarian national character of the Germans –
with much the same parochializing, marginalizing effect. Finally, and
perhaps most perversely, the strategy that results in the two-pronged effect
of marginalizing the crime and exonerating modernity is one of
exempting the Holocaust from a class of comparable phenomena, and
interpreting it instead as an eruption of pre-modern (barbaric, irrational)
forces, presumably long ago suppressed in 'normal' civilized societies, but
insufficiently tamed or ineffectively controlled by the allegedly weak or
faulty German modernization. One would expect this strategy to be a
favourite form of self-defence: after all, it obliquely re-affirms and rein-
forces the etiological myth of modern civilization as a triumph of reason
over passion, and an auxiliary belief in this triumph as an unambiguously
progressive step in the historical development of morality.

The combined effect of all three strategies – whether deliberately or
subconsciously followed – is the proverbial puzzlement of historians who
repeatedly complain that, however hard they try, they cannot understand
the most spectacular episode of the present century whose story they have
written so expertly and continue to write in ever-growing detail. Saul
Friedländer bewails the 'historian's paralysis', which in his (widely shared)
view 'arises from the simultaneity and the interaction of entirely heterogeneous phenomena: messianic fanaticism and bureaucratic structures,
pathological impulses and administrative decrees, archaic attitudes within
an advanced industrial society'. Entangled in the net of marginalizing
narratives we all help to weave, we fail to see what we stare at; the only
thing we are able to note is the confusing heterogeneity of the picture,
coexistence of things our language does not allow to coexist, the complicity of factors that, as our narratives tell us, belong to different epochs or
different times. Their heterogeneity is not a finding, but an assumption. It
is this assumption that gives birth to astonishment where comprehension
could appear and is called for.

In 1940, in the heart of darkness, Walter Benjamin jotted down a
message which, judging by the historians' continuing paralysis and the
sociologists' unperturbed equanimity, has yet to be properly heard: 'Such
an astonishment cannot be starting point for genuine historical understanding – *unless it is the understanding that the concept of history in
which it originates is untenable.*' What is untenable is the concept of our –
European – history as the rise of humanity over the animal in man, and as
the triumph of rational organization over the cruelty of life that is nasty,
brutish and short. What is also untenable is the concept of modern society
as an unambiguously moralizing force, of its institutions as civilizing

powers, of its coercive controls as a dam defending brittle humanity against the torrents of animal passions. It is to the exposition of this latter untenability that this paper, in line with the book on which it comments, has been dedicated.

But let us repeat first: the difficulty of proving untenable what by all standards are the commonsensical assumptions of sociological discourse derives in no small part from the intrinsic quality of the language of sociological narrative; as all languages, it defines its objects while pretending to describe them. The moral authority of society is self-provable to the point of tautology in so far as all conduct not conforming to the societally sanctioned rulings is by definition immoral. Socially sanctioned behaviour remains good as long as all action societally condemned is defined as evil. There is no easy exit from the vicious circle, as any suggestion of pre-social origin of moral impulse has been a priori condemned as violating the rules of linguistic rationality – the only rationality language allows. The deployment of sociological language entails the acceptance of the world-picture this language generates, and implies a tacit consent to conducting the ensuing discourse in such a way that all reference to reality is directed to the world so generated. The sociologically generated world-picture replicates the accomplishment of societal legislating powers. But it does more than that: it silences the possibility of articulating alternative visions in whose suppression the accomplishment of such powers consists. Thus the defining power of language supplements the differentiating, separating, segregating and suppressing powers lodged in the structure of social domination. It also derives its legitimacy and persuasion from that structure.

Ontologically, structure means relative repetitiousness, monotony of events; epistemologically, it means for this reason predictability. We speak of structure whenever we confront a space inside which probabilities are not randomly distributed: some events are more likely to happen than others. It is in this sense that human habitat is 'structured': an island of regularity in the sea of randomness. This precarious regularity has been an achievement, and the decisive defining feature, of social organization. All social organization, *whether purposeful* or *totalizing* (i.e., such as cut-out fields of relative homogeneity through suppressing or degrading – making irrelevant or otherwise down-playing – all other, differentiating and thus potentially divisive, features), consists in subjecting the conduct of its units to either *instrumental* or *procedural* criteria of evaluation. More importantly still, it consists in delegalizing all other criteria, and first and foremost such standards as may render behaviour of units resilient to uniformizing pressures and thus *autonomous* vis-à-vis the collective purpose of the organization (which, from the organizational point of view, makes them unpredictable and potentially de-stabilizing).

Among the standards marked for suppression the pride of place is kept by moral drive – the source of a most conspicuously autonomous (and hence, from the vantage point of the organization, *unpredictable*) behaviour. The autonomy of moral behaviour is final and irreducible. It escapes all codification, as it does not serve any purpose outside itself and does not enter a relationship with anything outside itself; that is, no relationship that could be monitored, standardized, codified. Moral behaviour, as the greatest moral philosopher of the twentieth century, Emmanuel Levinas, tells us, is triggered off by the mere presence of the Other as a *face*, that is, as an authority without force. The Other demands without threatening to punish or promising reward; his demand is without sanction. The Other cannot do anything; it is precisely his weakness that exposes my strength, my ability to act, as responsibility. Moral action is whatever follows that responsibility. Unlike the action triggered off by fear of sanction or promise of reward, it does not bring success or help survival. As, purposeless, it escapes all possibility of heteronomous legislation or rational argument, it remains deaf to *conatus essendi*, and hence elides the judgement of 'rational interest' and advice of calculated self-preservation, those twin bridges to the world of 'there is', of dependence and heteronomy. The face of the Other, so Levinas insists, is a limit imposed on the effort to exist. It offers therefore the ultimate freedom: freedom against the source of all heteronomy, against all dependence, against nature's persistence in being. Morality is a 'moment of generosity'. 'Someone plays without winning . . . Something that one does gratuitously, that is grace . . . The idea of the face is the idea of gratuitous love, the conduct of a gratuitous act.' It is because of its implacable gratuity that moral acts cannot be lured, seduced, bought off, routinized. From the societal perspective, Kant's *practical* reason is so hopelessly *impractical* . . . From the organization's point of view, morally inspired conduct is utterly useless, nay subversive: it cannot be harnessed to any purpose and it sets limits to the hope of monotony. Since it cannot be rationalized, morality must be suppressed, or manipulated into irrelevance.

The organization's answer to the autonomy of moral behaviour is the heteronomy of instrumental and procedural rationalities. Law and interest displace and replace gratuity and the sanctionlessness of moral drive. Actors are challenged to justify their conduct by reason as defined either by the goal or by the rules of behaviour. Only actions thought of and argued in such a way, or fit to be narrated in such a way, are admitted into the class of genuinely *social* action, that is *rational* action, that is an action that serves as the defining property of actors as *social actors*. By the same token, actions that fail to meet the criteria of goal-pursuit or procedural discipline are declared non-social, irrational – and *private*. The organization's way of socializing action includes, as its indispensable corollary, the privatization of morality.

All social organization consists therefore in neutralizing the disruptive and deregulating impact or moral behaviour. This effect is achieved through a number of complementary arrangements: (1) stretching the distance between action and its consequences beyond the reach of moral impulse; (2) exempting some 'others' from the class of potential objects of moral conduct, of potential 'faces'; (3) dissembling other human objects of action into aggregates of functionally specific traits, held separate so that the occasion for re-assembling the face does not arise, and the task set for each action can be free from moral evaluation. Through these arrangements, organization does not promote immoral behaviour; it does not sponsor evil, as some detractors would hasten to charge, yet it does not promote good either, despite its own self-promotion. It simply renders social action *adiaphoric* (originally, *adiaphoron* meant a thing declared indifferent by the Church) – neither good nor evil, measurable against technical (purpose-oriented or procedural) but not moral values. By the same token, it renders moral responsibility for the Other ineffective in its original role of the limit imposed on 'the effort to exist'. (It is tempting to surmise that the social philosophers who at the threshold of the modern age first perceived social organization as a matter of design and rational improvement theorized precisely this quality of organization as the immortality of Man that transcends, and privatizes into social irrelevance, the mortality of individual men and women). Let us go one by one through these arrangements that, simultaneously, constitute social organization and adiaphorize social action.

To start with the removal of the effects of action beyond the reach of moral limits, that major achievement of the articulation of action into the hierarchy of command and execution: once placed in the 'agentic state' and separate from both the intention-conscious sources and the ultimate effects of action by a chain of mediators, the actors seldom face the moment of choice and gaze at the consequences of their deeds; more importantly, they hardly ever apprehend what they gaze at as the consequences of their deeds. As each action is both *mediated* and 'merely' *mediating*, the suspicion of causal link is convincingly dismissed through theorizing the evidence as an 'unanticipated consequence', or at any rate the 'unintended result' of, by itself, a morally neutral act – as a fault of reason rather than ethical failure. Social organization may therefore be described as a machine that keeps moral responsibility afloat; it belongs to no one in particular, as everybody's contribution to the final effect is too minute or partial to be sensibly ascribed a causal function. Dissection of responsibility and dispersion of what is left results on the structural plane in what Hannah Arendt poignantly described as 'rule by Nobody'; on the individual plane it leaves the actor, as a moral subject, speechless and defenceless when faced with the twin powers of the task and the procedural rules.

The second arrangement could be best described as the 'effacing of the face'. It consists in casting the objects of action in a position from which they cannot challenge the actor in their capacity as a source of moral demands; that is, in evicting them from the class of beings that may potentially confront the actor as a 'face'. The range of means applied to this effect is truly enormous. It stretches from the explicit exemption of the declared enemy from moral protection, through the classifying of selected groups among the resources of action which can be evaluated solely in terms of their technical, instrumental value, all the way to the removal of the stranger from routine human encounter in which his face might become visible and glare as a moral demand. In each case the limiting impact of moral responsibility for the Other is suspended and rendered ineffective.

The third arrangement destroys the object of action as a self. The object has been dissembled into traits; the totality of the moral subject has been reduced to the collection of parts or attributes of which no one can conceivably be ascribed moral subjectivity. Actions are then targeted on specific units of the set, by-passing or avoiding altogether the moment of encounter with morally significant effects (it had been this reality of social organization, one can guess, that was articulated in the postulate of philosophical reductionism promoted by logical positivism: to demonstrate that entity P can be reduced to entities x, y and z entails the deduction that X is 'nothing but' the assembly of x, y and z. No wonder morality was one of the first victims of logical-positivist reductionist zest). As it were, the impact of narrowly targeted action on the totality of its human object is left out of vision, and is exempt from moral evaluation for not being a part of the intention.

Our survey of the adiaphorizing impact of social organization has been conducted thus far in self-consciously non-historical and exterritorial terms.

Indeed, the adiaphorization of human action seems to be a necessary constitutive act of any supra-individual, social totality; of all social organization, for that matter. If this is indeed the case, however, our attempt to challenge and to refute the orthodox belief in the social authorship of morality does not by itself offer an answer to the ethical concern that prompted the inquiry in the first place. It is true that society conceived of as an adiaphorizing mechanism offers a much better explanation of the ubiquitous cruelty endemic in human history than does the orthodox theory of the social origin of morality; it explains in particular why at a time of war or crusades or colonization or communal strife normal human collectivities are capable of performing acts which, if committed singly, are readily ascribed to the psychopathia of the perpetrator. And yet it stops short of accounting for such strikingly novel phenomena of our time as the Gulag, Auschwitz or Hiroshima. One feels that these central events of our century are indeed novel; and one is inclined (with justification) to suspect that they signify the appearance of certain new, typically modern, characteristics that are not a universal feature of human society as such and were not possessed by societies of the past. Why?

One: A most evident and banal novelty is the sheer scale of the destructive potential of technology that may be put today at the service of the thoroughly adiaphorized action. These new awesome powers are today aided and abetted in addition by the growing scientifically based effectiveness of managerial processes. Apparently, the technology developed in modern times only pushes further the tendencies already apparent in all socially regulated, organized action; its present scale conveys solely a quantitative change. Yet there is a point where quantitative extension augurs a new quality – and such a point seems to have been passed in an era we call modernity. It is true that the realm of *techne*, the realm of dealings with the non-human world or the human world cast as non-human, was at all times treated as morally neutral thanks to the expedient of adiaphorization. But, as Hans Jonas indicates, in societies unarmed by modern technology 'the good and evil about which action had to care lay close to the act, either in the praxis itself or in its immediate reach . . . The effective range of action was small', and so were its possible consequences, whether planned or unthought of. Today, however, 'the city of men, once an enclave in the non-human world, spreads over the whole of nature and usurps its place'. The effects of action reach far and wide in space and time alike. They have become, as Jonas suggests, *cumulative*, that is, they transcend all spatial or temporal locality and, as many fear, may eventually transcend the nature's self-healing capacity and end up in what Ricoeur calls *annihilation* which, unlike ordinary destruction that may yet prove to be a site-clearing operation in a creative process of change, leaves no room for a new beginning. Made possible by and arising from the eternal social technique of adiaphorization, this new development, let us observe, multiplied its scope and effectivity to the point where actions can be put in the service of morally odious aims over a large territory and protracted period of time. Their consequences may be therefore pushed to the point where they become truly irreversible or irreparable, without raising moral doubts or mere vigilance in the process.

Two: Together with the new unheard-of potency of man-made technology came the impotence of self-limitations men imposed through the millennia upon their own mastery over nature and over each other: the notorious *disenchantment of the world* or, as Nietzsche put it, '*death of God*'. God meant, first and foremost, a limit to human potential: a constraint, imposed by what man *may do* over what man *could do* and *dare do*. The assumed omnipotence of God drew a borderline over what man was allowed to do and to dare. Commandments limited the freedom of humans as individuals; but they also set limits to what humans together, as a society, could legislate; they presented the human capacity to legislate and manipulate the world's principles as being inherently limited. Modern science, which displaced and replaced God, removed that obstacle. It also created a vacancy: the office of the supreme legislator-cum-manager, of the designer and administrator of the world order, was now horrifyingly empty. It had to be filled, or else ... God was dethroned, but the throne was still in one place. The emptiness of the throne was throughout the modern era a standing and tempting invitation to visionaries and adventurers. The dream of an all-embracing order and harmony remained as vivid as ever, and it seemed now closer than ever, more than ever within human reach. It was now up to the mortal earthlings to bring it about and to secure its ascendancy. The world turned into man's garden but only the vigilance of the gardener may prevent it from descending into the chaos of wilderness. It was now up to man and man alone to see to it that rivers flow in the right direction and that rain forests do not occupy the field were groundnuts should grow. It was now up to man and man alone to make sure that the strangers do not obscure the transparency of legislated order, that social harmony is not spoiled by obstreperous classes, that the togetherness of folk is not tainted by alien races. The classless society, the race-pure society, the Great Society were now the task of man – an urgent task, a life-and-death matter, a duty. The clarity of the world and human vocation, once guaranteed by God and now lost, had to be fast restored, this time by human acumen and on human responsibility (or is it irresponsibility?) alone.

It was the combination of growing potency of means and the unconstrained determination to use it in the service of an artificial, designed order, that gave human cruelty its distinctively *modern* touch and made the Gulag, Auschwitz and Hiroshima possible, perhaps even unavoidable. The signs abound that this particular combination is now over. The passing of this combination is theorized by some as that of modernity coming of age; sometimes it is talked about as an unanticipated consequence of modernity; sometimes as the advent of the post-modern age; in each case, however, the analysts would agree with the laconic verdict of Peter Drucker: 'no more salvation by society'. There are many tasks human rulers may and should perform. Devising the perfect world order is not, however, one of them. The great world-garden has split into innumerable little plots with their own little orders. In a world densely populated with knowledgeable and intensely mobile gardeners, no room seems to be left for the Gardener Supreme, the gardener of gardeners.

We cannot here go into the inventory of events that led to the collapse of the great garden. Whatever the reason, however, the collapse is, I would suggest, good news in a great number of respects. Does it, however, promise a new start for the morality of human coexistence? In what way does it affect the topicality of our previous reasoning about the adiaphorization of social action – and, particularly, about the potentially disastrous dimensions given to it by the rise of modern technology?

There are few, if any, gains without losses. The departure of the great gardener and the dissipation of the great gardening vision made the world a *safer* place, as the threat of salvation-inspired and salvation-seeking genocide had faded. By itself, however, this was not enough to make it a *safe* place. New fears replace the old ones; or, rather, some of the older fears come into their own as they emerge from the shadow of some other, recently evicted or receding. One is inclined to share Hans Jonas's premonition: to an ever growing degree, our main fears will now relate to the apocalypse threatened by the nature of the unintended dynamics of technical civilization as such, rather than to custom-made concentration camps and atomic explosions, both of which require that grand purposes are spelled out and, above all, purpose-conscious decisions are taken. And this is so because our present world has been freed from the white man's, proletariat's or Aryan race's missions only because it has been freed from all other ends and meanings, and thus turned into the universe of means that serve no purpose but their own reproduction and aggrandizement. As Jacques Ellul observed, technology today develops *because it develops*; technological means are used because they are there, and one crime still deemed unforgivable in an otherwise value-promiscuous world is not to use the means that technology has already made, or is about to make, available. It we can do it, why on earth should we not? Today, technology does not serve the solution of problems; it is, rather, the accessibility of a given technology that redefines successive parts of human reality as *problems* clamouring for *resolution*. In the words of Wiener and Kahn, technological developments produce means beyond the demands, and seek the demands in order to satisfy technological capacities. . . .

The unconstrained rule of technology means that causal determination is substituted for purpose and choice. Indeed, no intellectual or moral reference point seems to be conceivable from which to assess, evaluate and criticize the directions technology may take except for the sober evaluation of possibilities technology itself has created. The reason of means is at its most triumphant when ends finally peter out in the quicksand of problem-solving. The road to technical omnipotence has been cleared by the removal of the last residues of meaning. One would wish to repeat the prophetic warning of Valéry written down at the dawn of our century: 'On peut dire que tout ce que nous savons, c'est-à-dire tout ce que nous pouvons, a fini par s'opposer à ce que nous sommes'. We have been told, and have come to believe, that emancipation and liberty mean the right to reduce the Other, alongside the rest of the world, to the object whose usefulness begins and ends with its capacity for giving satisfaction. More thoroughly than any other known form of social organization, the society that surrenders to the no-more challenged or constrained rule of technology has effaced the human face of the Other and thus pushed the adiaphorization of human sociability to a yet-to-be-fathomed depth.

This, however, is but one side of the emerging reality, its 'life-world' side, one that towers above the daily experience of the individual. There is, as we have briefly noted before, another side as well: the fickle, haphazard and erratic development of technological potential and its applications which, given the rising potency of tools, may easily, without anyone noticing, lead to the 'critical mass' situation in which a world is technologically created but can no longer be technologically controlled. Much like modern painting or music or philosophy before it, modern technology will then finally reach its logical end, establish its own impossibility. To prevent such an outcome, Joseph Weizenbaum insisted, no less is needed than the appearance of a new ethics, an ethics of distance and distant consequences, an ethics commensurable with the uncannily extended spatial and temporal range of the effects of technological action. An ethics that would be unlike any other morality we know: one that would reach over the socially erected obstacles of mediated action and the functional reduction of human self.

Such an ethics is in all probability the logical necessity of our time; that is, if the world that has turned means into ends is to escape the likely consequences of its own accomplishment. Whether such an ethics is a practical prospect is an altogether different matter. Who more than we, sociologists and students of social and political realities, should be prone to doubt the mundane feasibility of the truths that philosophers, rightly, prove to be logically overwhelming and apodeictically necessary. And yet who more than we, sociologists, are fit to alert out fellow humans to the gap between the necessary and the real, between the survival significance of moral limits and the world determined to live – and to live happily, and perhaps even ever after – without them.

Amalfi Prize Lecture
delivered on 24 May 1990

The Duty to Remember – But What?

Afterword to the 2000 Edition

> *Who controls the past controls the future,*
> *Who controls the present controls the past.*
>
> George Orwell

When ten years ago I started to write up the study of *Wahlverwandschaft* between the Holocaust and Modernity, I did not wish to explain the Holocaust – but to better understand modernity. I thought then that in terms of the ordinary meaning of the idea of explanation (presenting an event as a chain of causes and effects) all that was to be done to explain the Holocaust as an event in history had been done already. Thanks to the gigantic efforts of many formidable, scrupulous and dedicated historians, the train of events, decisions and deeds had been put on the record and everyone who wished to know could know who the perpetrators, the victims and the horrified, self-congratulating or just indifferent bystanders were. One could of course go on, perhaps without end, digging into certain heretofore untouched archives and diaries, adding a few names of the perpetrators here or there, and otherwise enlarging the huge library of monographic studies of the episodes which combined into the most purposeful, systematic, targeted and comprehensive mass murder in human history. But such further research could only be of the 'more of the same' nature. The volume of facts would grow, but not necessarily the knowledge or the comprehension of the process.

On the other hand, while thanks to the historians our knowledge of the Holocaust's *wie es ist eigentlich gewesen* had been growing apace over the years, the effort of the sociologists and social thinkers to grasp the meaning which that knowledge carried for the orthodox and still prevalent image of modern society lagged far behind; more exactly, that effort had never started in earnest since solitary writers like Theodor Adorno or Hannah Arendt first called for it to be undertaken. It was my intention to proceed from the point to which Adorno or Arendt had brought what has remained a blatantly unfinished task. I wished to exhort fellow social thinkers to consider the relation between the event of the Holocaust and the structure and logic of modern life, to stop viewing the Holocaust as a bizarre and aberrant episode *in* modern history, and think it through instead as a highly relevant, integral part *of* that history; 'integral' in the sense of being indispensable for the understanding of what that history was truly about, what it was capable of and why — and the sort of society that has emerged from it, and which we all inhabit.

I realize now that I made a mistake. Not because my appeal was wrongly addressed or bound to fall on deaf ears; not because there was something in the nature of contemporary social thinkers and their work that made it difficult to accept and to follow through the significance of the Holocaust for the nature of modernity. I was mistaken for quite a different reason. Contrary to my opinion, whenever the Holocaust is mentioned in contemporary social thought, nothing else is at stake but precisely that significance which I thought was left, heedlessly, out of consideration. As a matter in fact, most of the scholars who speak and write about the Holocaust are — overtly or covertly, consciously or subconsciously — concerned with little else but that significance: with the presence or the absence of the link between the Holocaust and the inner essence of modernity, and thus with the right to salvage or the obligation to revise some of the most coveted assumptions which modernity has made about the nature of its own enterprise and to which it has to cling if that enterprise is to continue in its historically shaped and prevailing form.

In other words, what I did not fully realize a decade or so ago but what seems clear to me now is that the silences spoke in unison with the voices. Whenever the issue of the Holocaust crops up in the social-scientific discourse, the true topic of debate — and certainly the one most likely to arouse the strongest emotions and to inspire the most pugnacity — is not so much the question of what did happen in history, but the nature of the world we inhabit today. The hidden agenda of all the current Holocaust discourse is the question of what, if anything, the facts of the Holocaust are capable of telling us about the hidden capacities of present-day life. Once the problem of the guilt of the Holocaust perpetrators has been by and large settled, and with the passage of time lost a good deal of its urgency and practical edge, the one big remaining question is the innocence of all the rest – not least innocence of ourselves.

Social production of guilt and innocence

In more ingenuous times, when the tyrant razed cities for his own greater glory, when the slave chained to the conqueror's chariot was dragged through the rejoicing streets, when enemies were thrown to wild animals in front of the assembled people, before such naked crimes consciousness could be steady and judgement unclouded. But slave camps under the flag of freedom, massacres justified by philanthropy or the taste of the superhuman, cripple judgment. On the day when crime puts on the apparel of innocence, through a curious reversal peculiar to our age, it is innocence that is called on to justify itself.[1]

That much Albert Camus, in 1951, before the book *Eichmann in Jerusalem* appeared in New York and before Eichmann, its hero, appeared in Jerusalem. The possibility that crime is logical, that 'murder has rational foudations', is 'the question put to us by the blood and strife of our century', Camus insisted. 'We are being interrogated.' We may refuse to listen to the question and console ourselves with the eternity of evil and the perpetuity of murder only at our peril; and first and foremost peril to our humanity, which is, in its innermost essence, our non-animality, the *ethicality* of our being.

Camus recalls that Heathcliff of *Wuthering Heights* would kill everybody to win Cathie – 'but he would never think of saying that murder is reasonable or theoretically defensible'. Heathcliff had no makings of a theoretician: he did not theorize, nor did he need a theory. He loved Cathie, he wanted Cathie and that was the only reason he needed in order to kill – that is, if reason he needed. Murder, were Heathcliff to commit it, would have been a *crime of passion*, and acting out of passion means putting reason to sleep; passion is, by definition, the unreason. When we speak of passion, we also speak of the non-being of reason. Passion and reason are at loggerheads: one wilts and fades in the face of the other.

Modernity declared war on passion and inscribed Reason, in the boldest of letters, on its banners: *in hoc signo vinces*. The modern mind shuns passion, denigrates and disdains passion, and in every manifestation of passion sniffs evidence of its own failure. By doing so, it refuses, not unjustly, to bear responsibility for the crimes of passion. Whoever kills for love or hatred is out of modern bounds. There is indeed nothing particularly modern about the crime of passion. And it is hardly the fault of modern ambition that some men and women refuse or fail to listen to the voice of reason and remain slaves to their passions. For the crimes of passion, modernity has no need to apologize. And if it does apologize – it could only be for slackness, for negligence, for not doing its modernizing job thoroughly enough.

As long as one can ascribe crimes to the passions of their perpetrators, crime may be condemned without awkward questions being asked about the nature of modern life. Reason, after all, leans over backwards to argue away blind hatred together with blind love. Most people – people like us – listen to reason and stop short of letting their aversions and hard feelings guide their actions and dissolving their bad blood in the blood of their neighbours. Not all, though, have been ennobled, 'civilized' in such a way. Some go on doing evil things. When it comes to explaining their evil deeds, the modern mind curiously forgets its declaration of its own omnipotence. Why do some people do evil? Because they are evil people. Why are they cruel? Because they are cruel people. Why do they perpetrate monstrous deeds? Because they are monsters. Why did some of them kill Jews? Because they liked killing people, or they hated the Jews, or both – and so killing people who happened to be Jews gave them particular pleasure.

These are all blatantly pleonastic statements, and tautology is a crude error of logic which does not square well with the self-proclaimed self-discipline of reason. Why did Hitler's executioners kill Jews? Because they were antisemites. How do you know they were antisemites? Because they killed Jews (forget the 250,000, which is more than a third of the total population of Gypsies, and the 360,000 mentally retarded and 'sexually perverted' Germans who followed or preceded the Jews on the road to the gas chambers and crematoria). If sentences like these go on being offered as explanations, something else, more important than the logic of scientific inquiry, must be the motive. This 'something else' is the distribution or redistribution of guilt and innocence. The issue is how to condemn the criminals while making sure that the innocence of modern men and women at large, together with the kind of society which made them what they are, emerge from the trial with their reputation unscathed and untarnished. Exoneration is the other face of the coin, and it is by that other side that the value of the coin is appreciated and the coin is made attractive and desirable. In the resulting scramble, Camus's noxious questions about slave camps under the flag of freedom and massacres in the name of philanthropy are, conveniently, all but forgotten.

Neither Hitler nor Stalin was yet born, *Arbeit macht frei* was not yet written above the gates of Auschwitz, and large sections of population had not yet been murdered wholesale for the love of mankind; but modern life was already in full swing when Nietzsche noted down the baffling — and horrifying — paradox of our civilization:

> The same men who are held so sternly in check *inter pares* by custom, respect, usage, gratitude, and even more by mutual suspicion and jealousy, and who on the other hand in their relations with one another show themselves so resourceful in consideration, self-control, delicacy, loyalty, pride, and friendship — once they go outside, where the strange, the *stranger* is found . . . emerge from a disgusting procession of murder, arson, rape, and torture, exhilarated and undisturbed of soul, as if it were no more than a student's prank, convinced that they have provided the poets with a lot more material for song and praise.[2]

It is not just that the paradox defies all easy explanation — it is, let me repeat, terrifying. What is the case here? Are these beasts of prey relishing their escape from the stuffy and stifling cage called civilization and falling back, with a deafening sigh of relief, on their true nature, as Nietzsche seems to suggest? Or, rather, are they once resourceful, now hapless humans, thrown out of their element, their ken and wits, cast into the eerie world where their habits can no longer guide them and with the rules by which they played their games officially declared null and void or simply no longer applicable? Both answers are as plausible as they are unprovable, and there is little point in arguing their substantive (as distinct from instrumental) merits. One conclusion, though, seems to be beyond reasonable doubt. It has been recently spelt out with exemplary clarity by Roberto Toscano:[3]

> what is at stake here is not an attempt to explain individual violence that finds its roots in personal passions, desires, hate, greed. On the contrary, it is significant that the mechanisms of the two kinds of violent action (individual and group) are different and manifest themselves differently in the same individuals, who may have a radically different propensity to have recourse to group versus individual violence.

And Toscano spells out what makes the two situations, and so also the deceptively similar acts of violence that occur in their contexts, so radically different; and the reason why they call for altogether different explanations. Unlike individual violence, 'group violence is by definition abstract'; 'real individual neighbours are not necessarily loved, but they are loved or hated for concrete, not abstract reasons... On the contrary, in order to apply group violence to the neighbour as belonging to a category, the concrete individual's face has to be erased: the person must become an abstraction.'

Categorial murder

Indeed: abstraction is one of the modern mind's principal powers. When applied to humans, that power means effacing the face: whatever marks remain of the face serve as badges of membership, the signs of belonging to a category, and the fate meted out to the owner of the face is nothing more yet nothing less either than the treatment reserved for the *category* of which the owner of the face is but a *specimen*. The overall effect of abstraction is that rules routinely followed in personal interaction, ethical rules most prominent among them, do not interfere where the handling of a category is concerned, including every entity classified into that category just on account of having been so classified.

Nazi legislation, propaganda and management of social settings took care to separate the one and only 'abstract Jew' from the many 'concrete Jews' known to the Germans as neighbours or workmates; and to cast all 'concrete Jews', through exclusion, deportation and confinement, into the position of abstract ones. Genocide differs from other murders in having a *category* for its object. Only the abstract Jews could be subjected to genocide – the kind of murder oblivious to differences of age, sex, personal quality or character. For genocide to be possible, personal differences must first be obliterated and faces must be melted into the uniform mass of the abstract category. Julius Streicher, the infamous editor-in-chief of the equally infamous *Der Stürmer*, had a hard time trying to make the exceedingly popular stereotype of the 'Jew as such', forged and disseminated by his paper, stick to the concrete Jews the readers knew from their daily intercourse; while Himmler found it necessary to reprimand even the selected and tested elite of his SS henchmen: ' "The Jewish people is to be exterminated," says every party member. "That's clear, it's part of our programme, elimination of the Jews, extermination, right, we'll do it." And then they all come along, the eighty million good Germans, and each one has his decent Jew. Of course the others are swine, but this one is a first-class Jew.'[4] Decent Germans were forbidden to have their own decent Jews – decent *because* 'their own': the next-door neighbours, caring doctors or friendly shopkeepers. Up to six million Jews were murdered wholesale not for what any of them had done but for how they had all been classified – just as, quite recently, in another hour of ultimate triumph of all-defining, all-classifying modern bureaucracy, the armed gangs of Hutus and Tutsis of Rwanda set off their victims from the others who shared the same look, language and religion, but who were meant to kill rather than be killed, simply *according to the entries in their passports.*

Jock Young coined the name of *essentialization* for the tendency to 'categorize' the others – the tendency perhaps extemporal as far as the human species goes, but most certainly aided and abetted, as Georg Simmel already noted, by the modern powers' knack for abstraction, and practised with particular zeal and put to the widest range of uses in modern times.[5] 'Essentialism', Jock Young writes, 'is a paramount strategy of exclusionism: it separates out human groups in terms of their culture or their nature. The advantages have always been there throughout human history but there are obvious reasons why the above strategies should appeal as we enter the late modern period.' Among the reasons Young lists for essentialization becoming a favourite modern strategy are the provision of an otherwise sorely missing ontological security, a legitimation of privilege and deference otherwise jarring with the modern promise of universality and equality, proffering the facility to shift the blame onto the other and to project onto the other inner fears and suspicions about one's own ability to match the standards of adequacy and decency that one professes. Treating others as separate beings endowed with personal virtues or vices would fail to serve such purposes: essentialization is indispensable, and the modern power of abstraction comes in handy. The abstracting powers simultaneously underlie and top up the other accoutrements of modernity without which the Holocaust, that exquisitely modern form of genocide, would have been inconceivable.

Some of those other necessary conditions available solely in the modern setting are well known and have been repeatedly discussed. Technological tools just as necessary for mass murder as they are indispensable for mass industrial production are perhaps the most frequently mentioned. Scientific management as embodied in bureaucratic organization – the ability to coordinate the actions of a great number of people and make the overall result independent of the personal idiosyncrasies, convictions, beliefs and emotions of individual performers – comes a close second. These two traits of modernity make it *possible* for the genocide, if and when it occurs, to be conducted with a cold and ethically indifferent efficiency and on a scale akin to that which set the Holocaust apart from all past, however cruel and gory, cases of mass murder.

What may lift that possibility to the level of reality is, however, the characteristically modern zeal for order-making; the kind of posture which casts the extant human reality as a perpetually unfinished project, in need of critical scrutiny, constant revision and improvement. When confronted with that stance, nothing has a right to exist just because of the fact that it happens to be around. To be granted the right of survival, every element of reality must justify itself in terms of its utility for the kind of order envisaged in the project. This is, as I suggested elsewhere,[6] an ambition which can best be grasped with the help of a 'gardening' metaphor (uprooting the weeds to enable useful plants to grow and preserve the elegance of overall design). Medicine (cutting out the diseased parts to secure the health of the organism) and architecture (eliminating from the design every out-of-place and redundant element) offer equally useful metaphors.

Genocide as order-building

This last point needs particularly strong emphasis when the affinity between modern life and holocaust-type murder is pondered. Indeed, this point is crucial if one wishes to comprehend the true nature of modernity as *modality of being* rather than any particular, concrete state of affairs already constructed, projected or adumbrated. Modern modality of being is characterized first and foremost by its endemic unfinishedness; by its orientation towards a state of affairs not yet in existence. To speak of modernity as an unfinished project is to commit a tautology. Modernity is by definition forever on the run, always (and incurably) *noch nicht geworden*. What is modern about any project is precisely its being a step, or two, or a hundred steps ahead of reality; what is modern about modernity is its inbuilt capacity to self-transcend, to push the finishing line further on in the course of running, and so to bar itself from ever reaching it.

Modernity is an inherently transgressive mode of being-in-the-world. Visions of order are born out of dissatisfaction with the existing state of things, and attempts to make them into flesh give birth to new disaffections and new, revised — and so deemed to be improved — visions. Modernity rolls and blends into one the act of drawing a frontier and the resolve to transcend it. All orders constructed under the aegis of modernity are therefore, even if only unintentionally, local, temporal, until further notice — bound to be reshaped before reaching fulfilment. 'Modernization' is not a road leading to a station called 'modernity'. Modernization — continuous, unstoppable, obsessive and in many ways self-propelling modernization — is the very human condition the concept of 'modernity' stands for; obsessive modernization *is* modernity. Were the modernizing thrust ever to grind to a halt, this would not augur the completion of modernity, but its demise or bankruptcy. Ulrich Beck has captured that state of affairs splendidly in his portrayal of our times as a process of the perpetual 'modernization of modernity' or 'rationalization of rationality'.[7]

Referring to the endemically precocious and precarious nature of all partial, local and temporary order-making efforts, Ulrich Beck introduced another by now household term — that of the *Risikogesellschaft* or risk society: ours is a kind of society in which the order-making urge results in the generation of a new series of disorders, imbuing all order-making endeavours with risks which can perhaps be roughly calculated in probability terms, but are never avoidable. What is especially relevant to our topic is that living in a *Risikogesellschaft* is, and is bound to remain, a *Risikoleben*. A life full of risks, an incurably risky life without any trustworthy knowledge of what the future may bring and without any possibility of controlling the outcome of one's own actions (that *conditio sine qua non* of all rational choice), is an unnerving, disturbing, anxiety-generating condition. Perhaps modern life started, as Sigmund Freud suggested, from surrendering a large slice of individual freedom in exchange for collectively endorsed security. In its present-day phase, though, the offer of social guarantees of individual security has been withdrawn or is no longer to be trusted. This state of affairs is a recipe for a life of insecurity and anguish; and also for a desperate search for a — genuine or putative, but trustworthy-looking — promise of a great simplification of a world too complex to walk safely through.

We may say that the modern order-making urge is thereby self-perpetuating and self-propelling: the state of affairs to be put in order is as a rule the leftover (the waste, the unanticipated and unwanted consequence) of an ordering bustle of the past. Modernity can be defined as *compulsive modernization*. And this means that there is no end to the tension saturating society, seeking desperately to be unloaded and an outlet through which to unload. As things stand now, in our postmodern or late modern times, there is little the political powers, which remain as local as they were in the times of high modernity, can do about the essentially global causes of rising uncertainty and insecurity. Of the three dimensions of that *Unsicherheit* that haunts the privatized individuals of our time, there becomes only one, that of safety (bodily safety and the safety of the extensions of the body – personal possessions, home, the street, the neighbourhood, the environment), in which the political states can show themselves to be resolute, resourceful, active and useful, and in which electoral support may be sought and gained. The constantly replenished supplies of anxiety and the pent-up aggression it generates are therefore channelled into concerns with 'law and order': into fighting crime and rounding up the criminals, or into control over the suspicious, unreliable and thus feared elements – mostly foreigners, people of different or opaque customs and lifestyle, who are presently filling the place vacated by the 'dangerous classes' or 'polluting races' of yore. In the age when mobility is fast turning into the major factor of stratification, privilege and discrimination, a growing section of law-and-order concerns focuses on the figures of the prowler, stalker, traveller, migrant – on whom the diffuse fears of increasingly alien, wayward and erratic *Umwelt* converge; and on a tough police force, long prison sentences, high security prisons and capital punishment, as well as on the isolation and deportation of 'undesirables' – on these and other deemed remedies for the novel, off-putting and disturbing experience of the fluidity of space.

There is a lot of political capital lodged in the present-day obsession with safety. And there is no shortage of political players eager to deploy that capital in the power game. To be sure, thanks to the late modern surfeit of mutually cancelling authorities and due to the irredeemable polyvocality which goes together with political democracy and the weakening grip of state powers, the chances of such players gaining an upper hand and deploying the absolute powers of the state to set a Holocaust-style 'solution' in motion are slim and remote. Yet to say with any degree of self-assurance that the forces eager for an *Endlösung* type of action, and either the necessary or the sufficient conditions for them acting in that way, are no longer present today would be equally premature and imprudent.

Living with the memory of the Holocaust

Not much more than half a century ago the Holocaust was unimaginable; half a century ago it was still, for most people, unbelievable. Today, one cannot imagine a world in which 'a holocaust' is impossible. And if a vision of such a foolproof and safe world were painted, one would not quite – not unreservedly – believe the picture. After all, everyone knows now that vexing problems may have their 'final solutions', that setting people apart, rounding them up and deporting or physically destroying them, 'cleansing' whole territories of great masses of people, is one of the options whenever a confused and messy reality clashes with the image of the orderly world, the world 'as it should be'; and that – if one only plays one's hand right (and better still, if one manages to secure a hand stronger than the hand of the next player) – this is quite an attractive option, considering that one can get away with it until the job is done, and even forever after, as long as one stays strong, avoids defeat and so escapes trial by the victors. In such a world, we can all guess now, there can be someone, somewhere, who is contemplating another genocide at this very moment – and such a world cannot be a safe place to live in. In this remarkable turnaround consists, in a nutshell, the profound and durable – social, political, cultural and psychical – significance of the Holocaust.

George Steiner remarked once that Voltaire's or Matthew Arnold's privilege was their ignorance of what we know and can hardly forget: the hidden potential and the aftermath of the great modern adventure. After the Holocaust and the Gulag, we cannot any longer claim ignorance. We cannot hide behind the naivety which used to be the age of innocence's redeeming grace. But having lost our innocence, we are not certain about the content of the knowledge we have acquired instead. This content remains a moot and hotly contested matter. But like the Holocaust itself, the way in which it is remembered is a matter of life and death.

By comparison with its *posthumous* life, the *reality* of the Holocaust seems in retrospect simple and straightforward: certain people methodically and systematically murdered certain other people whom some other people yet had earmarked for extermination, while still other people watched – whether in despair, with indifference or with barely concealed joy – but did too little or nothing at all to stop the murder. There were evil murderers, innocent victims, and bystanders of varying degrees of evil and innocence. Except for the lunatic fringe of 'revisionist historians' and Nazi mourners, a broad consensus has been reached about who was who and who did what in Auschwitz. Today, however, things look much more confused. The most confused of them all is the question as to what is to be learned from the Holocaust, who is to learn it and to what effect. Today, the lines dividing evil from innocence, guilt from good reason, a clear conscience from a dirty one are anything but straight and uncontested.

Mind-boggling and spine-chilling as the Holocaust was, one could still measure the scale of its fiendishness by counting the corpses and weighing the ashes. But how can one measure the damage done by the *memory* of gas chambers and crematoria? Half a century later that memory pollutes the world of the living, and the inventory of insidious poisons seems anything but complete. We are all to some degree possessed by that memory, though the Jews among us, the prime targets of the Holocaust, are – understandably – more so than most. Among the Jews, in the first place, living in a world contaminated with the possibility of a holocaust rebounds time and again in fear and horror. To many, the world appears suspect to the core; no worldly event is truly neutral – each event is burdened with sinister undertones, each contains an ominous message aimed especially at the Jews, a message that can be overlooked or played down only at the Jews' own peril. As the late E. M. Cioran put it,

> to be afraid is to think of yourself continually, to be unable to imagine an objective course of events. The sensation of the terrible, the sensation that it is all happening *against* you, supposes a world conceived without *indifferent* dangers. The frightened man – victim of an exaggerated subjectivity – believes himself to be, much more than the rest of his kind, the target of hostile events... [He has attained] the extremity of a self-infatuated consciousness; everything conspires against the one...[8]

The instinct of self-defence prompts the victim to learn the lesson of history, though in order to learn it, the victim needs to decide first what the lesson is. The precept of staying alive as the sole thing that counts, as the supreme value that dwarfs all other values, is among the most tempting, and the most common, interpretations of the lesson. As the direct experience of the victims recedes and fades, the memory of the Holocaust thins down and condenses into a simple precept of survival: life is about surviving, to succeed in life is to outlive the others. Who survives wins.

This reading of the Holocaust's lesson has been recently displayed – to worldwide acclaim and huge box-office success – in Spielberg's, now well-nigh canonical, image of the Holocaust. According to the *Schindler's List* version of the Holocaust experience, the sole stake of the tragedy was to remain alive – while the quality of life, and particularly its *dignity and ethical value*, was at best of secondary importance and above all of no consequence; it was never allowed to interfere with the principal goal. The goal of staying alive took care of moral concerns and dwarfed and pushed out of sight such moral concerns as could not be consumed. What counted in the last resort was to *outlive the others* – even if the escape from death required being put on a separate, and unique, list of the privileged (offered by the commandant of Birkenau a replacement for '*his* Jewesses', Schindler refuses; it was not the saving of lives that counted, but the saving of specific, selected lives). The value of staying alive was not diminished by the fact that others, less fortunate, travelled to extermination camps; the viewers of *Schindler's List* are invited to rejoice in the sight of Schindler's master of works pulled out in the nick of time – he alone – from the train destined for Treblinka. Through a wilful travesty made of the Talmud's precepts, Spielberg's film translates the issue of the salvation of humanity into the decision as to who is to live and who to die.[9]

That elevation of survival to the rank of the supreme, perhaps the only value, is not Spielberg's invention; neither is it a phenomenon confined to artistic representations of the experience of the Holocaust. Soon after the end of the war psychiatrists coined the concept of 'survivor's guilt' – a complex psychical ailment which they ascribed to the survivors' asking themselves why they had stayed alive when so many of their near and dear had perished. According to that interpretation, the joy of escaping death was permanently and incurably poisoned among the survivors by uncertainty about the propriety of sailing safe out of the sea of perdition – with disastrous consequences for the survivors will to live and to succeed in life after their rescue. Many practising psychiatrists acquired fame and fortune treating 'survivor's syndrome' so construed. Whether the syndrome was rightly spotted and the psychiatric treatment well aimed is perhaps debatable; what is rather obvious, though, is that in the course of time the 'guilt' aspect, so prominent in the original diagnoses, has been progressively exorcized from the model of the 'survival complex', leaving behind the pure and unalloyed, unambiguous and no longer contested approval of self-preservation for self-preservation's sake. It is just the haunting pain left by the sufferings that staying alive required that is now blamed for the persistence of the 'syndrome'.

Such a shift brings us dangerously close to the spine-chilling image of the survivor as painted by Elias Canetti – as the person for whom 'the most elementary and obvious form of success is to remain alive'. For Canetti's survivor, the survival – unlike the mere self-preservation – is targeted on the other, not on the self: 'they want to survive their contemporaries. They know that many die early and they want a different fate for themselves.' At the far end of the obsession, Canetti's survivor

> wants to kill so that he can survive others; he wants to stay alive so as not to have others surviving him... The survivor's most fantastic triumphs have taken place in our own time, among people who set a great store about the idea of humanity... The survivor is mankind's worst evil, its curse and perhaps its doom.[10]

The wider repercussions of the cult of survival contain dangers of potentially formidable proportions. Time and again, in this place and that, the lessons of the Holocaust are reduced for popular consumption to a simple formula, 'who strikes first, survives'; or to an even simpler one, 'the stronger lives'. The awesome, two-pronged legacy of the Holocaust is, on the one hand, the tendency to treat survival as the sole, or at any rate the topmost value and purpose of life, and, on the other, to the positing of issue of survival as that of competition for a scarce resource, and so of survival itself as a site of conflict between incompatible interests – a kind of conflict in which the success of some depends on the defeat of others in the race to survive.

Inadvertently, yet all the same ominously, such an interpretation of the Holocaust's lesson chimes with, and adds oblique support to, the most widespread and iniquitous arguments brandished nowadays around the globe in justification of recurrent new genocides: namely, of a new round of victimization being needed to revenge the past cruelty as well as to defend the victims of past persecution against the repetition of their sufferings. The reasoning behind such justification of new genocidal attempts eagerly resorted to by the 'political forces oriented towards the past' has been spelt out recently by Luc Boltanski in the following way: 'leaning on the memory of the suffering, misfortunes and sacrifices of the *past victims*, [they] legitimize appeals to the identity of peoples, classes and States.'[11] More often than not, such 'history lessons' are, in Boltanski's words, weapons of 'those in power who exploit past victims in order to take possession of the future while ignoring present suffering'.

There is another quality, though, claimed by the 'victim by proxy' – one of belonging to a *sui generis* 'aristocracy of victimhood' (that is, having a *hereditary* claim to the sympathy and ethical indulgence owed to those who suffer). That status can be, and often is, brandished as an equivalent of the medieval *indulgentia* or the contemporary 'blank cheque': a signed-in-advance certificate of moral righteousness. Whatever the legatees of the victims do is guaranteed to be moral (or at least *ethically correct*) as long as it can be shown that it was done in order to stave off a repetition of the lot visited on their ancestors; or as long as it can be shown to be psychologically understandable, nay 'normal', in view of the inherited trauma; the super-susceptibility of the hereditary bearers of victimhood to the threat of a new victimization.

The ancestors are pitied, but also blamed, for letting themselves be led, like sheep, to slaughter. How can one therefore blame their descendants for sniffing out a future slaughterhouse in every offensive-looking street or building? More importantly still, for taking preventive measures to disem-power the potential slaughterers? The people who need to be disempow-ered may have nothing to do with the perpetrators of the Holocaust and in no juridical or ethically sensible way could be charged with responsibility for one's own ancestors' perdition (it is, after all, the heredity of the 'hereditary victims', not the continuity of their assumed victimizers, which makes the connection and sustains the causal chain). And yet, in a world haunted by the memory of the Holocaust, those people are guilty in advance, guilty of *being seen* as prone or able to become, given a chance, the perpetrators of another genocide. Standing accused or just *being suspect*, true to the sinister message of Kafka's *Trial*, is already their crime, and the only crime needed to classify them as criminals and to justify harsh punitive measures. The ethics of hereditary victimhood reverses the logic of the law: the accused remain criminals until proved innocent. And since it is the accusers and the prosecutors themselves who conduct the hearings and decide the validity of the argument, the defendants have slim chance of their arguments being accepted by the judges, but every chance of staying guilty for a long time to come, whatever they do.

The self-reproduction of victimhood

Thus the status of hereditary victim may take the moral reprobation off the new victimization – this time perpetrated in the name of erasing the hereditary vulnerability. It is a banal truth that violence breeds more violence; somewhat less banal, since not repeated enough, is the truth that victimization breeds more victimization. Victims are not guaranteed to be morally superior to their victimizers, and seldom emerge from the victimization morally ennobled.

Martyrdom – whether lived in a real or a virtual reality – is not a warrant for saintliness. Memory of suffering does not ensure a lifelong dedication to the fight against inhumanity, cruelty and pain infliction as such, wherever they happen and whoever the sufferers. An at least equally probable outcome of martyrdom is the tendency to draw an opposite lesson: that humankind is divided into victims and the victimizers, and so if you are (or expect to be) a victim, your duty is to reverse the tables. We come across that perverse logic time and time again: we watch it today (making little or no effort to cut the vicious loop) in the seesaw of violence in Rwanda; all over the part of Europe known until recently under the name of Yugoslavia; also in Sudan, Congo, Somalia, Angola, Sri Lanka, Afganistan and countless other places. It is this lesson that the spectre of the Holocaust whispers into many ears; some Israeli political leaders lifted that lesson to the rank of an official policy of the state and crowning argument of its diplomacy. And for this reason we cannot be sure whether the lasting legacy of the Holocaust was not the very opposite to that hoped for by many, and anticipated by some: a moral reawakening or ethical purification of the world as a whole or any part of it.

The pernicious legacy of the Holocaust is that today's persecutors may inflict new pains and create new generations of victims eagerly awaiting their chance to do the same, while acting under the conviction that they are avenging yesterday's pain and warding off the pains of tomorrow; while being convinced, in other words, that ethics is on their side. This is perhaps the greatest among the Holocaust's curses and Hitler's posthumous victories. The crowds who applauded Goldstein's massacre of Muslim worshippers in occupied Hebron, who flocked to his funeral and go on writing his name on their political and religious banners, are the most terminally afflicted but not the only bearers of that curse. They may count on a tacit, sometimes quite vociferous compassion from ruling political forces. Such forces want to keep reality conforming to the vision of hereditary victimhood and do their best to force it into conformity. Another bomb, another outbreak of intifada serves that purpose very well. But in a somewhat diluted but still malignant form the curse spilt far and wide, affecting a sizeable section of the Israeli population brought up to believe in living inside a besieged fortress.

At the end of his pioneering study of the ardour with which the ordinary folks enlisted in the 101st Police Reserve Batallion fulfilled the order to kill, Christopher R. Browning mused: if the men of the 101st batallion could become murderers, what human group cannot? Unlike his later Ph.D student Daniel Jonah Goldhagen, Browning was puzzled, and frightened, by the fact that ordinary people, like the rest of us, could turn into murderers given the right conditions. Browning did not seek consolation in the idea that it is antisemites who have the patent for the miraculous avatar of this kind and that therefore being free of antisemitism is a patent medicine against participation in categorial crime.

Pondering the poisoned afterhistory of the Holocaust, two Israeli scholars, Ariella Azoulay and Adi Ofir, wondered what the 'we' in the language of Israeli politics means these days:

> We are the last place in Europe where the Nazi past is still profit-able – because the State has converted the destruction of European Jewry into a national property, symbolic capital... We are a site of experiments for testing the universalizability of evil – the principle of universalizability being a European legacy and the practices for the production of evil imported from a Europe which no longer exists. The hypothesis to be corroborated (one that has not yet been refuted) is: 'it can happen to everyone'; the victims of yester-day may always become today's victimizers. Every person can find herself participating in the hatred, humiliation, and oppression of the 'Other', in racial discrimination, in ethnic cleansing of neigh-bourhoods and cities; everyone may end up cooperating with a regime that produces and distributes evil systematically.[12]

'Hereditary victimhood' is the principal socio-psychological device serving the systematic production and distribution of evil. One should beware of confusing the phenomenon of hereditary victimhood with genetic kinship, or with family tradition preserved through parental influence over the educational setting. Heredity in this case is mainly imagined, acting through the collective production of memory and through individual acts of self-enlisting and self-identification. Thus the status of the 'Holocaust children', that is, of hereditary victim, is open to every Jew, whatever his or her parents might have been 'doing in the war' or whatever was done to them during that war.

Psychiatrists have conducted ample studies of the biological descen-dants (and/or educational objects) of the inmates of concentration camps and the dwellers in ghettos; but the swelling numbers of the 'sons and daughters of the Holocaust' who *are not children of either*, still await a comprehensive study. There are many clues, though, of what such a study might reveal. It may well transpire that the complexes of such 'imagined children', children-through-self-assignment (and, for the same reason, 'children *manqués*'), are no less severe and vicious, and perhaps burdened with more sinister consequences, than those the psychiatrists have described thus far. One may say: this stands to reason (whatever 'reason' may mean in our world gripped by the Holocaust memory). For the children *manqués*, the site they occupy in the world, from which they view the world and in which they want to be viewed by the world, is that of martyrdom; but it so happens that they are not, nor have been, personally, the butt of anybody's wrath and wrongdoing. The world seems reluctant to harm them and make them suffer, and under the circumstances such a world is too good to be true – since the reality of a harmless world means the irreality of a life which derives its sense from the harm done to it and the harm yet to be done.

Living in a world that is not hostile and harmless, let alone in a hospitable and comfortable world, means the betrayal of the sense-giving pedigree. To reach completeness, to fulfil their destiny, to get rid of their present deficiency, to efface the qualification '*manqués*' from the status of offspring and heir, they would need to reforge their own imagined continuity of victimhood into the real continuity of victimization in the 'world out there'. That can be done only through acting *as if* their present site in the world was really and truly a site of the victims; through abiding by a strategy that would be rational only in a victimizing world. The children *manqués* cannot be fulfilled unless the world they live in reveals its hostility, conspires against them – and, indeed, contains the possibility of another holocaust.

The awesome truth is that, contrary to what they say and think they wish, the children *manqués* – the 'flawed children' – are unfit to live in, and they feel out of place in, a world free of that possibility. They would feel more comfortable living in a world more like that other world, populated by the Jew-hating murderers who would not stop short of including them among their victims if their blood-soaked hands were untied. They draw a sense-giving reassurance from every sign of hostility towards them; and they are eager to interpret every move of those around them as an overt or latent expression of such hostility (a recent study reporting the disappearance of antisemitism in the USA has been reviewed in the American Jewish bimonthly *Tikkun* under the thoughtful title that tells it all – 'Can the Jews Take It?'). The macabre paradox of being a hereditary victim is to develop a vested interest in the hostility of the world, in fomenting the hostility of the world and keeping the world hostile. One can almost hear a sigh of relief exhaled by some political leaders of the country, and the many thousands of men and women who voted for them, whenever a new terrorist bomb is planted by their victims pushed to the end of their endurance.

The flawed children of the martyrs do not live in homes; they live in fortresses. And to make their homes into fortresses, they need them besieged and under fire. Where else can one come closer to one's dreams than among the famished and destitute, despairing and desperate, cursing and stone-throwing Palestinians... Here, the comfortable and commodious, all-mod-con houses are unlike the houses the children *manqués* have abandoned – those comfortable and commodious, all-mod-con houses over there, in the stale and dull, too-safe-for-comfort American cities, where the children would be bound to stay as they are, *manqués*. Here, one can tightly wrap the houses with barbed wire, one can build watchtowers in every corner and one can walk from one house to another proudly caressing the gun hanging from one's shoulder. The hostile, Jew-baiting world once forced the Jews into ghettos. By making a home in the likeness of the ghetto (this time round, though, a heavily armed ghetto), one can make the world look once more hostile and Jew-baiting. In that fully and truly flawed world, the children, at long last, would be no longer flawed. The chance of martyrdom missed by the generation would have been repossessed by its chosen representatives, who want to be seen as its spokespeople as well.

Whichever way you look at it, the ghost of the Holocaust appears self-perpetuating and self-reproducing. It has made itself indispensable to too many to be easily exorcized. Haunted houses have acquired an added value, and being possessed has turned for many into a valued, meaning-bestowing life formula. In this one can spy the greatest posthumous triumph of the *Endlösung* designers. What Hitler and his henchmen failed to accomplish when alive, they may yet hope to achieve after death. They did not manage to turn the world against the Jews, but in their graves they can still dream of turning the Jews against the world, and thus – one way or another – making the Jewish reconciliation with the world, their peaceful cohabitation with the world, all that much more difficult, if not downright impossible. The prophecies of the Holocaust are not quite self-fulfilling, but they do fulfil – render plausible – the prospect of a world in which the Holocaust may never stop being prophesied, with all the deleterious and disastrous psychical, cultural and political consequences which such prophesying is bound to bring forth and propagate.

Living in a one-dimensional world

Jean-Paul Sartre proposed that the Jew is a person whom others define as a Jew. What Sartre must have meant was that the act of such defining is also the act of reductive selectiveness: one of the manifold traits of an irretrievably multifaceted person is hereby given prominence, rendering all other traits secondary, derivative or irrelevant. In the practice of the possessed, the Sartrean procedure is conducted once more, though in the opposite direction. The others, the non-Jews, emerge as every bit as one-dimensional as the Jews appeared in the vision of their haters. The others are not benign or cruel *patri familiae*, caring or selfish husbands, benevolent or malicious bosses, good or bad citizens, peaceful or pugnacious neighbours, oppressors or oppressed, objects or culprits of injustice, in pain or pain-inflicting, privileged or dispossessed, threatening or threatened; more precisely – they may be all that, but the fact that they are all that or more is of but secondary or minor importance and does not count for much. What truly counts – perhaps the only thing that counts – is their attitude towards the Jews. And the stance taken to every person who happens to be *also* a Jew is read out as a manifestation of, and derivative of, the attitude taken towards the Jews as such. Like hereditary victimhood, so the one-dimensionality of the worldview has a self-perpetuating propensity.

It is tremendously difficult to square with the one-dimensional world view the fact that in the course of Hitler's war against the Jews many declared antisemites stoutly refused to cooperate with the perpetrators of the Holocaust; and that, on the other hand, the ranks of the executors were full of law-abiding citizens and disciplined functionaries who happened to be free of any peculiar resentment against the Jews as such and in particular bore no grudge whatsoever against the concrete Jews they shot or gassed (Nechama Tec, that indefatigable and remarkably perceptive student of the 'ordinary humans' cast in inhuman conditions, reports that, according to a witness of one mass execution, among thirteen policemen one stood out for his beastly cruelty, three did not participate in the Jewish action and the rest saw the operation as 'unclean' and refused to talk about it). It is similarly hard to come to grips with the fact that 'the deportation of the Jews' (as the annihilation of European Jewry was officially defined) derived its meaning in Nazi thinking from the overall, audacious plan of wholesale *Umsiedlung* – the vision of a European continent in which well-nigh everyone would be transported from their present, contingent site to the place where reason orders them to be[13] (and that could entail nothingness; as the Holocaust progressed, even Jewish graveyards were proclaimed out of order and replaced with chimney smoke). Or to accept that the extermination of the Jews was conceived in the framework of a total 'cleansing operation' (which also included people who were regarded as mentally deficient, physically handicapped, ideologically deviant and sexually unorthodox) by a state powerful enough, and sufficiently protected and immune from all opposition, to afford such total plans and to execute them without fear of effective dissent. Finally, to comprehend that the Nazis behind the Holocaust, whatever creatures they must have been otherwise, were *also* 'Bürger', who like all *Bürgers* then as much as now, here as much as there, had their 'problems' which they dearly wished to 'resolve'.[14]

All that has been said thus far does not intend to imply that warnings about the possibility of another holocaust are totally unfounded, that the world we live in now differs from the world of the Holocaust to an extent that makes the present-day world completely Holocaust-proof. But it does mean that the threat of such holocausts as may yet come is all too often sniffed out and searched for in the wrong places; the scrutiny is diverted from the ground in which *genuine threats* are rooted. A sinister trait of the one-dimensional worldview is that, while concentrating our attention in one direction, we close our eyes to the manifold nature of the real dangers.

The acclaim accorded to Daniel Goldhagen's version of the Holocaust as primarily a story of voluntary and Jew-hating helpers of Hitler adds to such risks. Goldhagen's thesis, as well as the poorly concealed satisfaction with which it has been received in so many circles, can be only fully comprehended in the context sketched above; the context which entails, as its primary ingredients, the phenomenon of hereditary (yet *manqué*) victimhood, intertwined with the one-dimensional worldview.

This view of mine sems to be shared, as a matter of fact, by Goldhagen himself and the most zealous of his eulogists and defenders. When Ruth Bettina Birn and Norman Finkelstein published a scathing critique of the one-sided uses Goldhagen made of the archives,[15] the criticized author, rather than owning up to his mistakes or defending his version of the facts, charged his critics with perfidious political intentions and resorted to argument *ad hominem*, dismissing the critics as 'crusaders of anti-Zionism'; by the same token, he obliquely admitted that the dispute – ostensibly about his rendition of the Holocaust – is, ultimately at least, a matter of defending certain quite contemporary political causes. Others who rushed to Goldhagen's rescue were more outspoken yet. And so Abraham

Fox, speaking on behalf of the Canadian branch of the Anti-Defamation League, declared that the problem is not to find out whether Goldhagen's thesis is justified or not – but whether the critique applied to it is 'legitimate' and does not cross the border of the permissible.[16]

Such a perception of Goldhagen's manifesto was more than justified. The message of the book, after all (to quote Goldhagen's own words from *Hitler's Willing Executioners* of 1996), was quite straightforward: 'with regard to the motivational cause of the Holocaust, for the vast majority of the perpetrators, a monocausal explanation does suffice' – that is, 'a demonological antisemitism'. Historians who wished to acknowledge more complex aspects of the Holocaust's mechanism were, in Goldhagen's view, mistaken; they should get rid of the idea that Germans (of Hitler's Germany at least) were 'more or less like us', that 'their sensibilities had remotely approximated our own'.[17] The reader would easily conclude that it was precisely because the Germans were *not* 'more or less like us' that the Holocaust happened. And since 'being unlike' is a symmetrical relation, the next conclusion is equally easy: because all the rest of us are not 'more or less like Germans', nothing 'remotely approximating' the Holocaust-style genocide can be perpetrated by anybody else and anywhere else. Holocaust was, is, and will remain the *German problem*, and so the rest of the world has nothing to fear, can put conscience to rest and stop the vexing soul-scratching. In other words, nothing that we can possibly learn from the event called 'the Holocaust' can teach us anything about ourselves, the world we live in, or, indeed, anything else – except German guilt. *Quod erat demonstrandum.*

Tom Segev of the Israeli daily *Haaretz* has been right on target, summing up the sense of the ongoing debate in the following words: 'The Jewish establishment embraced Goldhagen as if he was Mr Holocaust in person. This is absurd, since the critiques raised against Goldhagen are well founded...'[18] This is, Segev explains, nevertheless understandable since what is at stake is the 'Zionist character' of Goldhagen's thesis. What truly matters is that, in the end,

> not just the Germans, but all Gentiles hate the Jews. Hence the need of unity and solidarity of the Jews. Hence also the need of ever more numerous books on anti-Jewish hatred, and the more simplistic and superficial they are, the better.

Christopher R. Browning, whose eye-opening findings Goldhagen borrowed only to twist them and stretch them beyond their capacity in order to sustain his verdicts, charges Goldhagen with inventing an artificial dichotomy between actions motivated by allegedly 'internal' factors permitting moral judgments (namely beliefs and values, which in effect Goldhagen limits to anti-Semitic or racist convictions) and actions 'compelled' by what he terms 'external' factors that, because of the compulsion, are devoid of a moral dimension involving choice. In reality, of course, there are numerous 'values and beliefs' that motivate people other than racist ones, such as perceptions of authority, duty, legitimacy, and loyalty to one's unit and country in wartime. And there are other personality traits such as ambition, greed, and lack of empathy that shape people's behaviour without absolving them of individual responsibility.[19]

This is precisely the point: it took quite a few formidable modern inventions, 'rational bureaucracy' prominent among them, to render certain murders and other acts of cruelty exempt from moral judgments and so in the eyes of the perpetrators 'morally neutral', and to deploy a wide range of human 'values and beliefs' in the service of murder. But one would research Goldhagen's book in vain to find any sign that the author is aware of this and prepared to see the complexity of the modern predicament of the moral man beyond the most crude of dichotomies.

That some of the participants in mass murder did enjoy their part in crime either because of their sadistic inclinations or of their hatred of the Jews, or for both reasons simultaneously – is not, of course, Goldhagen's fantasy; though it is not his discovery either. Taking that fact, however, as the explanation of the Holocaust, as its central point or deepest meaning, says a lot about the contemporary political uses to which the memory of the Holocaust is being put, while turning the attention away from what is the most sinister truth of that genocide and what is still the most salutary lesson which our haunted world could learn – should learn, has the moral obligation to learn – from the recent history which contains the Holocaust as its major event.

The social production of killers

The point to remember is that for every villain of Goldhagen's book, for every German and non-German who killed his victims with pleasure and enthusiasm, there were dozens and hundreds of Germans and non-Germans who contributed to the mass murder no less effectively without feeling either way about their victims and about the nature of the actions involved. And the point is that, while we know quite well that prejudice threatens humanity, and we even know a little about how to fight and constrain the ill-intentions of the people tainted with prejudice, we know next to nothing about how to stave off the threat of a murder which masquerades as a routine and unemotional function of orderly society. At the same time, the other kind of knowledge – how to deploy people free of any murderous instincts in the service of 'legitimate killing', and the skills and technology needed to apply such knowledge in practice – is by now, thanks to the united efforts of psychologists, technologists and the experts in scientific management, considerable and continually growing.

Robert Johnson produced a meticulous, scrupulous and imaginative in-depth study of the dull daily routine of death row in the American penal system, notoriously fond of capital punishment; its suspended animation, and the festive routine of execution days; and also of the thoughts and feelings of the main actors in both. The huge amount of data Johnson elicited and gathered may serve as rich empirical evidence for the insights of the great Norwegian criminologist Nils Christie in his pioneering study of *Crime Control as Industry*.[20] All Christie's major insights find in Johnson's report ample empirical corroboration: the routinization of the killing procedure, the bureaucratic division of labour and 'agentic state' of all individuals involved in the collective accomplishment, the thorough 'emotional disenchantment' of the whole process, neutralization of ethical concerns and moral scruples, depersonalization of the victims... The 'civilizing process', as Norbert Elias famously suggested, has made us all (or most of us at least) dislike and shun violence. But modern civilization has also invented the means to make this aversion and loathing of violence irrelevant when it comes to complicity in the commitment of violent acts – particularly when the acts are to be committed in the name of civilized values.

'Complicity is obvious in that the death row officers expressly hold the prisoners for the purpose of execution,' Johnson notes. The officers interviewed by Johnson are aware of that and cannot help feeling bad because of it. 'The reality of that last family visit really made me feel bad... It was depressing to be there,' admits one of them (please note: the guards of death row do not have the luxury that the Holocaust executors enjoyed – they have ample time to develop personal relations with the convicted: those earmarked for execution *have faces*). But then he adds, as an afterthought: 'It's supposed to be part of the job, like being a doctor or something. You lose a patient and that's just it, but it's not that easy. You never forget this type of thing, but you can put it behind you.' And 'behind' them he and his mates put it, most of them, most of the time. How does this feat get to be accomplished?

First of all, by pushing aside moral considerations, replacing ethical measures with technical ones which arouse no emotions and do not concern the moral person's beliefs, and repeating what the people in charge keep telling them and what everyone around keeps repeating after them: 'It's not a job I like or dislike. I try to go about every job in the most professional manner. If they would stop the death penalty, it wouldn't bother me. If we had ten executions tomorrow, it wouldn't bother me,' says one of the wardens. 'It's done professionally; it's not no horseplaying. Everything is done by documentation. On time. By the book,' adds another.

Secondly, all those people partake of the act of killing, but no one is (or, rather, needs to feel) a killer. At no point is there but one trigger to be pulled by one finger. As Johnson puts it, 'members of the deathwatch team referred to themselves...as simply "the team".' Working in 'the team' is salutary; it is the team that kills without making any of its members a killer. Johnson quotes one warden's words: 'We can honestly say that we did not do it.' Responsibility, as Hannah Arendt observed, is floating. And a floating responsibility is nobody's responsibility.

Thirdly, no member of the deathwatch team performs his job for the love of killing, or even out of enthusiasm for the death penalty. Motives or their absence have nothing to do with what is going on. 'Only a few members of the execution team support the death penalty outright and without reservation,' Johnson observes. When filling the vacancies, prison governors did not advertise for sadists or 'law and order' addicts, militants and vigilantes. Strong feelings of whatever kind would, if anything, interfere with the smooth running of the bureaucratic procedure. It is safer, and above all much more efficient, to put emotions aside. Were emotions not defused, too much would depend on erratic and bureaucratically uncontrollable shifts of mood. It is so much more effective when everything is done 'by the book'. In the bureaucratic organization of the killing industry, as in any other bureaucratic organization, personal sympathies and antipathies are better left in the cloakroom before clock-in time.

Some thoughtful people in supervisory positions go a step further: they are positively and firmly *against* employing men who betray a special inclination not for good performance *as such*, but for performing this *particular* kind of job because of what that job is like. 'I don't want nobody who would like to do it... And if I suspected or thought anybody on the team really's gettin' a kick out of it, I would take him off the team... I would like to think that every one of them on the team... is doing it in the line of duty.' This particular supervisor's idea is faithful to the modern spirit. When recruiting soldiers for the *Einsatzgruppen* ordered to round up and shoot on the spot the Bolsheviks and the Jews found on conquered Soviet territory, precautions were reputedly taken to eliminate rabid antisemites and people with sadistic inclinations. The power of modern ways and means consists precisely in making the success of the enterprise *independent* of the presence or absence of dedication.

Modernity would not have got where it has if it had relied on things as erratic, whimsical and thoroughly unmodern as human passions. Instead, it relied on the division of labour, on science, technology, scientific management and the power to make a rational calculation of costs and effects – all thoroughly unemotional stuff. Stephen Trombley's remarkable study[21] does for the 'execution industry' what the work of Götz Aly and Susanne Heim did for the murderous enterprise of the Nazis: it shows beyond reasonable doubt that the setting which in modern society renders mass or regular killing possible is indistinguishable from that which makes mass production and unstoppable technological rationalization possible. Aly and Heim documented the crucial role played by the thousands of high-class experts – engineers, architects, constructors, medics, psychologists and countless others – in making mass extermination on a previously unheard-of scale feasible.[22] And we learn from the carefully documented history of the electric chair written by Trombley that the first electrocution (of William Kemmler, held on 6 August 1890 in New York's Auburn State Prison) 'excited a great deal of medical interest, and of the twenty-five witnesses who watched Kemmler killed by electricity, fourteen were doctors.' We also learn that the invention of the electric chair became an occasion of thorough scientific debate about the respective advantages of alternating and direct currents, and caused a heated public argument between such supreme luminaries of modern technology as Thomas Edison and George Westinghouse. We learn in addition that the distinguished members of Governor Hill's commission charged with finding the proper methods of execution fell for the arguments that carried the authority of science and progress: what convinced them was that electricity, 'the invisible and imperfectly understood form of energy was quintessentially modern'; it was also clean and promised to be cheap — and the members of the commission were duly impressed.

Both Johnson's and Trombley's studies are priceless; their value lies in the information they supply and perhaps even more in the understanding they imply of modern human conduct and the way modern society works. That way renders ethical considerations and moral impulses by and large redundant, and the reviewed studies document that redundancy and show how it is achieved and, daily, indeed routinely, reproduced. They also list the gains derived from that redundancy; gains in the straightforward sense of profit and the profitable use of resources, but also in the not immediately noticeable sense of giving plausibility and feasibity to endeavours which would be unthinkable were they to depend on human motivations and impulses. Participants in the killing operations and the legions of scientists and engineers who supply them with the killing weapons and work out the procedures for efficient action are not evil people. Evil people did evil things at all times. But they are few and erratic, 'crazy' by modern standards of reason. It has been perhaps the unique achievement of modern civilization to enable ordinary folks, 'just good workers', to contribute to the killing — and to make that killing more comprehensive and thorough, cleaner, and morally antiseptic and efficient as never before.

Modernity contra *homo sacer*

As Enzo Traverso put it recently with reference to France, the causes of the Holocaust in general, and of that 'wall of indifference' which surrounded the mass slaughter of the French Jews, need to be sought not in the 'Jewish question', as Jean-Paul Sartre saw it, not even in the circumstances of the genocide itself, but in French pre-Vichy society.[23] There are unwanted strangers in any society, and in any society there are some people who wish such strangers not to be there; but it is not in any society that a genocide of the unwanted strangers can take place. The presence of a quantity of Jew-haters is not the only, not even a necessary, and certainly not a sufficient condition needing to be met to make that genocide a possibility.

Hannah Arendt pointed out a long time ago that, in the phenomenon of the Holocaust, antisemitism may explain at most the choice of the victims, but not the nature of the crime. Nothing has happened since then to invalidate Arendt's verdict, while the monumental memoirs of

Primo Levi, the monumental historical research of Raoul Hilberg and the monumental documentary of Claude Lanzmann, to mention but a few landmarks, did a lot to confirm and reinforce it.

A short time ago another important voice was added – that of the Italian philosopher Giorgio Agamben[24] – to our attempts to pierce through the mystery of genocide. Agamben recalled the legal concept of the *homo sacer,* coined in the archaic Roman Law: the concept of a human being who could be killed without punishment, but at the same time – being absolutely Other, alien, indeed inhuman – a kind of being who could not be used in ritualistic religious sacrifices: his murder had no religious significance. *Homo sacer* was totally 'useless', completely outside human society and exempt from all obligations and other considerations due to other humans on account of their humanity. *Homo sacer*'s life was 'nude' – that is, stripped of all social quality and political rights, and as such unprotected, made into a sitting target for every frustrated sadist or murderer, but also a recommended target for everyone seeking to conform and exercise their civic duty.

Homo sacer was a *legal* construction. As a legal construct, it was addressed to the loyalty and *discipline* of law-abiding subjects, not to their beliefs and sentiments. Like all legal constructs it bypassed or suspended feelings and personal beliefs, as well as moral emotions, and as far as the required action was concerned cast them into irrelevance. The point about law is that it is expected to be obeyed *whether or not* the law-abiding person likes it, dislikes it, or has no feelings about it. That particular legal construct of *homo sacer* was in Roman legal practice an exceptional, marginal and almost empty category. It is different in the modern state, as Agamben points out.

True, the concept of *homo sacer* is absent from modern law and is largely forgotten. But having appropriated a monopoly over the means of enforcement and violence, as well as over the means and the prerogative to offer or to refuse the right to live, over the entitlement to control the bodies of subjects, including the right to inflict pain – the state has expanded what used to be an extraordinary category into a potentially universal aspect of its subjects' existential status: it has thus no need to resort to a special, exceptional category to sustain what has now become a routine prerogative. Concentration camps, also a gruesome invention of the modern world, were a space where what is in other parts of the state realm but a potential was made into the norm and practical rule.

The invisible presence of the *homo sacer* as the potential of the modern state – the potential which can be made into reality once 'the conditions are right' – brings into relief once more the most terrifying, and still most topical, aspect of the 'Holocaust experience': that in our modern society people who are neither morally corrupt nor prejudiced may also still partake with vigour and dedication in the destruction of targeted categories of human beings; and that their participation, far from calling for the mobilization of their moral or any other convictions, demands on the contrary their suspension, obliteration and irrelevance.

This is by far the most important lesson of the Holocaust which needs to be learned and remembered. If Orwell is right that control of the past allows control of the future, it is imperative, for the sake of that future, that those who control the present are not allowed to manipulate the past in a fashion likely to render the future inhospitable to humanity and uninhabitable.

Zygmunt Bauman

Notes

Preface

1 David G. Roskies, *Against the Apocalypse, Response to Catastrophe in Modern Jewish Culture* (Cambridge, Mass.: Harvard University Press, 1984), p. 252.
2 Cynthia Ozick, *Art and Ardour* (New York: Dutton, 1984), p. 236.
3 Compare Steven Beller, 'Shading Light on the Nazi Darkness', *Jewish Quarterly*, Winter 1988–9, p. 36.
4 Janina Bauman, *Winter in the Morning* (London: Virago Press, 1986), p. 1.

Chapter 1   Introduction: Sociology After The Holocaust

1 Cf. Konrad Lorenz, *On Aggression* (New York: Harcourt, Brace and World, 1977); Arthur Koestler, *Janus: a Summing Up* (London: Hutchinson, 1978). Among many writings which attempt to deploy theories of immanent faultiness of human nature for the explanation of the Holocaust, Israel W. Charny, *How Can we Commit the Unthinkable?* (Boulder: Westview Press, 1982) occupies a prominent place. The book contains a comprehensive survey of theories of human nature, and considers such hypotheses as 'man is naturally evil', 'tendency to get drunk with power', 'projecting that we can bear least in ourselves onto a scapegoat', or 'killing the humanity of another to spare one's own'. Wendy Stellar Flory, 'The Psychology of Antisemitism', in *Antisemitism in the Contemporary World*, ed. Michael Curtis, (Boulder: Westview Press, 1986) explains the incidence of the Holocaust by tenacity of antisemitism, antisemitism by ubiquitous prejudice, prejudice by 'the most fundamental and intuitive of all human drives – selfishness', which in its turn is explained as 'the result of another human characteristic ... – the pride that makes us ready

to go to almost any length to avoid admitting to ourselves that we were in the wrong' (p. 240). Flory claims that the prevention of destructive effects of prejudice requires that society insists '(as it does with other kinds of self-ishness) that it must be rigorously monitored and restrained' (p. 249).

2 For instance, 'Angela Davis is transformed into a Jewish housewife en route to Dachau; a cut in the food stamp programme becomes an exercise in genocide; the Vietnamese boat people become the hapless Jewish refugees of the 1930s,' Henry L. Feingold, 'How Unique is the Holocaust?', in *Genocide: Critical Issues of the Holocaust*, ed. Alex Grobman & Daniel Landes (Los Angeles: The Simon Wiesenthal Centre, 1983), p. 398.

3 George M. Kren & Leon Rappoport, *The Holocaust and the Crisis of Human Behaviour* (New York: Holmes & Meier, 1980), p. 2.

4 Everett C. Hughes, 'Good people and Dirty Work', *Social Problems*, Summer 1962, pp. 3–10.

5 Cf. Helen Fein, *Accounting for Genocide: National Response and Jewish Victimization during the Holocaust* (New York: Free Press, 1979).

6 Fein, *Accounting for Genocide*, p. 34.

7 Nechama Tec, *When Light Pierced the Darkness* (Oxford: Oxford University Press, 1986), p. 193.

8 John K. Roth, 'Holocaust Business', *Annals of AAPSS*, no. 450 (July 1980), p. 70.

9 Feingold, 'How Unique is the Holocaust', pp. 399–400.

10 Edmund Stillman & William Pfaff, *The Politics of Hysteria* (New York: Harper & Row, 1964), p. 30–31.

11 Raoul Hilberg, *The Destruction of the European Jews* (New York: Holmes & Meier, 1983), vol. III, p. 994.

12 Richard L. Rubenstein, *The Cunning of History* (New York: Harper, 1978), pp. 91, 195.

13 Cf. Lyman H. Legters (ed.), *Western Society after the Holocaust* (Boulder: West-view Press, 1983).

14 In the words of the former foreign minister of Israel, Abba Eban, 'With Mr. Begin and his cohorts, every foe becomes a "Nazi", every blow becomes an "Auschwitz".' Eban continues: 'It is about time that we stand on our own feet and not of those of the six million dead.': quoted after Michael R. Marrus, 'Is there a New Antisemitism?', in Curtis, *Antisemitism in the Contemporary World*, pp. 177–8. Begin-style statements invite response in kind: and thus the *Los Angeles Times* ascribes to Begin 'the language of Hitler', while another American journalist writes about the eyes of Palestinian Arabs looking out at him from under the photos of Jewish children marched into gas chambers: cf. Edward Alexander in *Antisemitism in the Modern World*.

15 Kren & Rappoport, *The Holocaust and the Crisis*, pp. 126, 143.

16 Leo Kuper, *Genocide: Its Political Use in the Twentieth Century* (New Haven: Yale University Press, 1981), p. 161.

17 Christopher R. Browning, 'The German Bureaucracy and the Holocaust', in Grobman & Landes, *Genocide*, p. 148.

18 Kuper, *Genocide*, p. 121.

19 H. H. Gerth & C. Wright Mills (eds.), *From Max Weber* (London: Routledge & Kegan Paul, 1970), pp. 214, 215. In her comprehensive survey and partisan evaluation of the treatment of the Holocaust by the historians (*The Holocaust and the Historians* (Cambridge, Mass.: Harvard University Press, 1981)), Lucy S. Dawidowicz objects against equating the Holocaust with other cases of mass murder, like the wiping out of Hiroshima and Nagasaki: 'The purpose of the bombing was to demonstrate America's superior military power'; the bombing 'was not motivated by a wish to wipe out the Japanese people' (pp. 17–18). Having made this evidently true observation, Dawidowicz nevertheless misses an important point: the killing of the two hundred thousand Japanese was conceived (and executed) as a searched-for effective means to implement the set goal; it was, indeed, a product of rational problem-solving mentality.

20 Cf. Karl A. Schleuner, *The Twisted Road to Auschwitz* (University of Illionis Press, 1970).

21 Michael R. Marrus, *The Holocaust in History* (London: University Press of New England, 1987), p. 41.

22 Gerth & Mills, *From Max Weber*, p. 232.

23 Browning, 'The German Bureaucracy', p. 147.

24 Kren & Rappoport, *The Holocaust and the Crisis*, p. 70.

25 Hannah Arendt, *Eichmann in Jerusalem: a Report on the Banality of Evil* (New York: Viking Press, 1964), p. 106.

26 Arendt, *Eichmann in Jerusalem*, p. 69.

27 Hilberg, *The Destruction of the European Jews*, p. 1011.

28 Cf. Herbert C. Kelman, 'Violence without Moral Restraint', *Journal of Social Issues*, vol. 29 (1973), pp. 29–61.

29 Gerth & Mills, *From Max Weber*, p. 95. During his trial, Eichmann insisted that he obeyed not just orders, but the law. Arendt comments that he (and not necessarily he alone) travestied Kant's categorical imperative, so that instead of individual autonomy, it should support bureaucratic subordination: 'act as if the principle of your action were the same as that of the legislator or of the law of the land': Arendt, *Eichmann in Jerusalem*, p. 136.

30 Quoted after Robert Wolfe, 'Putative Threat to National Security at a Nurenberg Defence for Genocide',, *Annals of AAPSS*, no. 450 (July 1980), p. 64.

31 Hilberg, *The Destruction of the European Jews*, pp. 1036–8, 1042.

32 Hilberg, *The Destruction of the European Jews*, p. 1024.

33 John Lachs, *Responsibility of the Individual in Modern Society* (Brighton: Harvester, 1981), pp. 12–13, 58.

34 Philip Caputo, *A Rumour of War* (New York: Holt, Rinehart & Winston, 1977), p. 229.

35 Fein, *Accounting for Genocide*, p. 4.

36 Hilberg, *The Destruction of the European Jews*, p. 1044.

37 Franklin M. Littell, 'Fundamentals in Holocaust Studies', *Annals of AAPSS*, no. 450 (July 1980), p. 213.

38 Colin Gray, *The Soviet–American Arms Race* (Lexington: Saxon House, 1976), pp. 39, 40.

CHAPTER 2   MODERNITY, RACISM, EXTERMINATION I

1 Harry L. Feingold, *Menorah*, Judaic Studies Programme of Virginia Commonwealth University, no. 4 (Summer 1985), p. 2.

2 Norman Cohn, *Warrant for Genocide* (London: Eyre & Spottiswoode, 1967), pp. 267–8.

3 Feingold, *Menorah*, p. 5.

4 Walter Laqueur, *Terrible Secret* (Harmondsworth: Penguin Books, 1980).

5 Cohn, *Warrant for Genocide*, pp. 266–7.

6 I have written more fully on this topic in 'Exit Visas and Entry Tickets', *Telos*, Winter 1988.

7 Eberhard Jäckel, *Hitler in History* (Boston: University Press of New England, 1964).

8 Cf. *Hitler's Secret Book* (London: Grove Press, 1964).

9 Cohn, *Warrant for Genocide*, p. 252.

10 Quoted after Walter Laqueur, *A History of Zionism* (New York, 1972), p. 188.

11 Max Weinreich, *Hitler's Professors: The Part of Scholarship in Germany's Crimes against the Jewish People* (New York: Yiddish Scientific Institute, 1946), p. 28.

12 W. D. Rubinstein, *The Left, the Right, and the Jews* (London: Croom Helm, 1982), pp. 78–9. I would phrase this observation differently: it was not the particular violence which resulted from the conflation of different antisemitisms, but precisely the phenomenon of antisemitism which arose from the conflation of perspectives.

It must be stressed that the contradictory social placement of the Jews which persisted up to the Second World War is at present fast disappearing in virtually all affluent Western countries – with consequences so far difficult to fathom and calculate. Rubinstein supplies convincing statistical proofs of a massive movement of the Jews towards the upper-middle sector of the social ladder. Economic success coupled with the dismantling of political restraints finds its reflection in the political profile of the Jewish opinion: 'Jews are now generally conservatives en bloc' (p. 118), 'not all neo-conservatives are Jews but most of its leading members are Jewish' (p. 124), the once liberal-progressive *Commentary* turned into a militant organ of the

American Right, the romance between the Jewish establishment and the fundamentalist Right is getting progressively warmer. In a recent symposium on the 'End of the beautiful friendship' between Jews and Socialism (see *The Jewish Quarterly*, no. 2, (1988)), Melanie Phillips confided: 'I have great pleasure telling my socialist friends and acquaintances that "I am an ethnic minority" and seeing them roll around in hysterics. How can I be? I'm powerful. And it's the perception among socialists that Jews are in positions of power. They are in the government, are they not? They are running things, they are running industry, they are landlords.' While George Friedman asked, rhetorically: 'The Jewish members of the government have been associated with rather unpopular policies. When the current bubble finally bursts... what will happen then? Where will the Jewish community be at that time and where will we be in relationship to the collapse and to the frustrations of the working-class in this country?'

It is interesting to note that social placement of German Jews immediately before the Nazi period came very close to the present patterns typical of Western Europe and particularly the United States. About three-quarters of German Jews lived then from trade, commerce, banking and the professions, especially medicine and law (against a mere one-quarter of the non-Jewish population). What made the Jews particularly visible was their domination of the publishing industry, culture and journalism ('Jewish journalists were notable across almost the entire spectrum of the liberal and left-wing press' – Donald L. Niewyk, *The Jews in Weimar Germany* (Manchester: Manchester University Press, 1980), p. 15). For reasons of their class membership, German Jews were inclined to follow the rest of the middle classes to the conservative part of the political spectrum. If, despite these inclinations they retained an above-average attachment to liberal programmes and parties, it was mostly because the Germany right was outspokenly antisemitic and hence adamantly repulsed recurrent Jewish advances.

13 Anna Zuk, 'A mobile class. The subjective element in the social perception of Jews: the example of eighteenth century Poland', in *Polin*, vol. 2 (Oxford: Basil Blackwell, 1987), pp. 163–78.

14 Cf. Zygmunt Bauman, *Legislators and Interpreters* (Cambridge: Polity Press, 1987).

15 Quoted after George L. Mosse, *Toward the Final Solution: A History of European Racism* (London: J. M. Dent & Son, 1978), p. 154.

16 Joseph Marcus, *Social and Political History of the Jews in Poland 1919–1939* (Berlin: Mouton, 1983), pp. 97–8.

17 David Biale, *Power and Powerlessness in Jewish History* (New York: Schocken, 1986), p. 132.

18 Hannah Arendt, *Origins of Totalitarianism* (London: Allen & Unwin, 1962), p. 14.

19 P. G. J. Pulzer, *The Rise of Political Antisemitism in Germany and p. 331. Austria,* (New York, John Wiley & Sons, 1964), p. 311.

20 Arendt, *Origins of Totalitarianism,* p. 20.

21 Arendt, *Origins of Totalitarianism,* p. 22.

22 Jacob Katz, *From Prejudice to Destruction: Anti-Semitism 1700–1933* (Cambridge, Mass.: Harvard University Press, 1980), pp. 161, 87.

23 Pulzer, *Rise of Political Antisemitism,* pp. 138–9. One can sample the flavour of the Jewish predicament in such cases from the following example: 'In eastern Galicia and in the Lithuanian-Belorussian borderlands, the situation was far more complex and dangerous, for there the Jews found themselves caught between competing national claims, as they did in ,other ethnically mixed regions of Eastern Europe such as Transylvania, Bohemia and Moravia, and Slovakia. In Eastern Galicia the Jewish population was strongly identified with Polish culture and had certainly acquiesced in the granting of political supremacy in the prewar period to Poles. Most were ignorant, and perhaps also contemptuous, of the Ukrainian language and indifferent to Ukrainian national aspirations. On the other hand, the short- lived West Ukrainian Republic, proclaimed in Lwów in the fall of 1918, promised the Jews civil equality and national autonomy, while the Poles in the region made no effort to hide their antisemitic tendencies. Uncertain as to who the ultimate victor would be, and unwilling to alienate either the Poles or the Ukrainians, the local Jewish National Council proclaimed neutrality... [S]ome Poles regarded this as a sign of pro-Ukrainian feeling and took revenge on the Jews of Lwów after their capture of the city in November 1918. The Ukrainians also denounced Jewish neutrality, interpreting it as a continuation of the Jews' traditional pro-Polish attitude' (Ezra Mendelsohn, *The Jews of East-Central Europe Between the World Wars* (Bloomington: Indiana University Press, 1983), pp. 51–2).
The story repeated itself, almost to the letter, during the Second World War. The Jews of Eastern Poland welcomed the entry of the Red Army in 1939 as a protection against the overtly and vehemently antisemitic Nazis. Again, whatever remained of Polish Jewry after the Nazi occupation saw the advancing Soviet troops as, unambiguously, a liberating force. To many Poles, both Germans and Russians were first and foremost foreign occupants.

24 Geoff Dench, *Minorities in the Open Society: Prisoners of Ambivalence,* (London: RKP, 1986), p. 259.

25 Katz, *From Prejudice to Destruction,* p. 3.

26 Patrick Girard, 'Historical Foundations of Antisemitism', in *Survivors, Victims, and Perpetrators: Essays on the Nazi Holocaust,* ed. Joel E. Dinsdale (Washington: Hemisphere Publishing Company, 1980), pp. 70–71. Pierre-André Taguieff has recently published a comprehensive study of socio-psychological foundations of racism and related phenomena, among which the resentment of *métissage* (mixed breed) plays a focal role. Half- breeds differ

significantly from apparently similar cases of the 'boundary-blurring'. If social outcasts, the *déclassé* individuals, are, so to speak, decategorized, while immigrants tend to be a-categorized (they exist, as it were, outside the dominant classification and hence on the whole do not sap its authority), half-breeds are overcategorized; they force the overlap of semantic fields which need to be carefully fenced and kept separate if the dominant classification is to retain its authority: (cf. *La force du préjugé: essai sur le racisme et ses doubles* (Paris: Éditions la Découverte, 1988), p. 343).

27 Arendt, *Origins of Totalitarianism*, p. 87.
28 J. S. McClelland (ed.), *The French Right* (London: Jonathan Cape, 1970), pp. 88, 32, 178.

CHAPTER 3   MODERNITY, RACISM, EXTERMINATION II

1 Cf. Pierre-André Taguieff, *La force du préjugé: essai sur le racism et ses doubles* (Parish: La Decouverte, 1988).
2 Taguieff, *La force du préjugé*, p. 69–70. Albert Memmi, *Le racisme* (Paris: Gallimard, 1982) maintains that 'racism, not anti-racism, is truly universal' (p. 157), and explains the mystery of its alleged universality by reference to another mystery: the instinctive fear invariably inspired by all difference. One does not understand the *different*, which by the same token turns into the *unknown* and the unknown is a source of terror. In Memmi's view, the horror of the unknown 'stems from the history of our species, in the course of which the unknown was the source of danger' (p. 208). It is suggested therefore that the putative universality of racism is a product of species learning. Having thus acquired a pre-cultural foundation, it is essentially immune to the impact of individual training.
3 Taguieff, *La force du préjugé*, p. 91.
4 Alfred Rosenberg, *Selected Writings* (London: Jonathan Cape, 1970), p. 196.
5 Arthur Gütt, 'Population Policy', in *Germany Speaks* (London: Thornton Butterworth, 1938), pp. 35, 52.
6 Walter Gross, 'National Socialist Racial Thought', in *Germany Speaks*, p. 68.
7 Cf. Gerald Fleming, *Hitler and the Final Solution* (Oxford: Oxford University Press, 1986), pp. 23–5.
8 Alfred Rosenberg (ed.), *Dietrich Eckart: Ein Vermächtnis* (Munich; Frz. Eher, 1928). Quoted after George L. Mosse, *Nazi Culture: A Documentary History* (New York: Schocken Books, 1981), p. 77.
9 George. L. Mosse, *Toward the Final Solution: A History of European Racism* (London, J. M. Dent & Son, 1978), p. 2.
10 Mosse, *Toward the Final Solution*, p. 20.
11 Cf. Mosse, *Toward the Final Solution*, p. 53.

12 Max Weinreich, *Hitler's Professors: The Part of Scholarship in Germany's Crimes against the Jewish People* (New York: Yiddish Scientific Institute, 1946), pp. 56, 33.

13 H. R. Trevor-Roper, *Hitler's Table Talk* (London, 1953), p. 332.

14 Norman Cohn, *Warrant for Genocide* (London: Eyre & Spottiswoode, 1967), p. 87. There is ample evidence that the language used by Hitler whenever he discussed the 'Jewish question' was not chosen merely for its rhetoric or propagandistic value. Hitler's attitude toward Jews was visceral rather than cerebral. He indeed experienced the 'Jewish question' as a matter akin to hygiene – a behavioural code he felt strongly about and with which he was obsessed. One will probably understand how much Hitler's disgust for the Jews emanated from, and chimed in with, his genuinely puritan sensitivity to all matters of health and hygiene when one ponders the response he gave in 1922 to the question asked by his friend Josef Hell: what would he do with the Jews once he had full discretionary powers? Promising to hang all Munich Jews on the gallows especially erected along the Marienplatz, Hitler did not forget to stress that the hanged Jews would remain hanging 'until they stink; they will hang there as long as the principles of hygiene permit' (quoted after Fleming, *Hitler and the Final Solution*, p. 17). Let us add that these words were spluttered in a fit of rage, in a 'state of paroxysm', with Hitler apparently not in control of himself; even then – or perhaps particularly on that occasion – the cult of hygiene and health obsession revealed the tightness of the grip in which it held Hitler's mind.

15 Marlis G. Steinert, *Hitler's War and the Germans: Public Mood and Attitude during the Second World War*, trans. Thomas E. J. de Witt (Athens, Ohio: Ohio University Press, 1977), p. 137.

16 Raoul Hilberg, *The Destruction of The European Jews* (New York: Holmes & Meier, 1983), Vol. III, p. 1023.

17 Weinreich, *Hitler's Professors*, pp. 31–3, 34. The traditions of cattle breeders and other biological manipulators were deployed by the national-socialist science not only to the solution of the 'Jewish question'. They offered inspiration to the totality of social policy under Nazism. Andreas Walther, a sociology professor from Hamburg and the leading urban sociologist of Nazi Germany, explained that 'one cannot change human nature through education and environmental influence... National Socialism will not repeat blunders of the past attempts of urban improvement, by limiting itself to house building and hygienic improvements. Sociological research will determine who can be still saved... Hopeless cases will be eliminated [ausmerzen].' *Neue Wege zur Grossstadtsanierung* (Stuttgart, 1936), p. 4. Quoted after Stanisaw Tyrowicz, *Światio wiedzy zdeprawowanej* (Poznań: Instytut Zachodni, 1970), p. 53.

18 Mosse, *Toward the Final Solution*, p. 134.

19 Hannah Arendt, *Origins of Totalitarianism* (London: Allen & Unwin, 1962), p. 87.

20 Diary of Joseph Goebbels, in *Survivors, Victims, and Perpetrators: Essays on the Nazi Holocaust*, ed. Joel E. Dinsdale (Washington: Hemisphere Publishing Company, 1980), p. 311.

21 John R. Sabini & Maury Silver, 'Destroying the Innocent with a Clear Conscience: A Sociopsychology of the Holocaust', in *Survivors, Victims, and the Perpetrators*, p. 329.

22 Richard Grünberger, *A Social History of the Third Reich* (London: Weidenfeld & Nicholson, 1971), p. 460.

23 Lawrence Stokes, 'The German People and the Destruction of the European Jewry', *Central European History*, no. 2 (1973), pp. 167–91.

24 Quoted after Sarah Gordon, *Hitler, Germans, and the 'Jewish Question'* (Princeton: Princeton University Press, 1984), pp. 159–60.

25 Cf. Gordon, *Hitler, Germans*, p. 171.

26 Christopher R. Browning, *Fateful Months* (New York: Holmes & Meier, 1985), p. 106.

27 *Le dossier Eichmann et al solution finale de la question juive* (Paris: Centre de documentation juive contemporaine, 1960), pp. 52–3.

28 Gordon, *Hitler, Germans*, p. 316.

29 Klaus von Beyme, *Right-Wing Extremism in Western Europe* (London: Frank Cass, 1988), p. 5. In a recent study Michael Balfour surveyed conditions and motives which prompted various strata of German Weimar society to offer enthusiastic, mild or lukewarm support to the Nazi thrust for power, or at least refrain from active resistance. Many reasons are listed, general as well as specific to a given section of the population. The direct appeal of Nazi antisemitism figures prominently, however, in only one case (of the educated part of the *obere Mittelstand*, who felt threatened by the 'disproportionate competition' of the Jews), and even in this case merely as one of many factors found attractive, or at least worth trying, in the Nazi programme of the social revolution. Cf. *Withstanding Hitler in Germany 1933–45* (London: Routledge, 1988), pp. 10–28.

30 Cf. Bernd Martin, 'Antisemitism before and after Holocaust', in *Jews, Antisemitism and Culture in Vienna*, ed. Ivor Oxaal (London: Michael Pollak and Gerhard Botz, 1987).

31 *Jewish Chronicle*, 15 July 1988, p. 2.

32 Cf. Gérard Fuchs, *Ils resteront: le défi de l'immigration* (Paris: Syros, 1987); Pierre Jouve & Ali Magoudi, *Les dits et les non-dits de Jean-Marie Le Pen: enquéte et psychanalyse* (Paris: La Decouverte, 1988).

CHAPTER 4   THE UNIQUENESS AND NORMALITY OF THE HOLOCAUST

1 Raul Hilberg, 'Significance of the Holocaust', in *The Holocaust: Ideology, Bureaucracy, and Genocide*, ed. Henry Friedlander & Sybil Milton (Millwood, NY: Kraus International Publications, 1980), pp. 101–2.

2 Cf. Colin Legum in *The Observer*, 12 October 1966.

3 Henry L. Feingold, 'How Unique is the Holocaust?' in *Genocide: Critical Issues of the Holocaust*, ed. Alex Grobman & David Landes (Los Angeles: Simon Wiesenthal Centre, 1983), p. 397.

4 Feingold, 'How Unique is the Holocaust?', p. 401.

5 Leo Kuper, *Genocide: Its Political Use in the Twentieth Century* (New Haven: Yale University Press, 1981), pp. 137, 161. Kuper's forebodings found a most sinister confirmation in the words of the Iraqi ambassador in London. Interviewed on Channel 4 on 2 September 1988 about the continuing genocide of Iraqi Kurds, the ambassador indignantly replied to the charges that the Kurds, their well-being, and their fate were Iraq's internal affairs and that no one had the right to interfere with the actions undertaken by a sovereign state inside its borders.

6 George A. Kren & Leon Rappoport, *The Holocaust and the Crisis of Human Behaviour* (New York: Holmes & Meier, 1980), pp. 130, 143.

7 John P. Sabini & Mary Silver, 'Destroying the Innocent with a Clear Conscience: A Sociopsychology of the Holocaust', in *Survivors, Victims, and Perpetrators: Essays in the Nazi Holocaust*, ed. Joel E. Dinsdale (Washington: Hemisphere Publishing Corporation, 1980), pp. 329–30.

8 Sarah Gordon, *Hitler, Germans, and the 'Jewish Question'* (Princeton: Princeton University Press, 1984), pp. 48–9.

9 Kren & Rappoprt, *The Holocaust and the Crisis*, p. 140.

10 Joseph Weizenbaum, *Computer Power and Human Reason: From Judgment to Calculation* (San Francisco: W. H. Freeman, 1976), p. 252.

11 Kren & Rappoport, *The Holocaust and the Crisis*, p. 141.

12 Peter Marsh, *Aggro: The Illusion of Violence* (London: J. M. Dent & Sons, 1978), p. 120.

13 Norbert Elias, *The Civilising Process: State Formation and Civilization*, trans. Edmund Jephcott (Oxford: Basil Blackwell, 1982), pp. 238–9.

14 Robert Proctor, *Racial Hygiene: Medicine under the Nazis* (Cambridge Mass.: Harvard University Press, 1988), p. 4, 6.

15 Proctor, *Racial Hygiene*, pp. 315–24.

16 R. W. Darré, 'Marriage Laws and the Principles of Breeding' (1930), in: *Nazi Ideology before 1933: A Documentation*, trans. Barbara Hiller and Leila J. Gupp (Manchester: Manchester University Press, 1978), p. 115.

17 Weizenbaum, *Computer Power*, p. 256.

18 Weizenbaum, *Computer Power*, p. 275.

19 Weizenbaum, *Computer Power*, p. 253.
20 Jacques Ellul, *Technological System*, trans. Joachim Neugroschel (New York: Continuum, 1980), pp. 272, 273.

CHAPTER 5   SOLICITING THE CO-OPERATION OF THE VICTIMS

1 Hermann Erich Seifert, *Der Jude an der Ostgrenze* (Berlin: Eher, 1940), p. 82. Quoted after Max Weinreich, *Hitler's Professors: The Part of Scholarship in Germany's Crimes against the Jewish People* (New York: Yiddish Scientific Institute, 1946), p. 91. Casting the Jewish elites in a major role in the implementation of their long-term plans of the solution to the 'Jewish Question' stood in stark contrast to the treatment allotted to the elites of the conquered Slav nations, meant to be enslaved rather than exterminated. For instance, ethnically Polish educated classes were subjected to persecution and annihilation from the very first day of the German occupation, long before the extermination of the Polish Jews took off. This fact misled the Polish Government in exile and the Polish opinion in general into believing that the Jews had been accorded a privileged status by the Germans, in comparison with their Polish neighbours: cf. David Engel, *In the Shadow of Auschwitz* (University of North Carolina Press, 1987).
2 Quoted after Leo Kuper, *Genocide, Its Political Use in the Twentieth Century* (New Haven: Yale University Press, 1981), p. 127.
3 Richard Grüberger, *A Social History of the Third Reich* (London: Weidenfeld & Nicholson, 1971), p. 466.
4 Cf. Hans Mommsen, 'Anti-Jewish Politics and the Implications of the Holocaust', in *The Challenge of the Third Reich: The Adam von Trotta Memorial Lectures*, ed. Hedley Bull (Oxford: Clarendon Press, 1986), p. 122–8.
5 Ian Kershaw, *Popular Opinion and Political Dissent in the Third Reich* (Oxford: Clarendon Press, 1983), pp. 359, 364, 372.
6 Franklin H. Littell, 'The Credibility Crisis of the Modern University', in *The Holocaust: Ideology, Bureaucracy, and Genocide*, ed. Henry Friedlander & Lythel Milton (Millwood, NY: Kraus International Publications, 1980), pp. 274, 277, 272.
7 Alan Beyerchen, 'The Physical Sciences', in *The Holocaust: Ideology, Bureacracy, and Genocide*, pp. 158–9.
8 Léon Poliakoff, *The History of Antisemitism* (Oxford: Oxford University Press, 1985), vol. IV.
9 Joachim, C. Fest, *The Face of the Third Reich*, trans. Michael Bullock (Harmondsworth: Penguin Books, 1985), p. 394.
10 Richard Grünberger, *A Social History of the Third Reich*, p. 313.
11 Norman Cohen, *Warrant for Genocide* (London: Eyre & Spottiswoode, 1967), p. 268.

12　Raul Hilberg, *The Destruction of the European Jews* (New York: Holmes & Meier, 1985), vol. I, pp. 78–9, 76.

13　Hannah Arendt, *Eichmann in Jerusalem* (New York: Viking Press, 1964), p. 132.

14　Arendt, *Eichmann in Jerusalem*, p. 118. This judgement was not entirely fanciful; it reflected a long tradition of the host elites' views and practices, which only Hitler and Himmler – not without some resistance from their own ranks – dared to overthrow. As late as 16 December 1941 Wilhelm Kube, a tested, unscrupulous and seasoned Nazi dignitary, petitioned his superiors on behalf of the German Jews entrusted to his *Sonderbehandlung*: '[p]eople who come from our cultural sphere are quite different, I submit, from the native brutish hordes' (quoted after Weinreich, *Hitler's Professors*, p. 155). There is a bizarre document, issued by the *Geheime Sicherheitsamt* in Berlin on 1 March 1940, which appointed Dr Arthur Spier, the director of Hamburg Talmud Torah School, 'to create in the Jewish Reservation in Poland [then planned around Nisko] a system of general Jewish education similar to the established system of the Reich'. The latter was clearly seen as, by proxy, superior to everything the lesser Jews, untouched by German culture, could create: Solomon Colodner, *Jewish Education in Germany under the Nazis* (Jewish Education Committee Press, 1964), pp. 33–4.

15　Quoted after Lucjan Dobroszycki, 'Jewish Elites under German Rule', in *The Holocaust: Ideology, Bureaucracy, and Genocide*, p. 223.

16　Jacques Adler, *The Jews of Paris and the Final Solution* (Oxford: Oxford University Press, 1987), pp. 223–4.

17　Hilberg, *The Destruction of the European Jews*, vol. III, p. 1042.

18　Helen Fein, *Accounting for Genocide*, New York Free Press 1979, p. 319.

19　Isaiah Trunk, *Judenrat: The Jewish Councils in Eastern Europe under German Occupation* (London: Macmillan, 1972), p. 401.

20　Quoted after Trunk, *Judenrat*, p. 407.

21　Trunk, *Judenrat*, pp. 418, 419.

22　Thus Maimonides: 'If pagans should tell them "give us one of yours and we shall kill him, otherwise we shall kill all of you", they should all be killed and not a single Jewish soul should be delivered.' *The Fundamentals of the Torah*, 5/5. Also *Pirkei Abboth*: 'A man once came before Reba and said to him: "The ruler of my city has ordered me to kill a certain person, and if I refuse he will kill me". Reba told him: "Be killed and do not kill; do you think that your blood is redder than his? Perhaps his is redder than yours."' (Pes. 25b). The *Jerusalem Talmud* instructs: 'A company of Jews were travelling along the road when some gentiles met them and said, "Give us one of your number that we may kill him, otherwise we will kill all of you!" Even if all of them should be killed, they may not hand over one soul of Israel.' As to the case when the enemies themselves name a specific person they want to punish, the opinions of authorities are divided. Even this case, however, the Talmud advises to consider in the light of the following story: 'Ulla bar Koshev was wanted by the government. He fled for asylum to Rabbi Joshua ben Levi at Lod. The government forces came and surrounded the town. They said: "If you do not surrender him to us, we will destroy the town". Rabbi Joshua went up to Ulla bar Koshev and persuaded him to give himself up. Elijah used to appear to Rabbi Joshua, but from that moment on he ceased to do so. Rabbi Joshua fasted many days, and finally Elijah revealed himself to him. "Am I supposed to appear to informers?" he asked. Rabbi Joshua said: "I followed the law". Elijah retorted: "But is the law for saints?'" (*Trumot* 8: 10).

23 Quoted after Trunk, *Judenrat*, p. 423.

24 Quoted after Trunk, *Judenrat*, p. xxxii.

25 Quoted after Trunk, *Jewish Responses to Nazi Persecution: Collective and Individual Behaviour in Extremis* (New York: Stein & Day, 1979), pp. 75–6.

26 Mark Edelman, *Ghetto walczy* (Warszaw: C. K. Bundu, 1945), pp. 12–14.

27 Hilberg, *The Destruction of the European Jews*, vol. III, p. 1036.

28 Wadysaw Szlengel, *Co czytaem umarym* (Warszaw: PIW, 1979), pp. 46, 49, 44.

29 Quoted after Trunk, *Judenrat*, pp. 447–9.

CHAPTER 6 THE ETHICS OF OBEDIENCE (READING MILGRAM)

1 Stanley Milgram, *The Individual in a Social World* (Reading, Mass.: Addison and Wesley, 1971), p. 98.

2 Richard Christie, 'Authoritarianism Re-examined', in *Studies in the Scope and Method of 'The Authoritarian Personality'*, ed. Richard Christie & Marie Jahöda (Glencoe, Ill.: Free Press, 1954) p. 194.

3 Stanley Milgram, *Obedience to Authority: An Experimental View* (London: Tavistock, 1974), p. xi.

4 Milgram, *Obedience to Authority*, p. 121.

5 Milgram, *Obedience to Authority*, p. 39.

6 John P. Sabini & Maury Silver, 'Destroying the Innocent with a Clear Conscience: A Sociopsychology of the Holocaust', in *Survivors, Victims, and Perpetrators: Essays on the Nazi Holocaust*, ed. Joel E. Dinsdale (Washington: Hemisphere Publishing Corporation, 1980), p. 342.

7 Milgram, *Obedience to Authority*, pp. 142, 146.

8 Milgram, *Obedience to Authority*, p. 11.

9 Milgram, *Obedience to Authority*, p. 104.

10 Milgram, *Obedience to Authority*, p. 133.

11 Milgram, *Obedience to Authority*, p. 107.

12 Milgram, The Individual in a Social World, pp. 96–7.

13 Cf. Craig Haney, Curtis Banks, & Philip Zimbardo, 'Interpersonal Dynamics in a Simulated Prison', *International Journal of Criminology and Penology*, vol. I (1973), pp. 69–97.

14 Cf. Amitai A. Etzioni, 'A Model of Significant Research', *International Journal of Psychiatry*, vol. VI. (1968) pp. 279–80.
15 John M. Steiner, 'The SS Yesterday and Today: A Sociopsychological View' in *Survivors, Victims, and Perpetrators*, p. 431.

CHAPTER 7   TOWARDS A SOCIOLOGICAL THEORY OF MORALITY

1 Cf. Zygmunt Bauman, *Legislators and Interpreters* (Cambridge: Polity Press, 1987) ch. 3, 4.
2 In various receptions of Durkheim and elaborations of Durheim's themes, it has been widely accepted that the paradigm of 'social production of morality' does not apply just to the Society writ large, i.e. one that connotes the fully equipped nation-state society. Inside such 'grand society', the presence of more than one authoritative moral systems is acknowledged; some of them may even go against the grain of the moral system promoted by the institutions of the 'grand society'. For our problem, however, the relevant point is not the moral monism or pluralism or the 'grand society', but the fact that within Durkheim's perspective any morally binding norm, however minuscule in its application, must have a social origin and be enforced by socially operated coercive sanctions. Inside this perspective, immorality is always, by definition, anti-social (or, conversely, a-sociality is by definition a-moral); indeed, Durkheim's language does not allow for the articulation of other than social origin of moral behaviour. The alternative to socially-regulated conduct is one caused by non-human, animal drives.
3 Richard L. Rubenstein, *The Cunning of History* (New York: Harper, 1978), p. 91.
4 Richard L. Rubenstein & John Roth, *Approaches to Auschwitz* (San Franscisco: SCM Press, 1987), p. 324.
5 Hannah Arendt, *Eichmann in Jerusalem: A Report on the Banality of Evil* (New York: Viking Press, 1964), pp. 294–5. Germany lost the war; hence murders committed on the command of Germany have been defined as crimes and as violations of moral rules that transcend the authority of the state power. The Soviet Union was among the victors; hence murders sanctioned by her rulers, though hardly less odious than German, still await a similar treatment – and this in spite of the ever more thorough spade work of the *glasnost* era. Though only few of the awesome mysteries of Stalin's genocide have been uncovered, we know now that mass murders in the USSR were no less systematic and methodical than those practiced later by the Germans, and that the techniques used by the *Einsatzgruppe* were first tried on a massive scale by the formidable bureaucracy of the NKVD. In 1988, for instance, a Belorussian weekly, *Literatura i Mastactva*, published the findings of Z. Pozniak and J. Shmygaliev ('Kuropaty – the death road', later to be reprinted by the *Sovietskaya Estonia* and *Moskovskiye Novosti*) on mass graves discovered

around all the bigger towns of Belorussia, filled in 1937–40 by hundreds of thousands of corpses, all with bullet holes in their necks or skulls. Alongside the local 'enemies of the people', lay Polish citizens deported from the freshly annexed eastern territories of Poland. 'Most of the objects found in the grave N.5 must have belonged to intelligentsia. Among them, toiletries, spectacles, monocles and medicines were found in large quantities, together with high-quality shoes, often custom-made, fashionable ladies' shoes, elegant gloves. Judging by the inventory of found objects, and by the fact that in many cases they were carefully packed (as well as by other evidence – like the presence of food supplies or suitcases) one can conclude that the victims left their homes shortly before the murder, and were not kept in prisons on their way to death. One can surmise that they had been 'liquidated' (according to the then current expression) without trial' (Quoted after a Polish report 'Strzelano w ty gowy', *Konfrontacje*, November 1988, p. 19). For all we know, the findings of the two enterprising journalists are the proverbial tip of an iceberg.

6 Alfred Schutz, 'Sartre's Theory of the Alter Ego', in *Collected Papers*, vol. I (The Haag, Martinus Nijhoff, 1967), p. 189.

7 Emmanuel Levinas, *Ethics and Infinity: Conversations with Philippe Nemo*, trans. Richard A. Cohen (Pittsburgh: Duquesne University Press, 1982), pp. 95–101.

8 Hans Mommsen, 'Anti-Jewish Politics and the Interpretation of the Holocaust', in *The Challenge of the Third Reich: The Adam von Trott Memorial Lectures*, ed. Hedley Bull (Oxford: Clarendon Press, 1986), p. 117.

9 Arendt, *Eichmannn in Jerusalem*, p. 106.

10 Martin Broszat, 'The Third Reich and the German People', in *The Challenge of the Third Reich*, p. 90.

11 Cf. Karl A. Schleunes, *The Twisted Road to Auschwitz: Nazi Policy Toward German Jews 1933–39* (University of Illinois Press, 1970), pp. 80–8.

12 Cf. Ian Kershaw, *Popular Opinion and Political Dissent in the Third Reich* (Oxford: Clarendon Press, 1983).

13 Dennis E. Showalter, *Little Man, What Now?* (New York: Archon Books, 1982), p. 85.

14 Quoted after Joachim C. Fest, *The Face of the Third Reich* (Harmondsworth: Penguin Books, 1985), p. 177.

15 Kershaw, *Popular Opinion and Political Dissent*, pp. 275, 371–2.

16 Kershaw, *Popular Opinion and Political Dissent*, p. 370.

17 Mommsen, 'Anti-Jewish Politics', p. 128.

18 Raul Hilberg, *The Destruction of the European Jews*, vol. III (New York: Holmes & Meier, 1987), p. 999.

19 Cf. Helen Fein, *Accounting for Genocide: National Response and Jewish Victimization during the Holocaust* (New York: Free Press, 1979).

20 Mommsen, 'Anti-Jewish Politics', p. 136.

21 Mommsen, 'Anti-Jewish Politics', p. 140.

22 Philip Caputo, *A Rumour of War* (New York: Holt, Rinehart & Wisdom, 1977), p. 229.

23 John Lachs, *Responsibility and the Individual in Modern Society*, (Brighton: Harvester, 1981), pp. 12, 13, 57–8.

24 Christopher R. Browning, *Fateful Months: Essays on the Emergence of the Final Solution* (New York: Holmes & Meier, 1985), pp. 66–7.

25 Christopher R. Browning, 'The Government Experts', in *The Holocaust: Ideology, Bureaucracy, and Genocide*, ed. Harry Friedlander & Sybil Milton (Millwood, NY: Kraus International Publications, 1980), p. 190.

26 Browning, *Fateful Months*, pp. 64–5.

27 In his conversations with Charbonnier, Claude Lévi-Strauss defined our modern civilization as *anthropoemic* (as distinct from *anthropophagic* 'primitive' cultures); they 'devour' their adversaries, while we 'vomit' them (separate, segregate, evict, exclude from our universe of human obligations).

28 Assignation by the legitimizing myth of Western Civilization of all natural (i.e. pre-social) drives (and thus also the 'responsibility for the other' under conditions of proximity) to the category of the 'animal instincts', and by the bureaucratic mentality to the category of irrational forces, is more than casually reminiscent of the defamation of all locally-and communally-based traditions during the cultural crusade which universalistic and absolutistic pretentions. Cf. Zygmunt Bauman, *Legislators and Interpreters* (Cambridge: Polity Press, 1987), ch. 4.

29 Raul Hilberg, 'The Significance of the Holocaust', in *The Holocaust: Ideology, Bureaucracy, and Genocide*, pp. 98, 99.

AFTERWORD FOR 2000

1 Albert Camus, *The Rebel*, trans. Anthony Bower (London: Penguin Books, 1971), pp. 11–12 (original published 1951 under the title *L'Homme révolté*).

2 Friedrich Nietzsche, *Basic Writings*, ed. Walter Kaufmann (New York: Modern Library, 1968), p. 476.

3 See Roberto Toscano, 'The Face of the Other: Ethics and Intergroup Conflict', in *The Handbook of Interethnic Coexistence*, ed. Eugene Weiner (New York: Continuum, 1998), pp. 63–81.

4 See p. 187 above.

5 See the chapter 'Essentialising the Other: Demonisation and the Creation of Monstrosity', in Jock Young, *The Exclusive Society: Social Exclusion, Crime and Difference in Late Modernity* (London: Sage, 1999). Here quoted from the MS.

6 Zygmunt Bauman, *Legislators and Interpreters* (Cambridge: Polity Press, 1987).

7 See, for instance, the chapter 'What Comes after Postmodernity? The Conflict of Two Modernities', in Ulrich Beck, *Democracy without Enemies* (Cambridge: Polity, 1998), pp. 19–31.

8 E. M. Cioran, *A Short History of Decay*, trans. Richard Howard (London: Quartet Books, 1990), p. 71.

9 'The Talmud', pointed out the late Gillian Rose, sublime philosopher and Judaic scholar in her last public lecture, recorded in *Modernity, Culture and the Jew*, edited by Brian Cheyette and Laura Marcus (Cambridge: Polity Press, 1998), 'is ironic – the most ironic holy commentary in world literature: for no human being can save the world.' Rose spoke of the 'ruthlessness of saving one or one thousand' and comments that while Keneally's original book, *Schindler's Ark*, 'makes clear the pitiless immorality of this in this context', Spielberg's film *Schindler's List* 'depends on it as congratulation'.

10 Elias Canetti, *Crowds and Power*, trans. Carol Stewart (Harmondsworth: Penguin, 1973), pp. 290–3, 544.

11 Luc Boltanski, *Distant Suffering* (Cambridge: Cambridge University Press, 1999), p. 192.

12 Ariella Azoulay & Adi Ofir, '100 Years of Zionism; 50 Years of Jewish State', *Tikkun*, 2 (1998), pp. 68–71.

13 Nechama Tec, *When Light Pierced the Darkness* (Oxford: Oxford University Press, 1986).

14 Frank Chalk & Kurt Jonassohn, *The History and Sociology of Genocide: Analyses and Case Studies* (New Haven: Yale University Press, 1990), p. 23.

15 Norman Finkelstein & Ruth Bertina Birn, *A Nation on Trial: The Goldhagen Thesis and Historical Truth* (New York: Henry Holt, 1998).

16 As quoted in *New York Times*, 10 Jan. 1998.

17 Daniel Goldhagen, *Hitler's Willing Executioners* (New York: Knopf, 1996), pp. 416, 279, 269.

18 *Haaretz*, 15 May 1998. See Dominique Vidal, 'Nouvelles polémiques autour d'un livre sur la Shoah', *Le Monde Diplomatique*, Aug. 1998, p. 58.

19 Christopher R. Browning, 'Victims' Testimony', *Tikkun* (Jan.–Feb. 1999).

20 Robert Johnson, *Death Work: A Study of the Modern Execution Process* (Belmont: Wadsworth, 1998); Nils Christie, *Crime Control as Industry* (London: Routledge, 1993).

21 Stephen Trombley, *The Execution Protocol: Inside America's Capital Punishment Industry* (New York: Anchor, 1993).

22 Götz Aly & Susanne Heim, *Vordenker der Vernichtung: Auschwitz und die deutsche Pläne für eine neue europaischer Ordnung* (Hamburg: Hoffmann & Campe, 1991).

23 Enzo Traverso, *L'Histoire déchirée* (Paris: Cerf, 1996).

24 Giorgio Agamben, *Le Pouvoir souverain et la vie nue* (Paris: Seuil, 1997).